The Last Voyage of Captain Cook

★

The Last Voyage of Captain Cook

The Collected Writings of John Ledyard

✦

Edited by James Zug

National Geographic
Adventure Classics

Washington, D.C.

Library of Congress Cataloging-in-Publication Data

Ledyard, John 1751-1789
    [Selections. 2005]
    The Last Voyage of Captain Cook: the collected writings of John Ledyard/ edited by James Zug.
    p.cm.

ISBN 0-7922-9347-9
    1. Ledyard, John, 1751-1789—Travel. 2. Ledyard, John, 1751-1789. Journal of Captain Cook's Last Voyage to the Pacific Ocean. 3. Ledyard, John, 1751-1789. Journey through Russia and Siberia, 1787-1788. 4. Voyages around the world—Early works to 1800. 5. Russia—description and travel—Early works to 1800. I. Zug, James, 1969- II. Title.

G226.L5A25 2005
910'.9164—dc22   2004063234

One of the world's largest nonprofit scientific and educational organizations, the National Geographic Society was founded in 1888 "for the increase and diffusion of geographic knowledge." Fulfilling this mission, the Society educates and inspires millions every day through its magazines, books, television programs, videos, maps and atlases, research grants, the National Geographic Bee, teacher workshops, and innovative classroom materials. The Society is supported through membership dues, charitable gifts, and income from the sale of its educational products. This support is vital to National Geographic's mission to increase global understanding and promote conservation of our planet through exploration, research, and education.

For more information, please call 1-800-NGS LINE (647-5463) or write to the following address:

NATIONAL GEOGRAPHIC SOCIETY
1145 17th Street N.W.
Washington, DC 20036-4688 U.S.A.

Visit the Society's Web site at www.nationalgeographic.com.

Contents

★

Captain Cook's
Third Voyage: 1776-1780
to the North Pacific
in the *Resolution* and *Discovery*

⟵——— Outgoing voyage

----▶ Return voyage
after Cook's death

*Oblique Azimuthal Equidistant Projection
central latitude: 40° N
central meridian: 90° W*

RETURN VOYAGE AFTER CAPTAIN COOK'S DEATH

Indian Ocean

1780

Batavia
(Jakarta)

Macao

A S I A

Siberia

EUROPE

*Arctic
Ocean*

*North
Sea*

London
Plymouth

Petropavlovsk

60°

A F R I C A

Dutch
Harbor
(Unalaska)

Anchorage

Canary Is.

30°

1779

Nootka Sound

*Hudson
Bay*

*NORTH
AMERICA*

EQUATOR

1778

Atlantic Ocean

AUSTRALIA

*HAWAIIAN
ISLANDS*

*Kealakekua
Bay*
Christmas I.

1780

TONGA IS.
Tongatapu I.

*COOK
IS.*

Bora Bora

Tahiti

*SOUTH
AMERICA*

Cape of
Good Hope

TASMANIA

*NEW
ZEALAND*

30°

Prince Edward Is.

1776

*Crozet
Islands*

1777

Pacific Ocean

150° 180° 150° 120° 90° 60° 0°

30°

120°

60°

30°

ANTARCTICA

Kerguélen Is.
60°

90°

1777

Indian Ocean

John Ledyard's route across the Russian Empire 1786-88

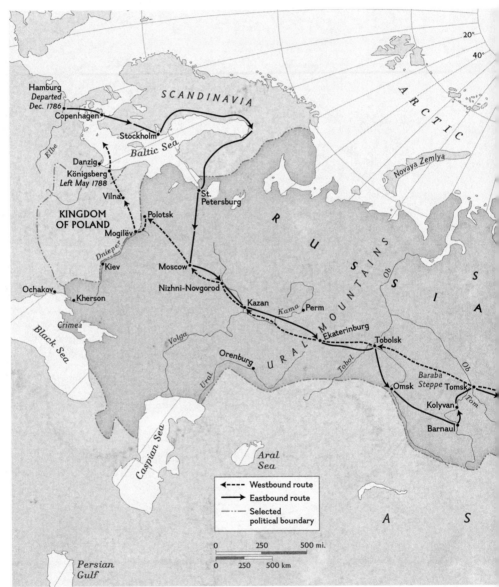

Primary Source: *John Ledyard's Journey Through Russia and Siberia 1787-1788, The Journal and Selected Letters*
University of Wisconsin Press, Madison, 1966
Edited by Stephen J. Watrous

INTRODUCTION

BY JAMES ZUG

✳

LIKE ALL CELEBRATED FIGURES from the epochal American Revolution era, John Ledyard embodied more than the facts of his curriculum vitae. In his lifetime he went from being a scapegrace and college dropout to a failed divinity student to a common seaman to a marine in the British Navy to a member of a famous expedition to a bold and stunningly well-publicized explorer who attempted to circumambulate the world.

Throughout these shifting personas Ledyard's character remained constant. He was restless, impervious to hardship, and hot-tempered. Above all, he developed a gift for marketing his schemes and cultivating relationships with the high and mighty in the Western world's capitals. He was an explorer who spent more of his time raising money and promoting his plans than out on the trail. At his height, he was famous for being famous.

After he died in Cairo in January 1789, John Ledyard was transformed into a doomed romantic hero. A halo of pioneering feats hovered like a gossamer cloud above him—the first American citizen to see the west coast of America, first to step on the future states of Alaska and Hawaii, first to get a Polynesian tattoo, first to start the China trade, first to attempt to cross the North American continent—but he was remembered more for his disappointments. He fled Dartmouth College after his freshman year; Catherine the Great arrested him in Siberia; on his way to discover the Niger River, he failed to get out of Cairo. His dreams were so large and impossible that people remembered the heartbreak more than mere distance traveled.

To gather for the first time his writings in a single volume is a powerful antidote to the Ledyard myth. Previously, rumors and distorted hyperbole, not the cold agate of words on a page, have served as the sources for his life. Even when confronted with his own original documents, historians have opted to romanticize. There have been three previous biographers of Ledyard: Jared Sparks in 1828, Kenneth Munford in 1939, and Helen Augur in 1946. Ledyard's mythical status weighed so heavily that all three revised, abridged, and edited his journals and letters, even creating imaginary scenes. Now, his collected writings will allow readers to see the unbowdlerized life of John Ledyard.

Nearly half of what follows is Ledyard's memoir of his voyage around the world with Capt. James Cook. The book, published in 1783, sold very well throughout the American states and helped cement his reputation as a thoughtful and articulate explorer. But until 1963 it was never reprinted, and now is out of print. The diary from his peregrinations across Russia was finally published in 1966, but again is now unavailable. His Egyptian diary has not reappeared since it was published in 1790. Many of his letters have never before been published. Placed together, it is a most extraordinary story.

COMPRESSING A SPECTACULARLY peripatetic life into 37 years, John Ledyard, fourth of name, was born to Abigail Hempstead Ledyard and John Ledyard, III, in November 1751 in Groton, Connecticut. After his father, a sea captain, died of malaria while trading in the Sugar Islands of the Caribbean, Ledyard moved with his mother and younger siblings to the Hempstead family home in Southold, Long Island. In three years' time, he joined his grandfather in Hartford, where Squire John, as he was known, ran a thriving mercantile business. Just before Ledyard's 20th birthday, Squire John died and young Ledyard learned that, contrary to tradition as the eldest son of the eldest son, he had been cut out almost entirely from the Ledyard family estate. His grandfather, however, had been friends with Eleazar Wheelock, and Ledyard used the connection to gain admittance to Wheelock's new university in the wilderness of New Hampshire, Dartmouth College.

Dartmouth, then in just its second year of operation, did not offer sufficient adhesive for the free-spirited Ledyard. He directed a play, led a midwinter camping expedition, and petitioned Wheelock to give dancing and fencing instruction. Confusion over his tuition bills—

Ledyard revealed early on his inability to hold onto cash—led to a rupture with Wheelock, and just over a year after his arrival, Ledyard departed in celebrated style. He carved a dugout canoe out of a pine tree and paddled 140 miles downstream to Hartford. (The epic trip is annually reenacted by members of his eponymous canoe club at Dartmouth.)

For three years Ledyard searched for his true calling. The family merchant business did not appeal to him. He tried to become a divinity student, but, because of his unsanctioned departure from Dartmouth, he could not find a permanent church. He shipped as a common seaman on a year-long trading voyage to Gibraltar, the Barbary Coast, and the Caribbean. On his next expedition, he abandoned his ship in England, but was soon impressed and forced to join the British Navy as a marine. He rusticated in barracks in Plymouth until June 1776 when Capt. James Cook sailed the *Resolution* into Plymouth harbor. Ledyard eagerly enlisted as a corporal of marines.

Cook had led two previous circumnavigations in which he charted large swaths of the southern Pacific Ocean, and now he was leading a two-ship, 180-man expedition to find the Northwest Passage from Alaska back to Newfoundland. Ledyard and the crew sailed via Cape Town to Tasmania and New Zealand, discovered the Cook Islands, and wintered in Tonga and Tahiti. On their way north to the American coast, they found what would be the voyage's most important geographical news, the Hawaiian Islands. On March 7, 1778, they sighted the coast of present-day Oregon and spent the next six months slowly tracing the Canadian and Alaskan littoral past Prince William's Sound, the Aleutians, and Bering Strait. On Unalaska in the Aleutians, Ledyard went on an arduous five-day hike to locate Russian fur traders, becoming the first Westerner to establish contact with what was already a burgeoning colonial system.

In Hawaii the following February, Cook was killed during a fracas with native islanders. The expedition spent a second summer exploring Alaska from the Siberian side. Turning toward home, they stopped for a month in China, where Ledyard and the crew sold their casually bought American sea otter furs for astonishing prices. They returned to England in October 1780.

Still a marine in the British Navy, Ledyard was sent back to Plymouth and over to North America to fight his countrymen at the tail end of the American Revolution. He deserted. Finding refuge in

Hartford, Ledyard sat out the last months of the war and wrote his *Journal of Captain Cook's Last Voyage*. Even before its publication in the summer of 1783, Ledyard was out promoting one of the book's startling pieces of news: A fortune was to be had trading furs in China. He formed a company with Robert Morris, the Philadelphia financier, and several of Morris's unscrupulous partners. Ledyard's plan was to purchase furs on the northwest coast of America, sell them at Canton, and return to the U.S. with Chinese silks and teas. He boldly predicted profits of one thousand percent. The plan was too ambitious, especially in a postwar depression, and Morris jettisoned Ledyard's fur-trading scheme in favor of a simple expedition directly to Canton. The voyage was successful, and the China trade soon ensued, leading the American economy into the Pacific.

Undeterred by his failure with Morris, Ledyard left the U.S. in June 1784 hoping to find backers in Europe. After attempts in Cadiz, Spain, and Lorient, France, Ledyard moved to Paris, where he thought he had secured the perfect partner in John Paul Jones. The celebrated sea captain, though, disappointed Ledyard when he also abandoned the fur-trading scheme in the face of British competition.

While in Paris, Ledyard struck up a friendship with Thomas Jefferson. They concocted a bold plan for Ledyard to walk around the world. He would travel across Russia, ship with Russian fur traders to the Alaskan coast, head down to Spanish California, and then hike overland to Kentucky. After numerous fits and starts, Ledyard departed from London in December 1786 with the financial support of the Marquis de Lafayette; Sir Joseph Banks, the celebrated botanist; and William Smith, John Adams's son-in-law.

From the beginning, his trip around the world was dramatic. He endured a two-day snowstorm on an open boat on the Elbe, gave away most of his money to a penniless American in Copenhagen, and marched alone through Lapland in midwinter darkness. He reached St. Petersburg with just two shirts and, as he told Jefferson, "more shirts than shillings." Via the German naturalist Peter Simon Pallas, Ledyard restored his health and situation and even fell briefly in love with a German woman. In June 1787 he left St. Petersburg, speeding across Siberia in post office carriages. In 11 weeks, he reached the far eastern Siberian village of Yakutsk before stopping for winter. There he met Joseph Billings, a fellow veteran of the Cook voyage, who was leading a large, imperial expedition launched in 1785 and focused on exploring the northeastern edge of

Siberia. Ledyard attached himself to Billings, and returned with him west to Irkutsk, the Siberian capital. In February 1788 Ledyard was arrested in Irkutsk on orders of Empress Catherine and banished, in a matter of weeks, back to the border with Poland. The cause of the arrest and banishment was unknown for 200 years until documents recently unearthed in Russian archives revealed that Ledyard had raised suspicions in Irkutsk that he was not an innocent traveler but a man bent on spying on the Russian fur colonies.

Returning to London, Ledyard serendipitously stumbled upon a new society, the African Association, looking for able-bodied explorers to go to Africa. Ledyard agreed to traverse the continent from the Red Sea to the Atlantic. In one month Ledyard went from a bedraggled vagabond smarting over his Russian failure to a lionized celebrity departing for Cairo. A protégé of Joshua Reynolds painted his portrait, and he was the guest of honor at formal farewell dinners.

In August 1788 he landed at Alexandria and spent the autumn in Cairo organizing his transportation. However, political instability delayed his departure, and in January 1789 a combination of dysentery and impatience caused a severe stomach ailment. He vomited so heavily that he burst a blood vessel. Alone in a monastery, he died and was buried in an unmarked grave. Newspapers in Europe and America mourned the passing of a great explorer.

WHETHER SCRIBBLING IN HIS uncle's law offices in Hartford, a dusty garret in Paris or a lonely hut in Siberia, Ledyard wrote with transcending passion. Incessantly inquisitive, he relished new experiences. He tasted a purportedly roasted human arm in British Columbia, got a tattoo in Tahiti, went to the slave market in Cairo, and sounded for the bottom of Lake Baikal in a driving rain. In a Whitmanesque, I-contain-multitudes style, Ledyard wrote, "I have a heart as big as St Pauls church."

His prose was ebullient and idiosyncratic. Well educated for the average American in the 18th century, he had attended grammar schools in Connecticut and Long Island and studied for a year at Dartmouth. He was well versed in the popular books of the time. Biblical language, especially from the Old Testament, frequently cropped up in his prose. He quoted or referred to Virgil, Calvin, Shakespeare, Confucius, Pope, Addison, Milton, Cervantes, and Sterne. He avidly read plays and directed and acted in one at Dartmouth, and there was a theatrical element to his storytelling—Shakespearean soliloquy, overheated rhetoric, a comic turn of phrase, and a conversational tone. He transmogrified his fur trading scheme into a donkey with whom he occasionally bantered. He peppered his paragraphs with spicy aphorisms: "An American face does nor wear well like an American heart" and "speak kind of Anthony ye who have not seen a Cleopatra."

His 1783 Journal was not a diary but rather a free-flowing memoir that regularly jumped the strict chronological tracks of the voyage. He was careless with grammar, spelling, punctuation, and syntax. He worshipped perhaps too fervently at the altar of the exclamation point and the colon, while far too often ignoring the sacred practice of starting a sentence with a capital letter. His book contained typographical errors and clumsy writing. Still, he has always attracted acolytes. Ledyard wrote so well that he startled friends who expected a much blunter pen. Thomas Jefferson wrote that Ledyard had "a talent for useful & interesting observation" and called him "a man of genius, of some science." Thomas Paine spoke about the reaction people had when first reading Ledyard's *Captain Cook's Last Voyage*: "His manner of writing had surprised them as they at first conceived him a bold but illiterate adventurer. That man, said Sir Joseph [Banks] one day to me, 'was all Mind.'" Thoreau and Melville were enraptured by Ledyard's writings.

Ledyard's 1783 Journal is notable for its perspectives. It was the only one from the 18th-century age of British circumnavigations written by an American. Furthermore, it is the only one from the third voyage written in English by a nonofficer. Unburdened by a fealty to the British crown which funded the trip, and with a different perspective as a common man, Ledyard constructed a divergent set of reasonings for Cook's death in Hawaii that blamed Cook as much as the islanders for the trouble that led to the captain's death. Historians have analyzed the events of January and February 1779 in Hawaii like almost no other period in the age of exploration, and at times Ledyard's descriptions, especially with his rendering of the infamous fence incident of February 4, seem at variance with other primary sources. Writing four years after the event without his own notes placed him at a disadvantage, as did the fact that he was a lowly marine not privy to information from the ships' officers or the island's leadership. Ledyard shaped his narrative in an honest attempt to make sense of a tumultuous and confusing event. Although he accused Cook of outrageous behavior, he bore little personal animus toward his former captain. In 1788 he wrote in his diary that he admired Cook's "Abilities & good Sense, [that he was] accustomed to think for himself & rely upon his own Opinion. It rendered him equally penetrating, cautious & bold." Even today, historians argue over what exactly happened those fateful weeks in 1779 and why, and Ledyard's account is rightfully considered one of the standard texts.

Regardless, Ledyard's *Journal* held a unique place in the Cook historical pantheon. For 200 years historians, missionaries, settlers and journalists saw Ledyard as the sole authentic eyewitness about Cook's last hours because he so brilliantly crafted his story that it appeared as if he was at his captain's side. Only in the 1960s did historians, led by Ken Munford, conclusively determine that Ledyard, in fact, had been on the beach a mile away rather in the detachment of marines accompanying Cook.

Valuable for their storytelling, the 1783 *Journal* and his letters and diaries, are equally fascinating for Ledyard's obsession with people. Unlike many of his contemporaries, he avidly catalogued social customs, diets, hunting equipment, vocabularies, and political systems. Although he sometimes resorted to stereotyping and racist comments, especially about Polish Jews in his Russian journal, he more often praised natives. Attempting to give a nuanced, rounded account of indigenous peoples' lives, he stepped out of his marine boots or traveler's shoes to see matters from their point of view. "Their charity to the dead is consistent with the real idea of this virtue, and breaths the purest spirit of philanthropy," he wrote about the islanders' burial ceremonies for a *Resolution* sailor who died in Hawaii. "It is an example that will put seven eighths of Christendom to the blush." His comments on native women attained near-cultlike status in the 19th century. Ledyard's motto—"the full exertion of extreme power is an argument of extreme weakness"—stemmed from his observations of native reactions to Cook's increasingly violent acts of punishment for theft.

Not content with compiling lists and facts, Ledyard mused on grand concepts like migration, beliefs, and the course of civilization. He argued that Native Americans had migrated from Siberia. Others had mooted it before, but as the first person to have personal knowledge of Native Americans on both sides of North America and Native Siberians, Ledyard's conclusions had tremendous force. More radical was that he reversed the accepted path of development. He suggested that civilization was the original state of existence and perhaps all societies originally started out civilized, with the natives he encountered having only slipped further from that original ideal than Europeans. He also declared that differences in skin color resulted from natural causes rather than being caused by God, thus debunking a common theory of the time that the different races had different origins and that all humans were not descended from common ancestors.

Strikingly modern in sensibility, Ledyard knew his limitations. He was proud of his storytelling ability and admitted, when recounting the reaction of Hawaiians to fireworks, that "I do think this part of the scene undescribable." Still, unlike his more judgmental contemporaries, he rarely made blanket generalizations and more than once declared that as a protoanthropologist he would, almost by definition, be unable to get the true story. Writing to Thomas Jefferson in February 1786, Ledyard said that "I had frequently observed that when a European queried a savage about a circumstance that perhaps he was totally ignorant of, that he was nevertheless unwilling that the European should know it or even think that he was ignorant and to divert his suspicions would make use of the most wily arts and rather than appear to be less informed of the common affairs of his country than the European would say any thing to make the European think favourably of him." Later in Siberia he discovered, much to his amusement, that an attempt to learn the language of the Aleuts on Unalaska Island in 1778 had made a mockery of his good intentions. Ledyard had pointed to a ship. An Aleut companion, Ledyard later learned, said the Russian phrase for "I know," but Ledyard wrote down an Aleut phrase next to "a ship." At the end of the session, he gave the Aleut some tobacco. The Aleut said the Russian word for "little," but Ledyard wrote down in his phrase book that the Aleut had said the Aleutian word for "more."

ALTHOUGH THIS COLLECTION bears John Ledyard's name as author, a surprisingly small amount can be confidently described as appearing exactly as he penned it. I have tried to reproduce the original texts as faithfully as possible. Yet it is maddeningly unclear if the ampersands, em dashes, and capitalized nouns, let alone his phrasing and vocabulary, are the choices of Ledyard or a transcriber.

The only text directly intended for publication was his 1783 *Journal*. Ledyard wrote the manuscript in the winter and spring of 1783 in the law offices of his uncle, Thomas Seymour. He left Hartford in early May. The printer, a Scot named Nathaniel Patten, issued the first half of the book in June and the second half in July. The final edition—a leather-bound, duodecimo edition numbering 208 pages in a small, 4-by-71/2 inch volume—sold very well. Booksellers in Philadelphia advertised it. Patten tinkered with the type and issued new editions. He also included a map of the voyage, to which an anonymous etcher added a decorative border of palm trees, harbors and ships. Enough copies circulated that more than two centuries later the 1783 Journal resides in dozens of libraries across the country and booksellers still regularly sell copies for around $2,000.

One of the beguiling aspects of the 1783 Journal is its place in the history of copyright. In a January 1783 letter to the Connecticut Assembly, Ledyard asked for "the exclusive right of publishing this said Journal or history in this State for such a term as shall be thot fit." In response, the assembly formed a committee that reported days later that "in their Opinion a publication of the Memorialists Journal in his voyage round the Globe may be beneficial to these United States & to the world, & it appears reasonable & Just that the Memorialist should have an exclusive right to publish the same for a Reasonable Term." The Connecticut Assembly not only accepted the report but expanded upon it and at the end of January issued an "Act for the encouragment of Literature and Genius," announcing that if a person was a resident of the United States he had sole power to publish a book for 14 years and had the right to apply for a second term of another 14 years. In March 1783 Massachusetts passed a similar act, in April Maryland did likewise, and by April 1786 all U.S. states had a copyright law. In May 1790 the U.S. Congress passed the first national law protecting copyright. Thus, A Journal of Captain Cook's Last Voyage, although it did not contain a notice of Connecticut's copyright in its front matter, had the historic distinction of being the catalyst for American copyright protection.

It was supremely ironic, therefore, that Ledyard's book was marred by plagiarism. On his desk he might have had copies of the official version of the second expedition, written by Cook and published in 1777, as well as unsanctioned versions from the first voyage (Magra, 1771 and Parkinson, 1773) and the second voyage (Marra, 1775 and Forster fils and pere, 1777 and 1778). He certainly had a copy of John Hawkesworth's three-volume An Account of the Voyages Undertaken by the Order of His Present Majesty for Making Discoveries in the Southern Hemisphere, published in London in 1773. Hawkesworth had mixed many officers' logs, including the journals of

Cook, to distill the Admiralty-sanctioned version of the first Cook voyage, as well as three previous expeditions from the 1760s. Ledyard borrowed fairly frequently from Hawkesworth. He used his Tahitian vocabulary list, lifted phrasing and ideas and occasionally a verbatim sentence. The most egregious theft, though, was from another account of the third Cook voyage: *Journal of Captain Cook's Last Voyage to the Pacific Ocean on Discovery; Performed in the Years 1776, 1777, 1778, 1779*, published anonymously in 1781 in London. Ledyard used the 1781 book for details—his dates, longitude and latitude measurements (which he sometimes miscopied) and bearings—that he would not have been able to remember without notes and probably, as a marine not on the quarterdeck, would not have known otherwise. He also reproduced a number of anecdotes and descriptive material. Most egregiously he took the final 38 pages of his book—the voyage from Kamchatka in June 1779 to London in October 1780—verbatim from the anonymous edition.

The theft of 11,000 words was noticeable within months of Ledyard's publication date. In the fall of 1783 Robert Bell, a Philadelphia publisher, saw the great sales of Ledyard's *Journal* and issued a version of the anonymous 1781 journal. With both Ledyard's and the 1781 book circulating, readers soon discovered that Ledyard had plagiarized. Because of his appropriations, Ledyard was considered the author of the anonymous 1781 edition; only in 1921 did a Canadian historian, F.W. Howay, take the trouble to decipher obvious clues that pointed decisively to John Rickman of the *Discovery* as its author.

It was never clear whether Ledyard or Patten was at fault. Ledyard was in a rush to start his fur-trading scheme. He left a number of blanks in the manuscript, clearly anticipating a time when he would return to the book before it was set in type. In such a state, he could have deliberately copied the text into his manuscript or could have asked Patten to fill out the story as he saw fit. Or Patten, holding a manuscript that ended 16 months earlier, could have, in Ledyard's absence, lifted the material himself. The only hint of self-awareness was in the subtitle of the book which included the years 1776 though 1779, but not 1780. Perhaps Ledyard or Patten, feeling guilty about the stolen pages, deliberately titled the book to disavow the Rickman selection. Yet, Rickman's book title also did not have 1780 in its list of dates. Either way, Rickman's words, often plodding and tedious, do not add much to the story of the voyage and it is best to remove the stain of plagiarism from Ledyard's memoir. Thus, the *Journal* reprinted here ends on June 17, 1779, the last sentence before a verbatim copy of Rickman begins.

Although the 1783 *Journal* is problematic because of the plagiarism, most of the other material included below suffers from a similar issue of authenticity. There are 62 extant letters of Ledyard's. Many exist only in someone else's hand. These were copied by his cousin, Isaac Ledyard, or by his cousin Ben's brother-in-law, Philip Freneau. In the 1790s Isaac Ledyard and Freneau compiled a *Life & Letters* manuscript of Ledyard. A copy of the three-volume, unpaginated manuscript resides at Dartmouth College. It contains 40 letters mostly written from Ledyard to Isaac, commentary by the compiler, and part of his Russian diary. (The Connecticut Historical Society holds a facsimile of the manuscript.) A few of the original letters used in compiling the manuscript exist, and an examination of both reveals that a somewhat heavy hand edited, rephrased, capitalized and cut out much of Ledyard's original prose. Of the 30 letters reprinted here, nine of them exist only in the *Life & Letters* manuscript; the rest are original.

Ledyard's journals also do not have a perfect provenance. His 1787-88 diary about Siberia is not positively as he wrote it. In the spring of 1788 Ledyard promised to make a copy of the Siberian journal for his cousin Isaac, but it appears he ran out of time. Before he left for Cairo, he gave the original journal (he lost part of it in Irkutsk when he was arrested) to Henry Beaufoy, one of his sponsors from the African Association. After Ledyard's death, Isaac Ledyard corresponded with Beaufoy and Sir Joseph Banks and eventually received the journal or a transcription of the journal. It covered the time from Ledyard's departure from St. Petersburg on June 1, 1787 to his arrival in Nizhni Novgorod on March 12, 1788. The compiler of the 1790s *Life & Letters* then copied the journal into the manuscript. The journal and other letters that were the basis of the *Life & Letters* were then lost at some point early in the nineteenth century, but copies of the *Life & Letters* manuscript remained extant.

Dartmouth owns another portion of Ledyard's Russian journal. It is a copy, not an original, made possibly under Ledyard's direction, but more likely under Henry Beaufoy's in the 1790s. The journal is 161 pages. The first 80 correspond to the *Life & Letters* journal section covering Ledyard's entries from his arrival in Yakutsk to his stay in Nizhni Novgorod; the rest concerns the journey from Moscow through Poland to just before he reached Konigsberg. The Beaufoy transcript has more flavor and texture than the *Life & Letters* version, though it appears that both of the tran-scripts enjoyed a transcriber's tamperings. Dartmouth bought the Beaufoy transcript for £85 in 1927.

A tiny, seven-page transcript of Ledyard's Russian journal is housed at the New-York Historical Society. It was presented to the Society in 1879 by a distant relative of Ledyard's. Not in Ledyard's handwriting, the journal overlaps with the *Life & Letters* transcript concerning Ledyard's initial observations in Yakutsk in September 1787.

Like Stephen D. Watrous in his thorough 1966 compilation of Ledyard's Russian journal, I have selected the entire Beaufoy transcript because of its more vivid, Ledyard-like language, supplementing it when appropriate with the *Life & Letters* and N-YHS transcripts.

Ledyard's Egyptian journal is taken from the *Proceedings of the Association for Promoting the Discovery of the Interior Parts of Africa*, a 1790 volume written by Henry Beaufoy. Ledyard's original journal from Egypt is lost, and the text, as printed by Beaufoy, is all we have left.

This litany of transcripts, plagiarism, and lost letters does not obscure the essence presented here of one of the most original and adventurous American explorers. "Mad, romantic, dreaming Ledyard"—that was how, according to Ledyard, his friends saw him. Two hundred and sixteen years after he died, we can finally see him for ourselves.

PART I

A JOURNAL OF CAPTAIN COOK'S LAST VOYAGE

✳

As a junior marine officer, John Ledyard sailed on the Resolution, Capt. James Cook's ship on Cook's third and final voyage around the world. Ledyard's memoir covers from the day of departure from England in July 1776 to his departure from Petropavlovsk in June 1779. The book, entitled A Journal of Captain Cook's Last Voyage To the Pacific Ocean, and in Quest of a North-West Passage, Between Asia and America; Performed in the Years 1776, 1777, 1778, and 1779 and "faithfully narrated from the original MS. of Mr. John Ledyard," was published in the United States in the summer of 1783.

Ledyard dedicated the book to Jonathan Trumbull, the governor of Connecticut, adding that "the affability and generosity I was honored with you at my first arrival in my native country, after a long absence, was truely worthy the distinguished character you always have had, and I sincerely hope ever will sustain in this country; I have received it as a testimony of that original urbanity and dignified familiarity which distinguishes the magistrate from the tyrant—the people from slaves, and is still the boon of which every son of this country participates. Such virtues, like the rose in the bud, are lovely in ordinary life; but when transferred to the bosoms of the fair and great, become amiable character alone naturally inspires an attachment and wish to participate of its favors. Under this influence I have presumed to dedicate the following work to your patronage; being fully sensible that let its intrinsic merit be what *it will, the approbation which I humbly hope for from your beneficence will be absolutely necessary to its prosperity."*

The chapterless text naturally falls into three sections. The first covers the time from when Ledyard left England in July 1776 until he sailed from the Society Islands in December 1777. The itinerary included landfalls at Cape Town, Kerguelen Island in the southern Indian Ocean, Adventure Bay in Tasmania, Queen Charlotte's Sound in New Zealand, the Cook Islands (Mangaia, Atiu, Takutea, and Palmerston), Tonga (Nomuka, Lifuka, Tongatapu, and 'Eua), Tahiti, Moorea, Huahine, and Raiatea.

PREFACE

THE IMPORTANCE OF NAUTICAL discovery has encreased so much since the voyages of Vasca de Gama, Columbus and Magellan, that at this day mankind have the highest esteem for the information they receive in matters of this kind, and read the accounts of such travellers with the most liberal approbation, and consumate satisfaction: The following voyage among many others it is presumed will share the praises of the civilized and enlightened world; the object was noble, it was gloriously concluded, and terminated happily. The discovery of a North-West Passage from Europe to the East-Indies has long been an object of emulation and enterprise, and competitors in fame have risen among every commercial nation in Europe to determine its existence or non-existence: It will be needless to recapitulate the various instances of this kind in this work since they are to be found in works of that kind published by those Navigators themselves: neither do the many other discoveries made at different times in the southern hemisphere come properly within the limits of our present history. It may however be thought necessary to observe that all the former voyages made in quest of a North-West Passage have been on the north east side of America whereas this was made on the north-west side of that continent. The voyage commenced on the 12th day of July, 1776, and terminated on the 6th day of October, 1780; the equipment consisted of two ships: the *Resolution* of about six hundred tons burthen, and the *Discovery* of about three hundred tons: the first commanded by Capt. JAMES COOK, and the latter by Capt. CHARLES CLERKE.

A VOYAGE PERFORMED IN HIS BRITANNIC MAJESTY'S SHIP RESOLUTION, IN COMPANY WITH THE DISCOVERY, UNDER THE COMMAND OF CAPT. JAMES COOK.

On the 12th day of July 1776 the *Resolution* unmoored, and dropt from Plymouth Sound into Corson-Bay: and on the 13th weighed again and came to sail, standing down the Channel. The *Discovery* who was to be our consort, was at this time detained at the Nore on account of her commander, Captain Clerke: uneasy at his delays and anxious to proceed, Captain Cook was determined to proceed and wait for him at the Cape of Good-Hope, and left instructions behind proper for the occasion to be delivered to captain Clerke when he should reach Plymouth.

Our present destination was the Cape of Good-Hope, and as it is seldom any occurrences happen in a passage so familiar as this, worthy the notice of an ingenious reader, I shall only observe that we touched at Teneriff, and looked into Porto Praya at St. Jago, and made the best of our way to the Cape. In general we had a very favorable passage, and arrived safe before the town in Table-Bay the middle of September following. The *Discovery* after a very tedious passage did not join us untill three weeks after our arrival. The *Resolution* in the mean time had nearly refited to renew the voyage, and was on that account able to assist in forwarding the *Discovery*, so that by the 27th of November both ships were in order for sea.

The Cape of Good-Hope is very romantic and some how majestically great by nature: the mountains that form the promontory are as rugged as lofty, they impel the imagination to wonder rather than admire the novelty. But the town and garrison at their feet display a contrast that molifies and harmonizes so as to render the whole highly finished. The land near the town was entirely barren until improved by the industry of the inhabitants, which has rendered it very fertile. The adjacent country is highly luxuriant, and no place can boast a greater plenty or variety of productions: their wines are very fine, particularly the Constantia so much celebrated and so seldom drank in its purity in Europe.

As this was the only port we had the least expectation of visiting that was possessed by Europeans until our return we improved it to the best advantage in accumulating the best stores and as great a quantity of them as possible, against the day of adversity, which we had a right to anticipate; but after our ships were already so filled that we could not stow in the whole above eighteen months provisions at full allowance: but reduced to an allowance of two thirds the estimate would be two years provisions, and this was the case as soon as we left the Cape, and continued so the whole voyage, unless relieved by the adventitious supplies of some fortunate Island. It was also expected that we should take with us a collection of the animal species in order to distribute among the remote Islands we should visit—we accordingly took on board four horses, six horned cattle, a number of sheep and goats, hogs, dogs and cats, besides, hares, rabbits and monkeys, ducks, geese, turkies and peacocks; thus did we resemble the ark and appear as though we were going as well to stock, as to discover a new world.

On the first day of December we took our departure from this great promontory and launched into that immense ocean which surrounds so great a part of the southern hemisphere. Our course from the Cape was about S.S.E. half E. and as we advanced to the southward the weather was not only very stormy and tempestuous, but rendered highly disagreeable when not so, by a constant series of foggs.

On the 13th we came in sight of land lightly covered with snow, which proved to be two islands discovered a few years since by Monsieur Marion, they are in lat. 46. 18. South.

On the 23d we discovered a distant resemblance of land.

On the 25th stood in to the land, and sent boats to reconnoitre the coast.

On the 26th having received a favorable report from the boats we entered a deep bay that afforded us a good retreat and came to anchor.

On the 27th as a number of our people were rambling about the shore in the bay, one of them found a glass bottle suspended by a wire between two rocks: it was corked and sealed over with a parchment within it. he brought it on board to be examined by the Captain, well imagining the circumstance to be very extraordinary.[1] Upon examination we found wrote in the French and Latin languages an account imparting that in the year 1772, this island was discovered by Mons. de Kergulen: that it contained plenty of water but no weed, that it was barren and without inhabitants; but that the shores abounded with fish, and the land with seals, sea-lions, and penguins &c.

The contents of the parchment were entirely true, and a short account of the voyager who left it may therefore be necessary to render our discoveries the more complete.

"Mons. de Kergulen, a lieutenant in the French service, had the command of 2 ships given him, the *la Fortune* and *le Gros Ventre*. He sailed from the Mauritius about the latter end of the year 1771, and on the 13th of January following he discovered the island we are now speaking of, and named it the Isle of Fortune. Soon after Mons. de Kergulen saw land, as it is said of a considerable extent, upon which he sent one of his officers in a boat to sound a-head; but the wind blowing fresh the Captain of the other ship (Mons. de St. Allouarn) in the *Gros*

Ventre, shot a-head and finding a bay to which he gave his ship's name, ordered his yawl to take possession. In the mean time, Mons. de Kergulen being driven to leward and unable to recover his station again, both boats returned on board the Gros-Ventre, and the one of them soon after cut a-drift on account of bad weather.

Mons. de Kergulen returned to the Mauritius, and Mons. de St. Allouarn continued for three days to take the bearings of the land, and doubled its northern extremity beyond which it trended S.E. After this he shiped his course to New-Holland, and from thence returned by the way of Timor and Batavia to the Isle of France where he died. Mons. de Kergulen was afterwards promoted to the command of a 64 gun ship, called the Rolland with the frigate l'Oiseau, in order to perfect the discovery of the pretended land; but returned with disgrace."[2]

That the land we now fell in with is the same discovered by Kergulen is certain, but that he ever saw a great country, such as he pretends near this, is very problematical.

This land lies in lat. 49. 30. south and in 78.10. east long. from the meridian of Greenwich: Mons. de Kergulen had laid it down very erroniously being nearly two degrees to the northward. It is ragged, detached, and almost totally barren; it seems to have been fitly appropriated by nature to be the residence of the innumerable herds of sea-dogs, and seals that cover its shores: there are also vast flocks of different kinds of sea-birds; it is without any kind of woods, or even shrubery, and the only plant we could find of the culinary kind was a species of wild cabbage, which was as wretched as the soil it was indigenous to.

On the 30th we took leave of this forlorn land and proceeded to the southern extremity of New-Holland called Van Diemans Land, from a Dutch navigator of that name.

From the 1st of January 1777 to the 19th we had a succession of hard gales of wind in which we lost one of our topmasts, and were otherwise very roughly dealt with.

On the 24th the Discovery made the signal for seeing land, which proved to be New-Holland.

On the 26th we stood off and on, to find the bay called by Tasman, Frederick Henry's Bay.

On the 27th entered Frederick Henry's Bay and moored both ships. We remained at this place only a few days, in which time we procured a good recruit of wood and water, and such grass for the animals on board as the country afforded; we caught a tolerable supply of fish with our seins, and this joined with our exercises refreshed the people.

The accounts given by Capt. Cook in a former voyage of New-Holland are so full and perfect, and our present visit was so partial that it entirely excludes any of my observation: Yet I cannot but remark the disparity which is so obvious, between a noble country and its ignoble inhabitants: The island of New-Holland (for its boundaries are now ascertained) is by much the largest now known, and most eligably situated in the map of nature, about one half within and the other without the tropic of Capricorn, and its extent is fully sufficient to gratify the most ambitious with—even the Empress of Russia might be gratified with such a portion. From its northern extremity opposite New-Guinea to its southern called Van Dieman's, it comprehends above 30 degrees of lat. and from east to west about 43 degrees of longit. The vicinity of its northern boundaries to the most commercial parts of the East-Indies is also a most glorious circumstance: and yet with all these advantages, the New-Hollander is a mere savage, nay more he possesses the lowest rank even in this class of beings—at least those I saw to the southward were such. They are the only people who are known to go with their persons entirely naked that have even been yet discovered. Amidst the most stately groves of wood they have neither weapons of defence, or any other species of instruments applicable to any other of the various purposes of life; contaguous to sea they have no canoes and exposed from the nature of the climate to the natural inclemancies of the seasons as well as from the anoyances of the beasts of the forest; they have no houses to retire to, but the temporary shelter of a few pieces of old bark laid transversely over some small poles: They appear also to be inactive, indolent and unaffected with the least appearances of curiosity, they are of a middling stature, but indifferent in their persons, of a dark complexion bordering on black, their hair a little wooly, their features discordant and without any kind of ornament or dress. As we had observed no quadrupedes of the domestic kind here we left a boar and a sow, which were presented to an elderly man among them: We also distributed as presents among them several medals to perpetuate the memory of the voyage. Our botanical researches were tolerably successful.

On the 1st of February we left New-Holland, and on the 10th were off Charlotte-Sound at New-Zealand.

On the 12th we entered a cove, and both ships moored. New-Zealand consists of two islands separated by a narrow strait called Cook's Straits: Taken collectively they are about six hundred miles long, but very equal in breadth: They are situated between the 35th and 47th degrees of southern lat. and between 166th and 179th degrees of long. east from Greenwich; and as the climate is admirable, so is the appearance of the soil, but near the sea-coast the land is inclined to be mountainous: It is almost every where covered with stately forests and almost impenetrable thickets: The country appears to be but thinly inhabited, and we conjecture that this failure in population originates chiefly from the constant state of warfare that subsists among the inhabitants, their feeble advancements in agriculture, and the desultory manner of their lives in general. The New-Zealanders are generally well made, strong and robust particularly the chiefs, who among all the savage sons of war I ever saw, are the most formidable. When a New Zealander stands forth and brandishes his spear the subsequent idea is (and nature makes the confession) there stands a man. It is their native courage, their great personal prowess, their irreversible intrepidity, and determined fixed perseverance that is productive of those obstinate attacks we have found among them when we have appealed to the decisions of war. In the article of dress among them there is but little diversification: In common they wear a clout about the loins, fabricated from a species of grass, which they twist and unite together so as to resemble our manner of weaving, but if the season or their caprice requires; they add what they call the Bugabuga or the Toga, and sometimes both. The Bugabuga is a very coarse covering made with little trouble, and affords a good shelter from cold or wet weather: The Toga is different and is equally calculated for use and elegance: The Bugabuga is formed round and converging to the top where there is an apperture just sufficient to admidt the head to pass through, and when on, covers the body as low as the hip: If it storms, or they have occasion to stop where they have no other shelter they squat down upon their hams, and then the bottom of the Bugabuga reaching the ground, forms a shelter to the whole body (the head excepted) which looks in that situation as if it had been severed from a human form, and fixed upon a hay-cock. The Toga is their ne plus ultra in this sort of manufactory: It is in size and form like a common blanket; its texture is simple, but the industry and ingenuity bestowed upon it in other respects renders it compact, strong, and handsome: The materials of the manufacture are the grass before-mentioned, which is a kind of silk-grass, said to be indigenous to the country, and the hair of the dogs blended together. This garment they wear mantlewise, commonly leaving the right arm and breast uncovered, carrying a spear in the right hand from thirty to forty feet long. They paint their faces with a coarse red paint, and oil or grease the head and upper part of the body: The hair in both sexes as well as their dress is wore much alike, and being generally long and black, it is tied up in a knot upon the top of the head. They are very curiously tatowed or punctuated in different parts of the body, particularly in the face. The food of the New-Zealanders is chiefly fish, some of which they dry and some they eat raw: They have also some yams upon the northern Island, but not in plenty: They have no hogs or other animals, except a few small dogs, which they eat occasionally, They have fine large strong canoes, some of which will carry upwards of an hundred men, and in these they generally fight their enemies.

Notwithstanding New-Zealand has been visited several times by different voyagers, and particularly by Cook, yet their ferocious manners have prevented their visitants from being otherwise than very partially acquainted with their manners and customs: Put in general they may be said to resemble those who have no other guide to knowledge or improvements, but the strong dictates of nature and necessity, and the direction of a few traditionary precepts, and these rendered imperfect by time and the imperfection of the mind: After a labored enquiry on our part with regard to their ancestors and the original population of the country, the only information we have obtained, is, "That their fore-fathers at some very remote period, but how remote they knew not, came from a far distant island called Hawyjee." This is imperfect, but as we afterwards actually discovered an island called by its inhabitants Owyhee, or rather as they pronounce it Hawyhee. I cannot think the information useless, but highly fortunate, as will be remarked hereafter.

As to the religion of the New-Zealanders we know little about it, however this I shall not hesitate to observe, that they have some idea that respects a God, and they are not ashamed of him, and if marriage is a religious ceremony with them, they also do that great honor; for here, as well as among the tropical islands, adultry is punished with death, and the spurious offspring of such an intercourse shares the same fate; but this last piece of policy, for I cannot call it virtue, will not I think redound to their honor; it seems however to be the case with all uncivilized beings to be actuated by extremes. They are susceptable of the tender passions, and their women of communicating as well as receiving the most ardent love. Belonging to the *Discovery* there was a youth, with whom a young Zealander girl, about fourteen years of age, fell desperately in love, nor was he wholly indifferent to this engaging Brunett; what time he would spare he generally retired with her, and they spent the day, but oftener the night in a kind of silent conversation, in which, though words were wanting, their meaning was perfectly understood; the language of love among all the languages in this sublunary world is the soonest comprehended.[3] But though our sailor appeared amiable in her eyes in the habit of a stranger he was conscious that to ornament his person in the fashion of New Zealand would recommend him more to his mistress and the country he was in, he therefore submitted himself to be tatowed from head to foot, nor was she less solicitous on her part to set herself off to the best advantage. She had fine hair, and her chief pride was in the dressing of her head. The pains she took, and the decorations she used would perhaps have done honor to an European beauty, had not one thing been wanting to render it still more pleasing.

Gowannahee, (that was her name) though young, was not so delicate but that the traits of her country might be traced in her locks, to remedy this misfortune she was furnished with combs and taught by her lover how to use them. After being properly prepared he would by the hour amuse himself with forming her hair into ringlets, rendering them fit for the residence of the little loves. The distaste arising from colour gradually wore off; their sentiments improved, and from imparting their passions, they became at last capable and desirous of communicating the history of their lives to each other. Love and jealousy directed her inquiries concerning the women in the country from whence he came, wishing at the same time that he would stay with her and be a Chief. He made her to understand that the women in her country were man-eaters, and if he should stay with her he might also be eat by them; she answered no, and said she would love him. He said the men would kill him when left behind and alone. She said no if he did not shoot them. He acquainted her that nine or ten of his countrymen had been killed and eaten by them though they did not shoot the men of her country. Her answer was, that was a great while ago, and the people who did it, came from the hills a great way off. This excited his curiosity to know if any of her relations were among the murderers; she sighed and appeared much affected when he asked her that question. He asked if she was at the feast when they broiled and eat the men? She wept, hung down her head and said nothing. He became still more pressing as she grew reserved; he tried every wining way that love and curiosity suggested, to learn from her what he found she knew and seemed inclined to conceal, but she artfully avoided his enquiries. He asked her why she was so secret? She pretended not to understand him. Finding all his persuasions ineffectual he turned from her, seemingly in great anger, and threatened to leave her; this had its intended effect, she caught him round the neck;—he asked her what she meant? She said her countrymen would kill her if she should divulge any thing; he said they should not know it; but won't you hate me said she? He said no, but love her more and pressed her to his breast; she grew composed, and finally informed him what she knew about the matter.

She gave him to understand that one Gooboa, a very bad man, who had been often at the ship and had stolen many things, when he came to understand she was about to sail went up into the hill country and invited the warriors to come down and kill the strangers. They at first refused, saying the strangers were stronger than they, particularly insinuating the force of the fire arms, he told them they need not fear, for he knew where they must come before they departed, in order to procure grass for their cattle, and that on such occasions they left their fire-arms behind them in the ship or carelessly about the ground, while they were at work. They said they were no enemies but friends, and that they must not kill men with whom they were in friendship. Gooboa said they were vile enemies, and complained of their chaining him and beating him, and shewed them the marks and bruizes he had received at the ship: And told them besides how they might destroy their fire-arms by throwing water over them. Gooboa undertook to conduct them in safety to the place where the strangers were to come, and shewed them where they might conceal themselves until he should come and give them notice, which he did. And when the men were busy about getting grass and not thinking any harm, the warriors rushed out upon them and killed them with their Patapatows, and then divided their bodies among them. She added that there were women as well as men concerned, and that the women made the fires while the warriors cut the dead men in pieces; that they did not eat them all at once; the the warriors had the heads which were esteemed the best, and the rest of the flesh was distributed among the croud. Having by various questions in the course of several days obtained this relation of which he said he had no reason to doubt the truth, he forbore to ask her what part of her relations and herself bore in this tragedy as there was reason to believe they were all equally concerned. He was however very solicitious to learn if any such plot was now in agitation against the people that might be sent upon the same service to Grass-Cove or elsewhere. Her answer was, no; the warriors were afraid at first that the ships were come to revenge the death of their friends, and that was the reason why she was forbidden to speak of killing the strangers, or to confess any knowledge of it were she asked the question. She said she was but a child about ten years old, but she remembered the talk of it as a great achievement; and that they made songs in praise of it.

On the 25th of February the ships being ready for sea, the precaution of mustering the ships-company was taken, when it was found that one was missing: This was our adventurer who with his faithful Gowannehee had completely made their escape. A messenger was immediately dispatched on board the *Resolution* to know how to proceed: And when the message was delivered, the captains and officers were joyous over their bottle. At first it only furnished a subject of pleasantry; but it came at last to be seriously debated whether the man should be sent for back, or not. Most were for leaving him to follow his own humor: But Capt. Cook thinking it would be a bad precedent, and an encouragement to other enamoratoes, when they came to the happier climates to follow the example, was for sending an armed force and bringing the man back at all hazards. Of this opinion was his own Captain with whom he was a favorite, who gave orders for the cutter to be properly manned, a serjeant's guard of marines to be put on board, and his mess-mate to be a guide to direct them, for it was supposed he knew where he was. This was instantly done. It was midnight before the cutter reached the intended rendezvous, and two in the morning before the guard found the spot where the lovers were. They suprized them in a profound sleep locked in each others arms, dreaming no doubt of love, of kingdoms, and of diadems; of being the progenitors of a numerous family of princes to govern the kingdoms of Ea-kei-nommauwee and T'Avi-Poenammoo. Love like this is not to be found in those countries where the boasted refinements of sentiment too often circumscribe the purity of affection and narrow it away to mere conjugal fidelity. God of love and romance! this pair ought to have been better heeded by thee, and at least secluded from the pursuit of those who never did, and perhaps never will be able to offer to thy deityship one single sacrifice of pure, sublimated romantic sentiment. Turn thine eyes now and behold the predicament in which thy cruelty, thy caprice and thy ingratitude, thou hypocrite hath left the forlorn Gowannahee and her hapless Mate! Even the rugged guard when they came to bind their prisoner could not but wish they had never seen the unfortunate shipmate, who was not only rendered unhappy in his affections, but had still to abide the rigid sentence of a court very unlike to love. But the situation of the guard was critical least the cries and lamentations of Gowannahee should rouse the savages to slaughter under the advantages of a dark night and a thick wood, they therefore hastened to the cutter leaving this unfortunate girl the picture of most distressing anguish. It was noon the next day before they arrived at the ships, and the captains began to be anxious for the safety of the people. When they arrived the prisoner was carried on board the commodore, where he underwent a long examination, and made a full confession of all his views and the pains he had taken to bring them to perfection. That he had considered the hazard and reward, and that the ardent love for his Gowannahee had determined him, and would, had the dangers that might have ensued been greater. Capt. Cook astonished at the young man's extravagant notions, pleased at his frankness instantly forgave him and ordered him to his duty, telling him he was convinced that even his present situation and feelings must be a sufficient punishment for a much greater crime.

On the 27th of February both ships came to sail, and on the 28th cleared the land passing through Cook's Straits.

We took with us from New-Zealand two boys; the oldest called Tiberua, was about seventeen years old: The other called Kohaw was about ten. Tiberua was the son of a Chief, stout and well made, but of a ferocious gloomy aspect: Kohaw was a young lively agreeable child. It is said they were purchased from their parents; if they were, it was upon such conditions as were kept concealed. They were however intended by Captain Cook as servants to Omai (the native of Otaheite) and were to be left with him at that Island.

The cattle we had on board which we brought from the Cape Good-Hope were in good circumstances having been well refreshed by being on shore: and we had procured a good supply of such wild grass as New-Zealand afforded for their subsistance at sea. We had also made a considerably quantity of beer from the spruce of that country, which is good and in unbounded plenty. It is esteemed an excellent for beverage and a great anti-scorbutic While it lasted the allowance of spirits was withheld from the people. We also took wild celery and scurvy-grass with us to sea, both which are natural to the country. Our course from New-Zealand was generally E.B.N. March is ever a blowing month and we here felt its force having from the first of that month to the 20th experienced a succession of hard gales, and as we approached the tropic of Capricorn violent rains; but these were sent in mercy to us for we were much distressed for water.

On the 29th of March we made land, which proved to be a new-discovered island called by the natives Manganooanooa it lies in lat. 21.54.

south and in 201 59 east long. it is about eight leagues in length and four in breadth: It makes a delightful appearance and like other tropical islands in this ocean is covered thick with cocoanut, palm, bread-fruit and other trees, and productions common to the climate.

On the 30th we went in with the land, and being about a mile and an half from the shore saw 5 or 600 people armed with spears and clubs drawn up in a body upon the beach shouting and runing about, but whether they appeared here to oppose our landing or only in consequence of their surprize could not be determined, though the shore did not appear favourable, to see if we could find anchorage for the ships and some kind of a landing place for we were very short of water and the weather was hot but we were sometime withheld from doing this by the appearance of a canoe which we saw approaching the ship with one man in it. He approached the ship with diffidence but did not seem much terrified. As soon as he was near enough to us we shewed him several European trinkets and made such signs to him, as we thought he would best understand meaning to conciliate his good will and prevail upon him to come on board the ship. He accepted of some of the trifles offered him, particularly some shreds of scarlet broad cloth, but no iron. He would not come on board, but as he went away beckoned us to the shore and spoke to us: What we could understand of his discourse was a friendly assurance of good treatment, and that his country afforded both meat and drink. After this we sent three boats manned and armed to reconnoitre the shore, and determine if it was acceptable to the purposes of watering. They were absent the best part of the day, and finally returned with an account that the island was surrounded by one continued reef of coral rocks and could not be approached. This is much the case with all the tropical islands in the southern and northern pacific oceans. The boats during their absence had been incessantly surrounded by the inhabitants, some in canoes, others on floats made of bamboo, and some swiming. The most of them brought something with them: Some hogs, some fruit, and some the manufactures of the country, all of which were exchanged with us for almost nothing in our esteem, but highly pleasing to these new-found sons of Mur.[4]

The enterview we had with these people fully convinced us that they were (to appearance) the same people who inhabit the tropical islands in the two Pacifics. What these appearances are that constitute such an opinion will be amply treated of when it will be more agreeable to the historian and the reader to attend to them.

On the 31st we again discovered land, which proved to be another new-discovered island 20 leagues from Manganooanooa, called Awgadoo. This we passed without particular examination, judging from the tremendous surf upon its shores that it was equally inaccessable as Manganooanooa. On the 1st of April we were so fortunate as to fall in with another new-discovered island called by the natives Wastew, situate in lat. 19. 51. south, and long. 201. 28. east. This island we also found equally difficult to approach with our boats, but as their canoes are better calculated for a high surf, some of our officers were determined to land in them, and take a view of the island. Omai (the Otaheite Indian) was in their suite. When they landed they were for sometime unable to advance through the surrounding, wondering throng. They had not proceeded half a mile before they were plundered of every article they had about them: Some things were taken by mere dexterity, and others by force, which they thought prudent to submit to. After this they passed unmolested until they thought proper to return. When they arrived again to the sea-shore they found a number of people together round a large fire, and prepairing a roasted pig and some fruit for their entertainment. Our adventurers were rather perplexed when invited to the entertainment by the very people who had just robed them of every thing they had, and would have been glad to have excused themselves, but they thought it most prudent at this time to renounce their resentment, and give the smiters the other cheek: They therefore set down with them, and eat a most humiliating morsel—a thing badly digested in a British ship of war. They were however richly prepared for this misfortune by finding several natives of Heuheine among the company. Hueheine is one of the Society-Islands 500 leagues to the eastward of this. The circumstance was known as soon as the natives came to understand that Omai was one of that country. Our adventurers were all surprized at the information, but particularly Omai who impatient and transported flew into their arms in an excess of joy and wept for some time. It had its effect upon those who were less interested, and when the natives who had just plundered the strangers found Omai a former neighbour of these foreign inhabitants who were now chiefs among them, they returned every thing valuable they had taken from him and his companions, and loaded them with such presents as the country produced. As soon as these matters were settled Omai desired to be particularly informed how they came there; in this he was fully gratified, and related it afterwards to Capt. Cook in these words: "About twelve years from that time fourteen persons (including men, women and children) were removing with their effects from Hueheine to Otaheite (which both belong to a clutter of islands nearly in sight of each other called the Society-Islands) and were overtaken in a storm, blown off from the land and driven they knew not where for the space of thirteen days, during which time half their numbers had died through excessive fatigue and hunger, and that after that time they who had finally survived were rendered so extremely weak as to be insensible what happened to them until they found themselves on that island and in the hands of the people they were then among." Omai offered to interceed with the captains for his countrymen if they would accept of a passage and return to Otaheitee, which they declined. We had been laying to with the ships during this interview. And,

On the 4th of April we again came to sail.

On the 7th though we had caught several casks of rain water we were obliged to distil sea water into fresh for which purpose we had a machine on board. This water discoloured the meat that was boiled in it and tinctured other things with a disagreeable blackness, but was nevertheless equal to rain water which cannot well be caught in a ship without tasting of the tar communicated from the rigging. Our course was now about S.W. until the 18th when we fell in with a group of islands that were discovered about thirty years ago, called Palmerston-Isles. Some of these isles are uninhabited, low and without water; those which are inhabited are somewhat higher but inaccessable to our boats, and of consequence we did not visit them. The inhabitants according to the accounts of those who have visited them do not differ from those of the other islanders here abouts. We varied our course now from W.S.W. to N.W. Palmerston Isles are situate in lat. 18. 11. south, and 164. 14. east longit.

On the 25th we had hard gales of wind, thunder and fierce lightening. Hove to during the storm.

On the 26th at night we made sail and past an island called Savage-Island, discovered by Cook in a former voyage.

On the 29th we fell in with one of that group of islands called the Friendly Islands. This island by the natives is called Anamoca, but Abel Tasman a Dutch navigator who first discovered those islands called it Rotterdam: But I shall distinguish it by the name of Anamoca.

On the 30th we entered a road-stead on the north side of the Island and came to an anchor with both ships: we were immediately surrounded by the natives in their canoes as usual among all these islands, and without any ceremony entered into a free brisk traffic with them for their hogs and tropical fruits, which they exchanged very eagerly for little iron instruments or almost any thing of European manufacture, with which they were somewhat considerably acquainted from the visits of former voyagers.

On the 2nd of May we got such of our live stock on shore to graze as had survived the long and distressing passage we had undergone from New-Zealand hither, particularly for want of water. We also sent a guard on shore and people to wood and water. As this was the first opportunity we had hitherto had of a free intercourse with the inhabitants of the southern tropical islands, and as individuals were possessed of a plentiful supply of articles for traffic which they might dispose of to the natives for less than their real value and by that means hurt the trade that respected the supply of ships provision, Cook laid some restrictions on private bargains until further orders, which had a very good effect. We remained here until the 4th of May when after a most salutary refreshment of our people and the cattle we had on board besides having procured a considerable supply of pork which we salted, we set sail for a group of small islands, within sight to the northward called the Appy-Islands by the natives. I think we reckoned thirty-five of those islands, but, except four of them, they are very diminutive, and only resorted to occasionally from the larger ones the principal of which is called by the natives Calafoy, which is about thirty miles in circumference and thick inhabited. We were three days cruizing about among these islands. And,

On the 17th of May we anchored at Calafoy, where we remained until the 25th, and procured a fine supply of provisions, and had a very friendly interview with the inhabitants.

On the 26th we again came to sail, and returned to Anamoca, but having very bad weather we did not reach it until the 5th of June when we anchored in our old birth: We tarried here only four days, and,

On the 19th set sail for an island called by the natives Tongotaboo, and by Tasman Amsterdam, as being the largest island in all that group, which collectively we called the Friendly Isles. Tongotaboo lying S. W. about nine leagues from Anamoca we reached it the same night though we passed through very difficult navigation, and anchored in a fine harbour on the north side of the island about one fourth of a mile from the shore. The inhabitants who had heard of our arrival and expecting a visit from us came off to us to the number of two or three hundred canoes bringing large supplies of hogs and the provisions of the country.

On the 10th of June we carried two large tents, two astronomical tents and a markee a-shore accompanied by a strong guard of marines, and erected them on a spacious green encircled by a grove of tall trees about forty rods from the water-side, which lay north of our encampment on the east we had a beautiful lagoon that reached several miles into the country on the margin of which were dispersed some houses: On the south a branch of the same lagoon and on the west a thin tall woods in which was interspersed several more houses; after our tents were pitched and the guard appointed Cook went on shore attended by a chief called Polahow who was the supreme governor of all these islands and invited him to his markee. Polahow was a man about fifty-five years of age and about the middle stature, but excessive fat and corpulent, yet active and full of life; he was exceeding good natured and humane, very sensible and prudent, and remarkably timorous: He was attended by another chief called Phenow, who was one of the most graceful men I ever saw in the Pacific ocean. He was about 5 feet 11 inches high, fleshy but not fat, and completely formed: He was open and free in his disposition, full of vivacity, enterprizing and bold, expert in all the acquirements of his country, particularly in their art of navigation, over which he presided, and what is esteemed among them as a necessary ingredient in a great character was possessed of uncommon strength and agility; he was besides extremely handsome, he had a large prominent eye full of fire and great expression, an aquiline nose and a well formed face: His hair which was long, hung after the manner of the country in thick bushy ringlets over his shoulders: With all these accomplishments he was extremely popular among the people, and the idol of the fair, having himself one of the most beautiful brunetts for a wife that the hands of nature ever finished, but during our stay he was seldom with her or with us, his active soul was ever on the wing, and in his canoe which sailed exceedingly swift he would in twenty-four hours surround the whole group of islands, and almost visit them individually. If we lost any goods, and they were carried either in land upon Tongotaboo or to any of the detached islands our only confidential resource was Phenow; or if any other emergency required dispatch, policy, courage or force, Phenow was the man to advice and act. In short, without his particular assistance joined to that of Polahow our visit at this large populous island would have been one continual broil proceeding from the pilfering disposition of the inhabitants, our methods of obtaining satisfaction and their tumultuous and factious dispositions: But that my accounts of these two noble Indians may be entirely true and impartial. I must observe that notwithstanding this general attachment to our interest and friendship, which did them so much honor, and us so much essential service, they sometimes fell into temptation themselves and did as others did. How often, Phenow, have I felt for thee, the embarrassments of these involuntary offences against a people thou didst as well love and wouldst as soon have befriended when thou wast accused and stood condemned as when not, and at that instant would most willingly have shared with thee those distresses which resulted only from imputed guilt and a theory of moral virtue thou couldst be no farther acquainted with, than from the dictates of uncultivated nature or imagine from the countenances of strangers—more savage themselves with all their improvements than thou wert without a single one of them.

The conversations at the markee between Cook and these two Chiefs could be carried on but very indifferently from our ignorance of the language which though radically the same as at New-Zealand and Otaheitee yet differing in the dialect confounded us a good deal at first. It was however apparent that they were extremely friendly and disposed to do us all the good they could and as little ill as possible for Polahow intimated plainly to Cook that it did not lay in his power to do good at all times on account of his numerous subjects who would he said on such an occasion as our visit, even wrangle with one another and perhaps with the strangers, and when they went out of the markee Polahow to convince Cook in a stronger manner than he could by words of his sincerity led him accompanied still by Phenow to a snug commodious house of his own that was situated in a thick embowring shade about 20 paces from one of our tents and made him an offer of it: this Cook accepted, and afterwards made occasional use of, and sometimes Polahow lodged in it himself.

It was now near sun-set and Cook being desirous of teaching the natives (once for all) what he expected of them relative to their conduct at the tents, desired Polahow and Phenow to signify to their people that at the going down of the sun they must retire and by no means approach the ground they had given us until it again rose or his guard would kill them: Phenow instantly steped on to the green and proclaimed this intelligence to the natives that were present who all instantly retired; at the same time a picket marched while the drum beat a retreat to possess an advance spot that commanded a view of our encampment and the ships in the harbour; this well timed parade had a very good effect and was a means ever after of supporting that dignity and ostentation which much excells precept or force when applied to such wild untutored creatures as these were.

Cook invited Polahow and Phenow on board with him but only the latter went. Polahow declined the offer on account of a kind of asthmatic complaint that was particularly troublesome to him in the night, but chiefly from a view the good old man had in lodging in his house to observe the conduct of his people with regard to us. It was just dusk when they parted, and as I had been present during part of this first interview and was detained on shore by my duty I was glad he did not go off and asked him to my tent, but Polahow chose rather to have me go with him to his house, where we went and sat down together without the entrance; we had been here but a few minutes before one of the natives advanced through the grove to the skirts of the green and there halted, Polahow observed him, and told me he wanted him, upon which I beckoned to the Indians and he came to us; when he approached Polahow, he squated down upon his hams and put his forehead to the sole of Polahow's foot and then received some directions from him and went away and returned again very soon with some baked yams and fish rolled up in fresh plantain leaves and deposited in a little basket made of palm-tree leaves, and a large cocanut shell of clean fresh water and a smaller one of salt water, these he sat down and went and brought a mess of the same kind and sat them down by me.

Polahow then desired I would eat, but prefering salt, which I had in the tent, to the sea-water which they used, I called one of the guard and had some of that brought me to eat with my fish, which were really most delightfully dressed and of which I eat very heartily.

Their animal and vegetable food is dressed in the same manner here as at the southern and northern tropical islands throughout these seas, being all baked among hot stones laid in a hole and covered over first with leaves and then with mould. Palahow was fed by the chief who waited on him both with victuals and drink. After he had finished, the remains were carried away by the chief in waiting who returned soon after with two large separate rolls of cloth and two little low wooden stools. The cloth was for a covering while a sleep, and the stools to raise and rest the head on as we do on a pillow: These were left within the house or rather under the roof—one side being open. The floor within was composed of coarse dry grass, leaves and flowers, over which was spread large well wrought matts. On this Polahow and I removed and sat down while the chief unrolled and spread out the cloath; after which he retired and in a few minutes there appeared a fine young girl about

17 years of age, who approaching Polahow stooped and kissed his great toe, and then retired and set down in an opposite part of the house. It was now about nine o'clock and a bright moon shine, the sky was serene and the winds hushed. Suddenly I heard a number of their flutes beginning nearly at the same time burst from every quarter of the surrounding grove: And whether this was meant as an exhilarating seranade or a soothing soporific to the great Polahow I cannot tell, though in fact from the appearance of the young girl and other circumstances I must confess my heart suggested other matters; but my heart at that time was what Polahow's ought to have been and not what it was—I appeal to any one. Polahow immediately on hearing the music took me by the hand intimating that he was going to sleep and shewing me the other cloth which was spread nearly beside him and the pillow, invited me to use it. I pretended to acquiesce, but a bed of flowers only added to my uneasiness. As soon as Polahow had lain down, the girl approached him and spread the cloth over him after which she sat down behind him as he lay upon his side and began one of the most extraordinary operations I ever before had seen or heard of, which was pating him on the posteriors with the palms and back of her hands alternately in a constant and quick succession of gentle strokes which she continued with unremitted uniformity and celerity until she found her lord fast a sleep when she gently rose and went off. This performance lasted about three quarters of an hour and both the novelty of it and the situation I was in respecting a variety of objects and sentiments left me in a kind of listless reverie. Whether this ceremony respected Polahow merely as a mark of distinction, or whether the operation was applied as a provocative to certain passions— as a lulaby to sleep, or to assuage the embarrassments he was under in that altitude from his asthmatic complaints I cannot determine. It is true said I, rising from my reverie and walking out into the middle of the green in the full moon shine, where I could extend my prospects and where the sound that proceeded from the circumventulating flutes would more regularly pass the ear.—It is true, that of all the animals from the polypus to man, the latter is the most happy and the most wretched, dancing through life between these two extremes, he sticks his head among the stars, or his nose in the earth, or suspended by a cobweb in some middle altitude he hangs like a being indigenous to no sphere or unfit for any, or like these Indians he is happy because he is insensible of it or takes no pains to be so.

On the 10th we got what few sick we had on shore, and also brought our cattle on shore; we also established a mart upon the green before our encampment, and appointed particular persons to traffic with the natives for the provisions of the country, and that the trade should wholly centre there, nothing was purchased at the ships, by this means we had every day a regular fair exchange; the natives set down in a circle on the outside of the green with their goods, and our purveyors walked round and purchased; they came constantly every day by seven or eight in the morning and went regularly and happily away before sun-down in the evening. We had also our wooders and waterers and sail-makers on shore, and every body was busily employed and the utmost expedition made in getting ready for the sea again. After the markets were over there being generally an hour or two, and sometimes those before dark, the natives, to entertain us and exhibit their own accomplishments, used to form matches at wrestling, boxing, and other athletic excercises, of which they were very vain, and in which they were by far the best accomplished among all the people we had ever visited before or after. These exercises were always performed on the green within the circle, and among the Indian spectators there were a certain number of elderly men who resided over and regulated the exercise; when one of the wrestlers or combatants was fairly excelled, they finished it by a short sonorous sentence which they sung, expressing that he was fallen, fairly fallen, or that he was fairly conquered, and that the victor kept the field; from this there was no appeal, nor indeed did they seem to want it, for among their toughest exercises I never saw any of them choloric, envious, malicious or revengeful, but preserving their tempers, or being less irascible than we generally are, quit the stage with the same good nature with which they entered it; when they wrestle they seize each other by a strong plaited girdle made of the fibers of the cocoanut, and wore round the waist for that purpose, and describe near the same operations in this contest that we do in what we call huging or scuffling; in boxing their manoeuvres are different: They have both hands clinched and bound round separately with small cords which perhaps were intended to prevent their clinching each other when closly engaged and preventing foul play, or it might be to preserve the joints of the fingers especially the thumb from being dislocated: Perhaps the best general idea I can convey of their attitudes in this exercise is to compare them with those of the ancient gladiators of Rome which they much resemble: They are very expert and intrepid in these performances, but as they are mere friendly efforts of skill and prowess they continue no longer than the purposes of such a contention is answered and the combatant as soon as he finds he shall be conquered is very soldom such an obstinate fool as to be beat out of his senses to be made sensible he is so, but retires most commonly with a whole skin: But the exercise of the club is not so, and as these contests are very severe and even dangerous they are seldom performed: We never saw but one instance of it, but it was a most capital one, as the performers were capital characters and though we expected the exhibition would be very short, yet it lasted near twenty minutes, protracted by the skill of the combatants in avoiding each other's blows, some of which were no less violent than artful: After being pretty well buffeted about the body, a fortuitous blow upon the head of one decided the matter and the conquered was carried off, while the victor elated with success stood and enjoyed the subsequent shouts of praise that proceeded from the spectators: When these shouts ended the young women round the circle rose, and sung, and danced a short kind of interlude in celebration of the hero.— But alas! what did this avail him when a son of Polahow's entered the lifts brandishing an enormous club and exposing his browny shoulders and that arm that had so long met with no rival, and that front which wore the marks of many a victory. This young chief was a spurious descendant of Polahow's and about twenty-four or five years old and was so well known not only at Tongotaboo but among all the neighbouring islands for his feats with the club that he could of late meet with no competitor which was the case now, and after he had waited on the green until he had received two shouts, he retired and the exhibition ended: He had one eye knocked out and his head and body had been at different times so beat that he was one intire piece of scarrification. When these exercises are meant to be full and well conducted Polahow is generally present, and when that is the case every pair who enter the lists walk up within 15 or 20 feet of their prince and compliment him after the manner of the country, which is by seting down crossleged before him, and instantly rising again, and whether victorious or otherwise, before they quit the lists repeat the same compliment. This exercise of the club seems in all its parts to resemble that of the gauntlet among the ancients and so indeed do the other games of wrestling and boxing.

These exhibitions on the part of the natives were considered by us in a kind of dubious light for though they evidently entertained us, we were not certain they were solely intended for that purpose, and if they happened to be numerous on any of those occasions we had always the guard under arms. The spectators on some of those occasions amounted to above ten thousand people. However we never let them know by any superfluity of parade or other means that we were jealous of their numbers or their boldness and skill, though we certainly were, and prudence demanded it. Our only defence was certainly our imaginary greatness, and this would unavoidably decline if not preserved by some studied means. It was therefore determined to preserve and if possible to promote this imaginary superiority; and as nothing could be more condusive to accomplish it than some extraordinary exhibition that would be incomprehensibly great to them, and without any hazard or miscarriage on our part, we were resolved to play off some of our fire-works that were brought from Woolwich for some such occasion; this was made known to the natives at the conclusion of one of their games, on which occasion they expressed great satisfaction, and a night being pitched upon, every thing was prepared for the occasion. The natives expected it would have been an heiva, as they call their games, at least somewhat like their own, and according to our personal appearance anticipated the satisfaction of finding us inferior to them; but in this they were totally mistaken, for when the first sky-racket ascended full one half of several thousand Indians ran off and appeared no more that evening; some of those who remained fell prone upon the earth with their faces downward and some in other attitudes, but all expressive of the most extreme surprize and astonishment. Polahow and Phenow who sat next to Cook and his officers with some other Indian Chiefs and women of distinction, were not less astonished than the multitude, and would instantly have worshiped Cook as a being of much superior order to themselves, and intreated him not to hurt them or their people, adding that they were friends and would always continue such; Cook assured Polahow that he nor any of his people should be hurt, and begged him to speak and pacify the people, and persuade them to stay and see the rest of the heiva. After this were exhibited some flower pots, horrizontal wheels, roses, water-rackets, crackets, serpents, &c. and it is hard to say whether they were upon the whole most terrified or delighted. When the entertainment ended and the assembly began to disappear nothing was heard but cries expressive of the wonders they had seen, the greatness of our heiva, and the poorness of their own; indeed this and the exhibition of our mathamatical and philosophical apparatus at our astronomical tents, confirmed them in the fear and admiration of our greatness; and these circumstances received a great addition from an eclipse of the sun which happened during our stay—this we foretold to them, and also acquainted them with the time it would disappear.

These circumstances joined with others secured us indeed from open insults but were ineffectual to prevent those of a more distant kind; thefts, and indeed robberies, when occasion offered, grew daily after the first week to disturb us. At first the interpositions of Polahow and particularly Phenow tended partly to aleviate these inconveniences by restoring our purloined property, or by making compensation for the defaults of their people by presents of hogs and the fruits of the country, which indeed went a great way with Cook, who, as he was purser of the ships, was often influenced more by acquiring a hog from the natives than the fear of losing the friendship of his hospitable allies, or the honor of being always nice in the distribution of impartial justice: but then it must be remembered that the ability of performing the important errand before us depended very much if not entirely upon the precarious supplies we might procure from these and other such islands, and he must of consequence be very anxious and solicitous in the concernment; but perhaps no considerations will excuse the severity which he sometimes used towards the natives on these occasions, and he would perhaps have done better to have considered that the full exertion of extreme power is an argument of extreme weakness, and nature seemed to inform the insulted natives of the truth of this maxim by the manifestation of their subsequent resentments; for before we quit Tongotaboo we could not go any where into the country upon business or pleasure without danger. It will be needless to particularize the instances of punishment inflicted upon the natives, or the instances of satisfaction made Cook on those occasions; but as one was something more curious and less disgustful than some others I shall mention it. We had two fine fowls, a peacock and hen, that we had brought from home at the expence of much care and trouble; and they had been too long admired and gazed at by the people not to wish them their own, and the opportunities that daily offered to take them, were too favorable not to determine them to make them such: The morning after they were missing, Cook perceived it would be a serious, if not an unfortunate circumstance without the exertions both of policy and dispatch, and therefore sent an officer from the ship to the tents with orders immediately to put poor Polahow under an arrest and the guard under arms, and upon the back of those orders came others to arrest Phenow too—but Phenow happened on purpose to be absent, and had in fact stolen the fowls, and we knew it was folly to pursue him, so were glad to secure Polahow, who really happened at this time to be innocent. It was a matter peculiarly aggravating to Polahow, to be confined by a stranger in his own dominions, in his own house, in the sight of his own people, and at the same time unconscious of any demerit: Increased still more by the weeping and distracted multitude about him, and the moving intreaties of his little grandson to the guard, and still more when he saw the angry Cook appear with another guard from the ships: But notwithstanding this conflict he saluted Cook to the greatest advantage and manifested a dignity that even did honor to his perplexed situation. An event of such importance soon collected a great concourse of people and a number of armed chiefs who formed in a body in the adjacent grove, and seemed determined to rescue their prince or perish in the attempt. Cook saw this with concern, particularly as it contradicted him in his opinion so agreeable to his importance that the natives would never dare attack him, and he was determined instantly to try it, but nevertheless to prevent the misfortunes that might arise from too much precipitancy, first desired Polahow to advise his people to withdraw, assuring him that as soon as the goods were restored for which he was confined he should be set at liberty, but if his people attempted to do it by force that he would instantly and could easily destroy them; and then ordered the drum to beat to arms and the guard to form, at the same time placed a number of men round them with their bayonets pointed at his body; this was too much, and the terrifying parade and pompous stile of the guard, and all the flourishes of our operations struck not only him but the chiefs. The old man rose and spoke to his chiefs, from which we could collect that the power of our fire-works were much insisted on, as well as the immediate danger of his own life which they could not rescue and the promises Cook had made him, for which reason he desired them to withdraw, which however they did with great reluctance. A partial peace being thus effected, Polahow's distress began to subside, and though he was not altogether indebted to Cook on that account, yet he was willing to express his gratitude, though it was only sacrificing to his timidity. He therefore desired the liberty to speak with some of his chiefs, whom he dispatched after a short conference to contrive some way to appease the threats of Cook, and if possible procure him his liberty.

The next day Phenow having heard of the situation of Polahow and finding himself circumvented by the very means that were most distressing to him, returned in spite of shame and all the contending passions that fluctuated in his manly heart to deliberate his lord and friend Polahow; when he came to the tents grief, sorrow, remorse and fear were so strongly delieneated in his whole appearance that it was impossible for Cook himself not to feel a sympathetic distress, especially from his interview with Polahow, whose feet he wet with his tears and wiped them with the hair of his head; as soon as these emotions had subsided he told Cook he should have the fowls before sun down, and begged him instantly to release Polahow, which Cook ventured to comply with, and the guard from this quarter was accordingly taken off. But Phenow, as prudent as valiant, perceiving by the methods Cook had taken in this matter that it was a circumstance of great importance in our estimation for them to make free with our property without our consent, and that it conferred the idea of shame and guilt on those who did, and that he himself being a chief of great distinction, it would render the shame, if imputed to him still more flagrant—was determined not only to throw off the odium of the imputation from himself by laying it at the door of some obscure persons but by a munificient present to Cook to prevent any enquiry who those unknown culprits were, or if they should finally be forgiven: these were Phenow's intentions, and he took care immediately to set them out to the best advantage with Cook; and he knew besides that he had many friends among the strangers, which was true, for every body loved Phenow. Accordingly he dispatched his swift sailing canoes to some of the nearest circumadjacent islands to procure what he knew would be highly delectable to Cook—a quantity of fine red feathers, and besides this they were to come loaded with provisions, which had for some time past from our feudes with the natives been getting scarce. On the other hand Polahow had dispatched numberless little troops into the country upon the same business. The news of this disturbance and the happy termination of it had now become very diffusive, and the next day we had a vast concourse of people as well as an accumulation of provisions, such as we had never before seen, nor could have concieved, for, besides the provisions that had actually been sent for, those who came merely as spectators of what they knew would produce some kind of entertainment—had also brought something, and hardly any body came empty handed. Cook anticipating the events of the day had made such regulations on board and on shore as he thought necessary, and having received the lost fowls according to Phenow's promise and being full of the idea of receiving the supplies of provision promised him by Polahow and Phenow—came on shore the next day dressed, with a number of his officers, attended by two French horns, and made it on his part a day of pleasure.

The two parties sent out by Polahow and Phenow arrived nearly together, about 11 o'clock in the forenoon, and their approach was soon known by the movements of the people. Polahow's party arrived first and entered upon the green before our encampment in pairs through an avenue among the people, and making a very formal and regular procession, they retired after they had disburdened themselves of their loads, by the same rout in which they entered. The manner of their bringing their loads was upon a short pole carried upon the shoulders of two men from the middle of which hung suspended the provisions, sometimes consisting of baskets of Fish, of bunches of yams, bread-fruit, plantains, bananas, shaddocks, cocoanuts, and every now and then a hog; and every couple as they retired turned towards Polahow as he and his chiefs set among Cook and his officers, and complimented him. This procession was not half over before Phenow's men entered the opposite side of the green in the same manner, but the first of them were so gorgeously set off with aprons and mantlets of red and yellow feathers that they entirely took of our attention for sometime to Polahow's men, who nevertheless were much more numerous than his. About two o'clock this procession of wealth ended, and Cook with his officers, Polahow, Phenow, and a numerous company of respective suits dined. In the mean time the natives were forming two lofty edifices, composed of sticks laid transversly over each other in four squares, beginning with a base about 12 feet, and contracting it gradually until it rose about 40 feet high: The one they called Polahow, and the other Phenow, and the former was the highest; these they filled with yams to the top, and to crown the oblation deposited on the summit of each two large barbacued hogs: After dinner there was a grand heiva, as they denominate all their games, but this was a kind of war-dance and different from any thing we had hitherto seen among them, but had nothing in it that deserves particular description, though it seems to be in the highest estimation among them. In the evening the people withdrew, but some of them living at too great a distance to return that night slept at a little distance in the woods.

The next day we were fully employed in carrying part of the provisions on board, nor did we complete this business under two succeeding days: Our decks were full of hogs notwithstanding we had been killing and salting night and day, and we had got full yams enough to last us two or three months. We were fully convinced that we were strangers to the unbounded plenty of those happy islands, and Cook not to be behind hand with those two munificent chiefs, presented them with a horse and a mare, a bull and a cow, and two goats, besides other things of the greatest value to them, and with which they were highly delighted.

We had now been at Tongotaboo 26 days and possibly should have remained there longer, but for the supply of provisions we received by this last present from Polahow and Phenow, which enabled us to sail immediately.

On the 7th of July we got every thing on board, when we invited Polahow, Phenow and several other chiefs, and made them all rich presents, particularly the two first. In the afternoon we took our leave of them, and unmoored and came to sail plying to windward through a different passage to the eastward, but meeting with obstructions did not clear Tongotaboo until the morning of the 19th when we reached the Island Eaowhee: This also is one of the Friendly-Islands, and was called by Tasman Middleburgh. It is about 30 miles S.E. of Tongotaboo, and is a most beautiful island, thick inhabited, and between thirty and forty miles in circumference: We stayed here until the 18th, when we weighed, sailing E.S.E. as near as we could lay: Our appointed rendezvous in case of separation being the Island of Otaheite, and as we had nothing very interesting on our passage thence, the time may not be misapproved if we give some further description of Tongotaboo. This island lies in lat. 21 19 south, and longit. 184 20 east from the meridian of Greenwich, from which we always calculated: It is about 130 miles in circumference, but of an irregular form: It is very low and the soil beyond comparison rich and exuberant: It affords but very indifferent water, and is subjected to heavy dews, and we had while there the shock of an earthquake; the surrounding shores and the soundings near the land are all coral rocks; the internal parts of the island as well the outsides of it are covered with a kind of lava, which is the case with most of the islands in this ocean. The inhabitants like those of the other inhabited islands we visited in its neighbourhood are a very fine people, exceeding in beauty, in stature, strength, and the improvements of their mental capacities any of the great variety of people among the islands scattered throughout this ocean: If this can be an exception, they are indeed not quite so light coloured as at Otaheite and the Society-Isles: The manner of their cultivating their land exceeds even the inhabitants of some islands we afterwards discovered and called Sandwich-Islands: The pains they have taken to clear up the woods when we consider the disadvantages they must have labored under for want of husbundry implements, is astonishing, and as strong a proof of their unlimited industry, as the elegance in which they have laid it out and otherwise improved it, is of their rural taste and good judgment. These inclosures also indicate separate property among them, which was a certain intimation in my opinion of an energetic jurisprudence and increasing civilization.

Their language is radically the same as that which pervades all the tropical islands in this part of the ocean, and I may more particularly say so not only of their animals and the common productions of nature, but of their manners and customs throughout. A minute detail of their history in these respects would be unnecessary as that of Otaheite or of Sandwich-Islands, of which I shall treat more largely hereafter, will apply to them with the strictest propriety in every thing that concerns a reader who makes his speculations upon a more general and comprehensive scale than those who are pleased even with a repetition of things of now more consequence in their first relation.

On the 13th of August we made the island of Otaheite about 8 leagues distant.

On the 14th we stood in for the land and anchored in a small bay on the east side of the island called by the natives Otaheite-peha. We were immediately surrounded by the inhabitants in their canoes, and the little village within the bay was full of people dancing and runing about with joy at our arrival, which was encreased when they found it was Cook, or Tutee as they pronounce it, who was known among them from a former voyage here. A boat was soon hove out and Cook with other gentlemen and Omai went on shore, where they were very much surprized to find a large wooden cross about 9 feet high erected in the village, with an inscription in the latin language, importing that in February 1777 two Spanish ships had been there, and taken possession of the island in the name of his Catholic Majesty. This was also confirmed by many subsequent appearances as well as from the information of the inhabitants. At a little distance from this they found a house built with boards a little in the European stile, and within it a large mahogany chest with a Spanish lock to it, this the natives readily opened and showed us several Spanish garments, which they said belonged to a man the Spaniards had left there, who was now dead— and gave us furthermore to understand that the Spaniards had taken three of the natives with them when they went away, and when we asked where they came from they pronounced the word Rema, which we made no doubt was Lima in Spanish America.

We also found afterwards that the Spaniards had left several American hogs and a bull and a cow, among them, but the two latter were dead. What the purport of this visit from the Spaniards could be time must discover.

When our boat returned they brought off the cross the Spaniards had erected—eraced their inscription, and after putting on one in favor of his Britannic Majesty erected it again in the place from which we took it. The next day we had a number of visitors, among whom was a sister to Omai, who came to welcome her brother to his native country again; but the behaviour of Omai on the occasion was consonant to his proud empty ambitious heart, and he refused at first to own her for his sister; the reason of which was, her being a poor obscure girl, and as he expected to be nothing but king, the connexion would disgrace him.

On the 22nd of August we unmoored and came to sail steering for the old rendezvous, a bay called by the natives Mattavai, and by us Port-Royal, from its excellency as a harbour.

On the 23rd both ships entered and moved about noon in Mattavai-Bay. We were immediately visited according to custom by the natives in their canoes, who were almost frantic with joy to see us, and without any ceremony ran down between decks crying out for some of their old acquaintance, many of whom they found and embraced with the greatest affection. Capt. Cook and Lieut. Gore were particularly recognized, and found more old acquaintance than they knew how to dispose with; in short the ship was so crouded and confused that we could attend to no duty the remaining part of the day, Cook fairly gave it up as a day of festivity, not only to the Otaheiteeans but to his own people particularly those who had been there before who were apparently and many in reality as much and perhaps more pleased than if they had been moored in any part of Great-Britain.

On the 24th we sent all our tents, sails, water-crafts and whatever stores wanted airing or repairing; the tents were erected on the same spot where they formerly were, and a guard of marines set over the whole.

This island has so often been visited by the English, French and Spaniards, particularly by the former who first discovered it between twenty and thirty years ago, together with the islands in the neighborhood, its history now as far as could be obtained is almost universally known; but as every visiter furnishes some new additional circumstances, these ought not to be omitted, and are what I shall chiefly confine myself to, together with a general description of the country, its inhabitants and manners for the information of such as may not yet have been made acquainted with them.[5]

Mattavai-Bay is situate in latitude 17. 19. south and long, 211 east. The island taken collectively consists of two peninsulas, nearly of an equal magnitude, and is about 160 miles in circumference, the form being somewhat irregular: the internal parts of the island are high and craggy, but towards the sea the land either consists of gentle slopes or level plains that reach the sea, after which it protuberates in a continued bed of coral, which like a border surrounds the whole. This is the case with all the islands in the neighbourhood, and this invariable uniformity in their conformation is remarkable. The country is very fertile, particularly the plains where the inhabitants reside; it produces bread-fruit, cocoanuts, bananas of thirteen sorts, plantains, and fruit not unlike an apple, sweet potatoes, (though not in plenty) a few yams and sugarcanes; besides a number of curious plants, and the most of these the earth produces spontaneously. They have no European fruit, garden stuff, pulse, legums or grain of any kind; perhaps the bread fruit may deserve a particular description.—It grows on a tree of about the size of a middling oak with large leaves deeply sinuated, and when broken from the branch exubes a white milky juice, the fruit is about the size of a childs head and nearly shaped like it; it is covered with a skin the surface of which is reticulated, and it has a small core; it is quite white, and when roasted or boiled has the consistence of new wheat-bread, and resembles it in taste only it is sweeter. It abounds also (though in no great plenty) with hogs, dogs, and poultry, all which are tame; and upon the coasts are plenty of fish.

The inhabitants are of the largest size of Europeans, the men are tall, strong well limbed and fairly shaped. The women of superior rank among them are also in general above our middle size; but those of the inferior rank are below it, some of them are quite small; which defect in stature may probably proceed from their early commerce with the men in which they differ from their superiors. Their complexion is clear olive or brunette and the whole contour of the face quite handsome, except the nose, which is generally a little inclined to be flat. Their hair is black and course. The men have beards, but pluck the greatest part of them out; they are vigorous, easy, graceful and liberal in their deportment, and of a courteous hospitable disposition, but shrewd and artful.[6] The women cut their hair short, and the men wear theirs long. They have a custom of staining their bodies in a manner that is universal among all those islands, and is called by them tatowing; in doing this they prick the skin with an instrument of small sharp bones which they dip as occasion requires in a black composition of coal-dust and water, which leaves an indelible stain. The operation is painful, and it is some days before the wound is well.

Their cloathing consists of cloth made of the inner rind of the bark of three different kinds of trees: The Chinese-paper-mulberry, the bread-fruit tree, and a kind of wild fig-tree, which in the conformation of different sorts of cloth are differently disposed of by using one singly, or any two or all of them altogether. The principal excellencies of this cloth are its coolness and softness; its imperfections being pervious to water and easily torn; and they sometimes, especially if it is wet, wear fine mats of which they have a great variety. This cloth they wear in different ways just as fancy leads them, but very seldom cover any part of the body except about the loins, and there is little difference in this respect either with regard to sex or condition unless it be in the quantity put on, which is generally the greatest on the people of superior rank; neither do they cover their feet, or seldom the head, nor this part only with a temporary kind of bonnet made in a few minutes of palm-tree leaves, which they fling away an hour after. At one of their heiva's indeed or on some such occasion when the women are dressed, they wear a kind of turban on the head which they highly esteem; it consists of human hair painted in threads, scarcely thicker than sewing silk, and is when extenuated several hundred yards in length. The children of both sexes go quite naked until they are four or five years old.

The houses or rather dwellings of these people are simple structures, but have an air of neatness and elegance, and are very well calculated for the climate; they are generally of an oblong square, and one of a middling size is about 30 feet long and 10 broad; the roof is raised on three rows of pillows parallel to each other one on each side and the other in the middle; the roof consists of two flat sides terminating in a ridge, and is thatched with palm-leaves; the floor is covered with dry grass, over which is spread matts, on which they sit by day and sleep by night, and every thing is preserved exceedingly neat.

The food of the inhabitants is much the greatest part of it vegetables, of which the bread-fruit forms the principal part. The chiefs eat but little pork, the commonalty less and the women none, unless by stealth. Dogs and fowls are their most frequent dish, and the dogs are preferable to their fowls; they are indeed a very fine dish, especially cooked in their way. The process is simply this, while the animal is dressing they dig a hole about two feet deep, in which they kindle a fire and heat a quantity of stones, when they are sufficiently heated they take out about half of them leaving the rest to cover the bottom of the hole, the dog when cleaned and dressed is wrapped up with several folds of green plantain leaves and laid in the hole, then the remainder of the stones are laid around it and the lightest of them upon the top of it, then another quantity of leaves are laid thick over the whole, and last of all the whole is covered over with the mould. If the animal is large it will remain two hours, if smaller a less time before it is prepared. This is the only method they have of cooking their food, whether flesh, fish, fowl or fruit; but the smaller fish are eat raw, and salt-water is their only sauce.

For drink they have in general nothing but water or cocoanut-milk: But they mostly use water only. They have a drink compressed from the root of a plant they call ava; but this rather stupefies than exhilerates though it is used by them as a spirituous drink: This however is seldom drank by the poor sort, and never by the women, unless very secretly. They are neat both in cooking and in eating almost to an extreme. The men and women never eat together, though it be husband and wife, nor do the men generally eat out of the same dish: They eat with great voracity though they consume but a moderate quantity, and notwithstanding their mouths are crammed as full as they can contain, yet are they very conversible and full of talk at their meals. Preparatory to all their meals it is a custom to lay aside a little modicum of what they are eating in some by-place which they do as an offering to their god or gods. After meals at mid-day they generally sleep; indeed they are extremely indolent, and sleeping and eating is almost all they do.[7]

Their amusements are music, dancing, wrestling and boxing, all which are like those at Tongotaboo.

The language at Otaheitee is the same that is spoken throughout all the south-sea islands, and will therefore serve as a specimen for the whole; but how it should equally correspond with that of New-Zealand is still more remarkable, and I have on that account added a column of the New-Zealand language opposite to that which contains the Otaheitee language; the words in each column have their signification explained in English in a third column.

Otaheite.	New-Zealand.	English.
Earee	Eareete	A Chief
Taata	Teata	A Man
Ivahine	Wahinee	A Woman
Eupo	Eupo	The Head
Rooarooa	Macauwee	The Hair
Terrea	Terringa	The Ear
Erai	Erai	The Forehead
Mata	Mata	The Eyes
Paparea	Paparinga	The Cheeks
Ahew	Ahew	The Nose
Outou	Hangoutow	The Mouth

Tahei	Tahai	One
Rua	Rua	Two
Toron	Toron	Three
Hea	Ha	Four
Rema	Rema	Five
Ono	Onu	Six
Netu	Euta	Seven
Warou	Warou	Eight
Heva	Iva	Nine
Ahowrow.	Angahourow	Ten.

By this specimen without adding a great number of words it appears to demonstration that these two languages were aboriginally the same and will have its influence in supporting the conclusion that the people who make use of it were also originally the same.—That the inhabitants of the south sea islands are the same people with each other and all derived from the same common source is beyond doubt, but from what source is yet difficult to determine. If we endeavour to determine the question by reasons founded on the analogy of language, as well as manners we shall most certainly conclude that they all originally came from the westward, that is, from Assia; but if we give due weight to the thousand adventitious circumstances that attend a fortuitous emigration as well as the more solid and rational consideration of the situation of those isles, particularly respecting the winds, as well as a variety of other causes, it is as probable and perhaps more so they came from the eastward, which is America. It opens a wide field for speculation however, and as the object respects the ways of God to man upon a large scale of enquiry men of every cast will pursue it with equal curiosity. I never invite the misanthropist to the curious enquiry, but perhaps some future occurrences may elucidate the matter.

As to the religion, laws and government of the people much has been said about them by former voyagers, and in truth too much, especially about their religion which they are not fond of discovering, and therefore when urged on the matter have often rather than displease those who made the enquiry told not only different accounts, but such as were utterly inconsistent with what we knew to be true from occular demonstration. They assured us for instance that they never sacrificed human bodies, but an accident happened that contradicted it and gave us the full proof of it, its operation and its design; which were the same as I have mentioned at Sandwich Islands, and was an oblation to the God of war made previous to that undertaking. In short the only standard that seems justifiable to judge by is what we saw practiced, that was obvious and the inferences that naturally followed could not well be misunderstood.

They believe the immortality of the soul at least its existence in a separate state: But how it exists, whether as a mere spiritual substance or whether it is united again to a corporeal or material form, and what form is uncertain; it is supposed they have notions of transmigration: our conjectures originate from observing that universal, constant and uniform regard which they pay in a greater or less degree to every species of subordinate being, even to the minutest insect and the most insignificant reptile. This was never esteemed a philosophical sentiment, or a mere dictate of nature, because the people who entertain these notions are not led to embrace them from the unbiassed impulses of nature, which would lead them to regard their own species more than those of any other. It must therefore be from other motives, and know of none so probable as religion or superstition, which are indeed synonomous terms when applied to these people, besides it is well known to have been a religious sentiment among many other people both ancient and modern who claim the appellation of civilized. It exists now among several Asiatic sects both east and west of the Ganges particularly among the Bangans so called from abstaining from the use of all animal food: It is well known that some tribes in Asia have built hospitals for certain species of subordinate beings.

The Otaheiteans do indeed eat animal flesh: But it is certain they do not allow their women to eat much of it, and that either do not universally eat of it: We know of two certain instances wherein they do not, and those respect two birds: The Kingfisher and the Heron: They are besides very observant of the manner in which they kill the animals they do make use of, endeavoring to mitigate the pangs of the dying animal, and also to soften the act that deprives it of life: For which purpose they strangle or drown them, and having previously disposed of the animal so as they are sure it will die—they run out of fight, and leave it until expired. In other respects they extend this regard still further: There are a great many rats about their dwellings, but though a rat should steal into one of their dishes of food and destroy it, or should they eat their cloath or do any other of those mischevious tricks they are addicted to, and should they catch him in the fact he would only signify his displeasure by waving his hand to it very friendly and politely to be gone; and when they are stung by a fly or musketo they only frighten it away.

If the system of transmigration forms any part of the Otaheitean religion, it is likely to compose a considerable part, if not the whole of it; if it can be reduced to any system at all. One argument is its universality and strict observance among the people, and another is, that all the customs of mankind appear to be derivative and traditionary, and that this sentiment in religion exists in Asia, from whence it is probable it emigrated with the people, and that this sentiment, where it does exist, and originally did exist, does, and originally did form a system as materially distinct from any other as systems generally are and perhaps more so as the combination of those sentiments which form it were when primarily promulgated the most wild fanciful, innocent, mischievous, subtile, and therefore the most curious opinions that ever entered the head of that child of contradictions, so well known by the name of Man to conceive of: Why, what amazing quantities of beef, mutton, pork and fowl hath it saved in Indostan; and on the other hand how hath it increased the prolific generation of flies, musquetos, batts, tarantulas, toads and snakes: Are not the plains of Siam, Pegu and Aracan rendered the most delectable spots on earth by it?

They have other religious customs that as plainly indicate their source as this, but they are simple, detached, individual and various; they seem to be fragments of many different theories: To unite them if possible, would discover their absurdity, and they seem to be kept by the priests for charge; circumcision is one of them; though in Hawkesworth's compilation of a former voyage it is said not to be a religious custom: But if Cook had then taken it for granted that the Otaheiteans were the greatest lyars on earth especially when queried about their religion he would not have believed their report and to say that the prepuce of the male was abscinded merely from motives of cleanliness was to say nothing even suppose it had that effect. If it had been enjoined the Otaheiteans to cut of their noses for religion sake, and they had said the amputation was from motives of cleanliness, the story would have been much more plausible: And as for the particular form of the incision, it is not so different from that now used among the Jews, as theirs may be from the form of the operation by father Abraham: Besides, they have the finest instruments to perform the ceremony and the Otaheitean has only an oyster-shell; and the member is a delicate, a nervous and sensible member. Sacrificing is another of those religious ceremonies that is incompatable with the system of transmigration, and indeed as the oblation consists of a human being it is different from any civilized usuage, is a solitary wandering barbarous custom, and is therefore found no where but among a detached and scattered people, and though always found there does not appear to be comprized in any code or system of other customs where we find such; which indeed is seldom as the instance of transmigration here.

Their notions of a deity and the speculative parts of their religion is involved even among themselves in mystery and perplexed with inconsistences, and their priests who alone pretend to be informed of it have by their own industrious fabrications and the addition of its traditionary fables rolled themselves up in endless mazes and inextricable labyrinths: None of them act alike in their ceremonies and none of them narrate alike when enquired off concerning the matter: therefore what they conceive respecting a God we cannot tell; though we conclude upon the whole that they worship one great Supreme, the author and governor of all things, but there seems to be such a string of subordinate gods intervening between him and the least of those, and the characters of the whole so contracting, whimsical, absurd and ridiculous that their mythology is very droll, and represents the very best of the group no better than a harlequin.

The government at Otaheite resembles the early state of every government, which in an unimproved and unrefined state, is ever a kind of feudal system of subordination: Securing licentious liberty to a few, and a dependant servility to the rest. Otaheite, as I have had occasion to observe before, consists of two peninsulas, each of these are presided over by chiefs they distinguish by an appellation, signifying the great chief, and this is the first order among them: The lesser diversion of the island consists of circles or districts of which there are in the whole about one hundred: Over each of those districts a chief presides, whom they call chief without the affixa, Great: This constitutes the second order: The third order are those who occupy and improve certain portions of land in each district, for which he is accountable to the chief of the district: He is a kind of tenant. The fourth order are those who labor and cultivate the land and do other services under the tenant, which constitutes the fifth and last order. The priests are chiefs by rank though they do not immediately intermeddle in the civil department.

One Otoo was supreme chief of the northern peninsula, and was possessed of the government by a collateral right his predecessor the amourous queen Oberea dying without issue: The supreme chief is by every body much respected and reverenced: But he did not appear to me to hold any particular power without his own district any more than the other, except in these two instances, which are a negative respecting war and respecting peace.

With regard to distributive justice and the inostensible parts of their government we are little informed; but it cannot be supposed to be very regular. There is apparently but little opposition of interest, and every desire and every appetite being easily gratified their cannot be many crimes.

We left at this island two cows and a bull, two ewes and a ram, a pair of goats, several pair of geese, and a great variety of European seeds, which we planted, and while we stayed took care of.

On the 29th of September we came to sail, leaving Otaheite. And,

On the 30th anchored in a fine bay at the island called by the natives Imayo, where we continued until the 13th of October, and procured a considerable addition to our flock of provisions. From hence we proceeded to the island of Hueheine, where we arrived and came to anchor in a bay on the east side of the island on the 13th.

On the 14th finding our birth foul we hove up, warped nearer in shore and took fresh moorings.

As this was the native island of Omai and where he was finally to be left, and proposing to remain at it some time on that account particularly, we sent the tents on shore with the usual guards. Omai had ever since our arrival among these isles been declining not only in our estimation but in the opinions of the natives, among whom he was envied for undeserved riches and dispised for his obscure birth and impudent pretentions to rule and command, in short his ignorance and vanity were insupportable.

Captain Cook, however, was determined to support him while under his care, and leave him in as happy a situation after he was gone as possible; he accordingly purchased about an acre and a half of the best ground, of the chiefs, for which he gave them the usual articles of traffic—the axes, hatchets, saws, nails, knives, &c. and this he circumscribed with a deep ditch, hove up the ground within, and laid part of it out in a garden, wherein were planted and sown a variety of European garden seeds, and upon the corner of the garden fronting the beach he built him a small house, or rather box, for it was chiefly meant only to preserve his effects from the ravages of the people he was to be left among; it was about 20 feet by 15, composed of a slight frame and covered with boards we sawed in the country; there was no iron work about it for fear that should be a temptation to the natives to hurt the edifice on that account; it took 30 days to build it from the materials we made use of, and when finished all Omai's effects were put into it, and he went on shore and took possession of it. Cook also left the two New-Zealand boys here as companions and servants to Omai. we also left him a horse and mare, a cow with calf, sheep, goats, turkies, geese, a pair of rabbits, a monkey and two cats.

On the first of November being ready to sail Capt. Cook made an entertainment in behalf of Omai at his little house, and in order to recommend him still further to the chiefs of the island invited them also; everybody enjoyed themselves but Omai who grew more dejected as the time of his taking his leave of us forever approached the nearer, and when he came finally to bid adieu the scene was very affecting to the whole company. It is certainly to be lamented that Omai will never be of any service to his country from his travels, but perhaps will render them and himself too the more unhappy.

On the 2d, after getting every thing on board, we left the bay under an early sail, and saluted Omai with several guns as our last adieu, and at the same time to impress an idea of greatness on the natives and the consequence of our resentments should they hurt Omai after our departure.

On the 3d of November we reach the island of Ulietea. And,

On the 4th entered a deep bay in that island and came to an anchor close in with the shore.

We continued at Ulietea near a month, and were generally employed in augmenting some part of our stores or adding to our provisions which was one great concern as this was the last of these happy islands we should touch at for provisions, and where we should procure our next supply we knew not; we had ever since our arrival at the Friendly-Islands to this time, including nine months, eat no kind of the ships provisions, and had added to this salvage about nine months supply of pork more, and two or three of yams and plantains, to which we had become so habituated that we had in a manner lost the relish of our bisket, especially when we could get bread fruit.

As we were now about to take leave of these islands several of our people who had been waiting for the opportunity to make their escape and stay behind us, began to put their resolutions into execution. The first was one of the marines who quit his post when on centry at the tents about midnight and went off with his mistress; the consequence of this was, that armed boats were sent round the island in search of him; they were gone two days before they found him, and he was betrayed by powerful presents to those who knew where he was, or he would never have been found: he had quitted his military garb and assumed the dress of the country, and when taken was sitting with his girl, who was dressing his head with flowers in the house of her parents. She was a woman of good and numerous connexions, and when she found the desperate situation of her dear soldier she flew into the woods and collected a body of her male friends to assist her in rescuing him from the hands of his enemies, and in fact would have done it had we not hasted with the prisoner to the boats, where we had hardly arrived before two hundred and more appeared all armed coming down the hills: the young lad bore the fate he anticipated with fortitude; though he lamented the loss of his lover. He was confined at his return and expected a very severe punishment, but it did not happen so, and his remarkable good character finally excused him.

This circumstance added to some private hints alarmed Cook, and fearing as his departure grew nearer that his men might go off in a body, it determined him immediately to hawl off and lay at an anchor in the middle of the bay, where the means of escape would be less practicable, but the very night before this took place one of the midshipmen and a gunner's mate from the Discovery absented themselves; this was still more alarming, and as soon as the ships were removed out into the bay, Cook confined the son and daughter by marriage, of the chief of the island, on board the Discovery, and then published his reasons for doing it to the people, and desired them to inform the father of the young prisoners and other chiefs, that unless they returned the deserters they should never more see their young prince or his partner, he at the same time offered large premiums to those who should bring him back, for it was found that we could not interest ourselves in the pursuit of them, being convinced they were not upon the island. These measures were calculated to influence both the chiefs and the people, the affections of the former and the interests of both; but after waiting several days to no purpose, and being anxious to depart, Cook applied himself to another stratagem—He gave out that since he could not obtain his people, and not being willing that the innocent captives he had on board should so dearly suffer for the transgressions of his people, he had determined to deliver them from their confinement, and as he should then take his final farewel of them, and wanted to leave them upon friendly terms, invited the chiefs and people, as many as would, to pay him a visit, and bring if they had any thing to market, for which should end with a grand HEIVA on our part; this took, and the next day after it issued we were visited by the people of all denominations from different parts of the island: The chiefs, particularly the father of the young captives were in raptures, and their first interview was extremely affecting; nothing was seen or heard on board the ships and in the canoes but shouts of joy and merriment. Cook as soon as he saw the provisions pretty well purchased up and the people beginning to disperse hove out a private signal to the *Discovery* and the boats were all instantly out manned, armed and regularly detached in different parts of the bay; this appearance alarmed the natives, and they betook themselves to flight, and to compleat the alarm and inform the boats without to begin their duty one of the cannon was fired; this produced the desired confusion, and terminated in the capture of almost every canoe, and in the imprisonment of all the chiefs on board each ship. The great chief now found the measure of his misfortune to be compleat, and absorbed in grief fell upon his children and swooned upon their necks. I would not have been the author of such grief for two deserters. As soon as this tumultuous scene had a little subsided Cook informed them that he would never release either of them or the canoes that were taken or the people in them until he should recover his two fugitives. It was too late to temporize or evade in the matter. The great chief immediately informed Cook that if he would let any four of the chiefs then present go as he should order he would endeavour to get his men, but declared he was afraid he never should, for he said they were gone to the island Bolabola whether he was afraid to pursue them, but added that he would send to the chief of Bolabola and get his consent if he could; this accordingly done, and Cook taking advantage of every circumstance, sent by the same chiefs a small present to the chief of Bolabola accompanied by a threat that if he did not aid and assist in procuring his men, that he would come with his ships and destroy him and his people without mercy. In the mean time Cook took care by every art to mitigate the sorrow of his royal captives, and make their confinement sit as easy as possible, and finding it to add too sensibly to the other griefs of the principal chief, to see so many of the people confined, ordered them to be liberated, but kept their canoes, they were accordingly all put on shore but the chiefs. Two days were elapsed and we had no intelligence of the deserters or those that went after them, and at length a third.

On the fourth however a number of canoes were seen entering the bay shouting and expressing their joy, and as they approached we saw with our glasses our two men bound hand and foot by the Indians: A circumstance we were glad to observe as it extremely mortified them and discovered how

the crew spent the next six months carefully skirting the coast past pres-
ent-day British Columbia and Alaska, going through the Bering Strait
and reaching the Arctic ice pack at a latitude of 70° north. After retreat-
ing from the ice, Ledyard had a five-day adventure on Unalaska Island
in the Aleutians in search of Russian fur traders.

On the 22d we crossed the equator.

On the 23d we were by observation in lat. 2 north, longit. 203. 55 east.
In the evening we saw low land ahead.

On the 24th we came up with it and anchored within a cables length
of the shore. This is a low, small island, mostly a bed of coral rock, and
scarcely more than 15 feet above the surface of the water in the highest
part of it, but as it was our first discovery in the northern hemisphere, and
produced us a noble supply of turtle we kept a merry christmass at it. We
caught above 300 large turtle to one ship: But our people suffered much
in their enterprizes on shore for this purpose: The *Discovery* had nearly
lost two men in them. Besides the great quantity of turtle upon this
island it was covered with innumerable flocks of seabirds: The shores also
covered with fish, particularly sharks, of which none of us had ever seen
the like in numbers.

On the 1st of January, 1778, we unmoored and continued our course
to the northward, steering N. by E. and N.N.E.

On the 19th our lat. was 21 20 north, longit. 198 east, and about two
o'clock we discovered high land, bearing N.N.E. right a-head: This was
immediately determined from our position to be a new discovery and of
course gave every one joy: As we continued our course standing for the first
discovered land, which now appeared to be an island, we saw more land to
windward of the former, bearing N.E. by E. which had also the appearance
of an island. Towards evening the wind failing we could not get in with the
land, and therefore tacked and stood off S.by E. and S.S.E. under all the sail
we could set, hoping by a good board, the next morning to weather the windward island: Put in this we were much deceived finding as we approached
the first discovered island the next morning that we had fell to leward two
leagues owing to a lee-current: As we approached near the shore we could
discern the land to be cultivated, saw smokes, and soon after houses and
inhabitants: When we were near enough the shore to examine for a harbour we bore away and run down the coast westward and northward in quest
of one, and about four o'clock entered a shallow bay; it afforded but

indefferent prospect, but it was thought best not to risk a further pursuit and we accordingly run in and anchored in seven fathom water three fourths of a mile from a village we saw in the bite of the bay and one fourth of a mile from a reef that projected from the western extremity.

We had been approached several times by some canoes at a distance, but none of them would come near enough to converse with us or that we might see what sort of people they were until we anchored and furled our sails: They shook their spears at us, rolled their eyes about and made a variety of wild uncouth gesticulations: But we had exchanged but a few words with them before we found to our joy and surprize that with little variation their language was the same as that of our acquaintance at the southern islands. In a little while after we had anchored, a number of canoes were round and at length some of them came on board. They were exceeding wild: Ran up to us and examined our hands and faces, then striping up our shirt-sleeves and opening the bosoms of our shirts to view such parts of our bodies as were covered by our cloaths: They then enquired if we could eat, which we discovered by eating some biscuit: As soon as they observed this they run to the side of the ship and called to those in the canoes, who hove on board several little pigs and some sweet potatoes: Among other acts of hospitality exhibited on this occasion, was the presentment of an Indian's arm roasted, which they signified to us was very good eating: But our surgeon to whom this offer was first made imprudently prevented any thing curious that might have been discovered on this occasion by expressing the greatest degree of abhorrance at the action, which so frightened the Indian that he immediately went off with it, and we never after saw another instance of it while among them. They had no knowledge of iron or European articles, but the moment we discovered its obvious importance they were in raptures about it, and gave us any thing they possessed in exchange for it.

The next day we were visited by a great multitude of canoes, bringing yams, sweet potatoes, hogs, plantains and other tropical fruits, which they greedily exchanged for little bits of old iron, nails and other articles.

The third day after our arrival we went on shore and traded with them there, and viewed the country, of which I shall give a full account hereafter.

We remained at this place about a week, and then sailed to visit some other islands to the N.W. and passing two small barren islands anchored off the westernmost called Nehow. The island we left was called Ottowai. We traded with the natives at Nehow as we had done at Ottowai. We remained at Nehow untill the second of February.

The island we had seen to windward of that of Ottowai, the two barren islands and Nehow made five in number, and Cook was strongly of the opinion that there were more farther to the eastward, which proved to be true as we shall see in the sequel of the history. The group already known he collectively called Sandwich Islands. Nehow is situate in lat. 21 44 north longit. 199 east.

I have defered any particular account of these islands at this time not only because our stay was short among them, but because we afterwards visited them and others of the same cluster to the eastward on our return from the northward a twelvemonth after when we had a more extensive acquaintance with them, and consequently a better fund of information.

On the 2nd of February we again launched into that extensive ocean that separates America and Asia, and continued our course to the northward and eastward intending to fall in with America in about 40 degrees of north latitude.

We had in general a very comfortable passage until after we made the coast when we had a series of very bad weather.

On the 7th of March we fell in with the coast of America in lat. 49 deg. N. long. 233 E. a little below Cape Blanco, and tracing it northerly until the 28th we entered an inlet in 49° N. From the 7th to the 28th we had the ruggedest weather we had yet experienced. The weather was cold, the gales of wind were successive and strong, and sometimes very violent. Our ships complained. We were short of water, and had an unknown coast to explore. And the very day we purposed to reconnoitre for a harbour, the wind veered to the N.E. and forced us off the coast a full week. We entered this inlet about 4 o'clock in the afternoon. The extremes of the opening at the entrance were about 2 miles distant, and we had the prospect of a snug harbour. It was a matter of doubt with many of us whether we should find any inhabitants here, but we had scarcely entered the inlet before we saw that hardy, that intriped, that glorious creature man approaching us from the shore. As we advanced into the inlet we found it still more favorable, and perceived several small islands between the two shores. Night approaching we came to an anchor between one of those islands and the eastern shore about one quarter of a mile from each. In the evening we were visited by several canoes full of the natives; they came abreast our ship within two rods of us and there staid the whole night, without offering to approach nearer or to withdraw farther from us, neither would they converse with us. At the approach of day they departed in the same reserve and silence.

On the 30th we sent our boats to examine a small cove in the opposite island, which answering our wishes we moved with both ships into it and moored within a few rods of the surrounding beach.

This inlet proving to be a sound was called George's-Sound. It lies in lat. 49. 33. N. and in 233.16.E. long. and as it afforded excellent timber we furnished ourselves with a new mizen-mast, spare yards and other spars, besides wood. It also afforded us excellent water, a variety of good fish and the shores with some excellent plants. The country round this sound is generally high and mountainous, though further to the northward and eastward it appears more open and level. It is intirely covered with woods, such as maple, ash, birch, oak, hemlock, but mostly with tall well grown pine. We also found currant bushes, wild rasberry and juniper bushes, and little crabed apple-trees, but could not learn whether they bore any fruit, neither is it probable they do. We saw no plantations or any appearance that exhibited any knowledge of the cultivation of the earth, all seemed to remain in a state of nature; but as our observations did not extend three miles into the country they are imperfect. Neither did we explore the sound highest up than three leagues, as that satisfied us that it was of no great extent beyond. The light in which this country will appear most to advantage respects the variety of its animals, and the richness of their furr. They have foxes, sables, hares, marmosets, ermines, weazles, bears, wolves, deer, moose, dogs, otters, beavers, and a species of weazle called the glutton; the skin of this animal was sold at Kamchalka, a Russian factory on the Asiatic coast for sixty rubles which is near 12 guineas, and had it been sold in China it would have been worth 30 guineas. We purchased while here about 1500 beaver, besides other skins, but took none but the best, having no thoughts at that time of using them to any other advantage than converting them to the purposes of cloathing, but it afterwards happened that skins which did not cost the purchaser sixpence sterling sold in China for 100 dollars. Neither did we purchase a quarter part of the beaver and other furrskins we might have done, and most certainly should have done had we known of meeting the opportunity of disposing of them to such an astonishing profit.

On the 1st of April we were visited by a number of the natives in their boats, which resemble our batteaux, They are about 20 feet in length, contracted at each end, and about 3 feet broad in the middle, and 2 feet and an half deep from end to end: They are made from large pine-trees, and we suppose burnt out. This was the first fair opportunity after our arrival that I had of examining the appearance of those unknown aborigines of North-America. It was the first time too that I had been so near the shores of that continent which gave me birth from the time I at first left it; and though more than two thousand miles distant from the nearest part of New-England I felt myself plainly affected: All the affectionate passions incident to natural attachments and early prejudices played round my heart, and indulged them because they were prejudices. I was harmonized by it. It soothed a home-sick heart, and rendered me very tolerably happy.

I had no sooner beheld these Americans than I set them down for the same kind of people that inhabit the opposite side of the continent. They are rather above the middle stature, copper-coloured, and of an athletic make. They have long black hair, which they generally wear in a club on the top of the head, they fill it when dressed with oil, paint and the downe of birds. They also paint their faces with red, blue and white colours, but from whence they had them or how they were prepared they would not inform us, nor could we tell. Their cloathing generally consists of skins, but they have two other sorts of garments, the one is made of the inner rind of some sort of bark twisted and united together like the woof of our coarse cloaths, the other very strongly resembles the New-Zealand Togo, and is also principally made with the hair of their dogs, which are mostly white, and of the domestic kind: Upon this garment is displayed very naturally the manner of their catching the whale—we saw nothing so well done by a savage in our travels. Their garments of all kinds are wore mantle-wise, and the borders of them are fringed or terminated with some particular kind of ornament like it: Their richest skins when converted to garments are edged with a great curiosity. This is nothing less than the very species of wampum so well known on the opposite side of the continent: It is identically the same: and this wampum was not only found among all the aborigines we saw on this side the continent, but even exits unmutilated on the opposite coasts of North-Asia. We saw them make use of no coverings to their feet or legs, and it was seldom they covered their heads: When they did it was with a kind of basket covering made after the manner and form of the Chinese and Chinese-Tartars hats. Their language is very guttural, and if it was possible to reduce it to our orthography would very much abound with consonants.

In their manners they resemble the other aborigines of North-America, they are bold and ferocious, sly and reserved, not easily provoked but revengeful; we saw no signs of religion or worship among them, and if they sacrifice it is to the God of liberty.

When a party was sent to procure some grass for our cattle they would not suffer them to take a blade of it without payment, nor had we a mast or yard without an acknowledgment. They intimated to us that the country all round further than we could see was theirs. Water and wood they charged us nothing for. Capt. Cook would not credit this fact when he first heard it and went in person to be assured of it, and persisting in a more peremptory tone in his demands, one of the Indians took him by the arm and thrust him from him, pointing the way for him to go about his business. Cook was struck with astonishment, and turning to his people with a smile mixed with admiration exclaimed, "This is an American indeed!" and instantly offered this brave man what he thought proper to take; after which the Indian took him and his men to his dwelling and offered them such as he had to eat. This characteristic of theirs and having found but one instance of theft among them set these people high in Cook's opinion. The houses we saw near this cove appeared to be only temporary residences from whence it was supposed that in winter they retired into the interior forests, and in summer lived any where that best answered the purposes of fishing or hunting.

The food we saw them use consisted solely of dried fish and blubber oil, the best by far that any man among us had ever seen: this they put into skins. We purchased great quantities of it, and situated as we were with respect to butter or suet, it was a very good succedaneum to either, and was constantly used to fry with; besides it furnished our lamps, and answered many other purposes useful and necessary. Like all uncivilized men they are hospitable, and the first boat that visited us in the Cove brought us what no doubt they thought the greatest possible regalia, and offered it to us to eat; this was a human arm roasted. I have heard it remarked that human flesh is the most delicious, and therefore tasted a bit, and so did many others without swallowing the meat or the juices, but either my conscience or my taste rendered it very odious to me.

We intimated to our hosts that what we had tasted was bad, and expressed as we could our disapprobation of eating it on account of its being part of a man like ourselves. They seemed to be sensible by the contortions of our faces that our feelings were disgusted and apparently paddled off with equal dissatisfaction and disappointment themselves. We were complimented once before in the same stile, at our first discovery of Sandwich Islands.

The custom of eating human flesh is very extensive and pervades much the greatest part of the habitable earth, and as it seems aboriginally to have been derived from the antecedent custom of sacrificing human flesh, it would be curious to enquire into this matter.

The custom of sacrificing is very ancient. The first instance we have of it is in the lives of Cain and Abel, Their sacrifices consisted in part of animal flesh, burnt upon an alter dedicated to their God. This custom exists now among all the uncivilized and Jewish nations in the essential rites requisite to prove it analogous to the first institution. The only mutilation in the ceremony materially different, is that the barbarous nations have added human flesh. Whether this additional ingredient in the oblation took place at a remote subsequent period by the antecedent intervention of any extraordinary circumstance independent of the original form does not appear, unless we place the subsequent period below the time of Abraham or perhaps below the time of Jeptha. The circumstance of Abraham's intended sacrifice of Isaac to which he was injoined by the Deity, though he absolutely did not do it, yet was sufficient to introduce the idea that such a sacrifice was the most pleasing to God, and as it was an event very remarkable it probably became an historical subject, and went abroad among other tribes, and was handed down among them by tradition, and liable to all the changes incident thereto, and in time the story might have been that Abraham not only offered but really did sacrifice his own son. But perhaps the story of Jeptha, judge of Israel, is more to the point. It is said he sacrificed his daughters as a burnt-offering to the God who had been propitious to him in war; which does appear to be an act independent of custom or tradition, as it transpired wholly from the obligations of a rash vow made to the Deity in the fulness of a heart surcharged with hopes and fears. It is also a fact that after this, particularly in the reign of the wicked Ahaz, it was a general custom, especially among the heathen, to make their children "pass through the fire;" by which I suppose it is understood that they were sacrificed with fire. It seems then that the circumstance of adding human flesh in the ceremony of sacrificing did take place before the years antecedent to Christ, and most probably from the example of Jeptha. After this we find it shifting places, attending the duffusive emigrations of the tribes, and commixing with mankind in general, but especially with those disunited with the chosen descendants of the great Abraham; whose descendants being constantly favored with civil and religious instructions from Heaven itself, were not only preserved from superstition and barbarity themselves, but were the means of furnishing the detached heathen with a variety of customs and ceremonies, that from the mere light of nature they never could have thought of; nor could they preserve pure and uncorrupt after they had adopted them. Even the favored Israelites were perpetually deviating into schisms and cabals and frequently into downright idolatry, and all the vanity of superstition and unbridled nonsense from the imbecility of human policy when uninfluenced by heavenly wisdom and jurisprudence. No wonder then that the separate tribes from the house of Abraham, though they primarily received many of their principles of civil and religious government from a pure fountain, should debase and contaminate them by the spurious conjunction of things derived from their own imaginations. And this seems to have been the course of things to this day. There hath always been a part of mankind conspicious for knoledge, superior in wisdom, and favored by heaven, from whom others are separated; and these, like the moon, have only shone with borrowed light. Some customs may be local and indigenous to particular times and circumstances, both in the civilized and uncivilized world, but far the greater part are derivative and were originally bestowed on many by his supreme Governor; those that we find among the civilized and wise, measured on a philosophic scale, are uncorrupted, while those that we find existing in parts remote from civilization and knowledge, though they have a resemblance which plainly intimates from whence they came, are yet debased mutilated, and by some hardly known. But who, that had seen a human body sacrificed at Otaheite to their God of war, would not perceive an analogy to antient custom on those occassions, and attribute it rather to such custom than any other cause whatever, and the custom is not confined to Otaheite alone, it pervades the islands throughout the Pacific-Ocean. It was the case with the ancient Britons. The Maxicans depopulated society by this carniverous species of sacrifice. This could not be the effect of accident, want or caprice. It may be worth notice to remark furthermore: that in the time of Ahaz these sacrifices were made in high places. It was so in Mexico—is so at Otaheite and other islands. The Mexicans flung their victims from the top of their temple dedicated to their God of war. The Otaheiteans and the other Islanders prepare those oblations on their morass.

These people are possessed of a variety of impliments calculated for war, hunting, fishing and other purposes, some of which are remarkably analogous to ancient models, particularly the lance, which is every way similar to that used in ancient tournaments and feats of chivalry. They have also a kind of armor that covers the body from the breast downward to the knees; this consists of mooseskin, covered externally with slips of wood sewed to the leather transversly, and made short or long as best suits the part of the body it covers. They have also good bows and arrows, and stone hatchets; also a variety of snares both for fowl and quadrupedes. Their fishing geer is highly curious. I can give no adequate description of the variety and singularity of these matters: They have near a dozen different kinds of fish-hooks, and all made of wood, but was an European to see any one of them without any previous information of their design, he would as soon conclude they were intended to catch men as fish. They have a harpoon made from a mushel shell only, and yet they have so disposed of it as to subdue the great leviathan, and tow the unweildly monster to their shores. Let no man think meanly of himself, but claim that glorious rank his amazing powers so justly entitle him to. If Descartes and Newton from the improvements of ages could produce at last the magnificent system of Philosophy that hath immortalized them; why should not these glorious savages, who, without any of those great collateral assistances, without which THEY could have done nothing, have discovered such astonishing sagacity be intitled to equal veneration, and the name of Ben Uncus be as great as that of Isaac Newton.

We found a few copper bracelets and three or four rough wrought knives with coarse wooded hafts among the natives at this place, but could not learn from the appearance of either of those articles or from any information they could give us how they became possessed of them, but it was generally thought they came from a great distance and not unlikely from Hudson's-Bay. Commerce is defusive and nothing will impede its progress among the uninformed part of mankind, but an intervention of too remote a communication by water, and as this cannot be the case with regard to the inhabitants of a continent, it seems intirely conclusive to suppose no part of America is without some sort of commercial intercourse, immediate or remote.

On the 26th of April we towed out of the sound in a calm, about sun down we were favored with a breeze that gave us a tolerable offing, but before 12 at night the wind veered from N.N.W. to E.S.E. and was succeeded by a sudden and impetuous gale of wind that threw us into the utmost confusion from its unexpected approach and our unprepared situation to receive it. This gale continued with very little intermission until the 1st of May, when it abated and we had fair weather. We parted company with our consort the Discovery the first night and concluded from our own distresses some irrepairable misfortune had attended her. We lay to on that account the greatest part of the time, and she adopting the same plan occasioned our meeting again two days before the gale entirely subsided. This gale was very severe, and was the means of opening a defective place in the *Resolution's* bottom, which was of an alarming nature. We did not meet with an opportunity of repairing it untill some time after, when we found that the complaint originated from a hole eat through the bottom of the ship as far as the sheathing by the rats, and the sheathing being old gave way when the ship strained: we were surprized to find the apperture stoped up by some old shakings of yarns and oakum, that by some accident was washed into it.

We continued our course, after this the coast trending about N.W. untill the 10th of May being then in Lat. 59°. 33 N. and Long. 217. 23 E. without any particular occurrence.

On the 11th of May we found the coast abruptly trending to the westward of south appearing to be broken, detached and irregular in the height.

On the 12th at nine in the morning we entered an inlet, steering as it trended, which was about N.N.W. and N. At six in the evening perceiving bad weather approaching we run in with the land and both ships anchored, and finding the weather as yet to be tolerable we flung out the boats and sent them on shore to fish with the seine, but caught nothing. The pinnace of the *Resolution* with the first lieutenant, some other gentlemen and myself went to the opposite shore to shoot some wild fowl. We had some success, and being engaged in our sports, and not suspecting the country from its inhospitable appearance to be inhabited were surprized when we saw several large boats full of Indians already close upon us from behind a small island.

We had but three or four fowling pieces with us, and the Indians being numerous, and we being out of the sight of the ships our situation was mentioned to Mr. Gore (the first lieutenant) as being disagreeable. Mr. Gore confessed he was afraid the Indians would want to quarrel, which he should be sorry to do though under no apprehensions for our own safety, but for the lives of the savages, who must sacrifice their prowess to unequal force. He therefore gave orders to let them come within musket shot, and then row for the ships: We indeed suffered them to come nearer, and they hallooed to us, making signs that they wanted to trade, and we returned them for answer as well as we could to follow us, and we would trade. This they complied with, shouting, shaking their spears and using a variety of noises and gesticulations that we knew nothing of until they came within hail of the ships, soon after which they stopped. The people

on board as well as those on shore observing our situation, and miscon-
struing our drawing them to the ships to have some interview with them
to a flight we were making from them, were uneasy, and an armed boat put
off from each ship, the one to assist us and the other the people on shore,
who were without arms. But we soon got on board with the pennace,
rectified the mistake, and boats were sent to try if they could not by some
friendly means persuade the savages to the ships, but in vain—they turned
their boats about and were soon out of sight.

We could perceive them to be a different kind of people from those
on George's Sound, and to have skin-canoes.

On the 13th though the weather was bad we came to sail and pursued
our course up the inlet not without hopes of the dear Passage, which was
now the only theme. The weather increasing to be bad, about four in the
afternoon we came to and moored in a snug road-stead, convenient for water,
and what was of more importance for the purpose of examining and repairing the leak occasioned by the temptuous night we left George's-Sound.

On the 14th while we were employed in these several services we were
visited by the natives who were the same kind of people we had seen the preceding day. We continued here until the 20th, during which time we sent our
boats to explore the inlet, and found it to be a large sound without any communication to any other sea or water northward. We therefore called it
Sandwich-Sound. It lies in lat. 61 39 north longitude 214 east, about 1500 miles
from Georges's-Sound. The inhabitants seem to be a distinct tribe from those
at George's-Sound, and bear a very striking resemblance if not an exact one
to the Esquimaux. I need give no other description of them. Their skin-
canoes, their double bladed paddles, their dress and other appearances of less
note are the same as on the coast of Labrador and in Hudson's-Bay. We found
them possessed of a few knives and copper trinkets like those we had seen
at George's-Sound, and found the wampum among them, which proves the
commercial intercourse as universal as I before observed it to be.

On the 20th of April we came to sail again, having watered and
repaired the leak in the *Resolution*. We pursued the direction of the coast,
which trended from S. E. to S. meaning to get out to sea again.

On the 21st we opened the southern extreme seen yesterday, and
doubling it entered another opening very capacious trending full to the eastward. Course all night N.E. by E.

On the 22nd and 23d mostly calm.

On the 24th we had hard squalls with sleet.

On the 25th steered N. by W. the land to starboard trending N.E. high and mountainous. At noon passed some large islands bearing W.S.W.

On the 26th the land exceeding high on both sides—passed two vulcanoes.

On the 27th found ourselves in what we conjectured to be a vast river, having a strong southerly current—sounded 40 fathoms. This gave us hopes again of a Passage.

On the 29th we entered a large bay, and found the water brakish. Came to an anchor in 9 fathoms, and sent the boats to explore the coast. To the N.E. they entered a narrow opening trending N.W. which they pursued to 8 and 3 and a half fathoms water. They returned the same day. We were now in 62° 15 north 209° 55 east. The country here though it had some exceeding high mountains was in many places level, open, and well covered with wood, and inhabited. The inhabitants are the same as those we left in Sandwich-Sound. We called them the New-Esquimaux: They were also possessed of a little iron, and some European beads. It is remarkable that we distinctly heard pronounced the words YACUTA, YONEREE, which I very well remember to have heard pronounced by the American Indians from the frontiers of the northern American States. They have here as well as at the other parts of the coast we had hitherto explored a plenty and variety of rich furrs, which they exchanged with us upon the same terms we had hitherto practiced.

On the 1st day of June we came to sail, returning by the same rout we came, to the sea.

On the 6th we cleared the inlet which we called Hinchinbroke-Sound, the navigation of which had been very fatigueing.

On the 7th course S. by E. half E. coasting along the main. In the afternoon ran upou a sunken reef of rocks. But our good fortune still accompanying us got off without damage.

On the 11th we passed a great number of seals, seahorses and several whales.

On the 15th lost sight of land, and had blowing weather with sleet and rain.

On the 16th the weather abated, and we stood W. S.W. with a stiff breeze. Lat. 56° 23 long. 205 16.

On the 17th stood in and saw the land trend S.E. half E. 2 leagues from the land.

On the 18th our lat. was 55 long. 200 58 within one mile of the shore. At 3 in the afternoon we observed 3 canoes making to us from the shore in which were six Indians. When they came along side which they did without any hesitation they made signs to us to drop our anchors, and shewed us a pair of old plush breeches, and black cloth waistcoat. These circumstances were as curious as unexpected. We hove to, and the Indians came close along side, and made signs to us to give them a rope, which being done one of the Indians made the end of it fast to a little box made of bark and desired us to hale it on board, after which they returned to the shore. This box contained to our infinite surprize several separate notes written upon European paper, and in European characters, but we could not understand the language though we thought we saw the figures 1778 pretty plain. This occasioned much speculation but was not thought of sufficient consequence to detain the ships for a further enquiry by sending on shore after the Indians. We therefore continued our course along the coast.

On the 21st course S.W. and S.S.W. passed two lofty vulcanoes. The land covered with snow. Hove to and caught several hundred holybret, and cod-fish—an acceptable supply!

On the 24th altered our course S. by E.

On the 25th we changed our course S. by W. as the land trended. About 7 in the evening we saw distant land bearing nearly south. By 10 o'clock we had a thick fog; sited signal guns to the *Discovery* and burnt false fires. At 3 o'clock in the morning heard the noise of a surf, sounded 24 fathoms. The noise of the surf encreasing we were alarmed; fired a signal of distress and came to an anchor with the *Discovery* just under our lee.

On the 27th the fog cleared up, and we found ourselves embayed with rocks, reefs, and an island, all within two cables length. We were not only amazed to find ourselves in such a frightful situation, but were still more astonished to conceive how we got there, as the least accidental deviation from the course we had steered would have been fatal, and we did not steer uniformly to any particular point, but generally as we conceived the coast to trender from the bearings and distances taken the preceeding day. From this circumstance we named the island in view Providence Island. In the afternoon we entered a passage between Providence-Island and the main that opened to the northward, and finding a snug bay in the island we entered it with both ships and moored. This island with a few rocks to the S.W. forms the southern and western extreme of that part of the continent which took so abrupt a direction to the southward and westward from the lat. 59 33 north, and long. 217 33 east, Providence-Island in 55 18 north, 195 east.

While we were busied in watering in this harbour we were constantly visited by the natives, among whom we found other intimations like those we had seen lately of an European intercourse with this part of the world, and we doubted much if some Europeans were not actually at that time there. This, however, we deferred enquiring about at present as we expected to touch at the same island on our return to southward if unsuccessful in our future attempts for the Passage to the northward.

On the 2nd of July we came to sail, and passed through the remaining part of the streight between the island and the main, and pursued our course, steering E.N.E.

On the 5th steered N.N.E. The land low and trending very much eastward. Lat. 57 4 long. 199 40.

On the 6th we continued the same course, and finding the water shoal tacked and stood S.E. this leading us to 3 and a half fathoms tacked again and stood N. We were now in a laborious and perilous navigation, and continued so until the 15th, when we clea[r]ed a labyrinth of rocks, shoals, and spits of sand, but found ourselves again involved on the 16th and we were obliged to bring to an anchor, and send the boats out to explore. The nearest land about 7 leagues distant. Our boats were cut all night, sounded in different directions without being able to find a channel to the northward, eastward or westward.

On the 17th to crown our joys it came on to blow, and we parted our best bower cable in the bend and lost the anchor.

On the 18th the gale abating we spent the day in sweeping for our anchor which we finally recovered by the exertions of a mad-hardy Tar, who dived to the freezing bottom and hooked a grapling to the ring. The anchor was in five fathom water.

The 19th was spent in sounding without success.

On the 20th Captain Cook himself went out and found a channel with regular soundings from 8 to 10 fathoms, to the S.E. In consequence of this we weighed and came to sail. Lat. 59 37 longit. 197 16.

On the 21st the nearest land 5 leagues. Hove to having a head-wind and current setting southerly. In the afternoon were much surprized to see eight canoes full of Indians paddling full speed towards the ships. They did not hesitate to come near enough to the ships to converse and traffic, but would not come on board of us. They were tall, well made, wild fierce looking people, in skin canoes, and every way like all those we had seen since we left George's-Sound, except in the dress of their hair, which was exactly like the Mahometan Tartars.

On the 22nd deepened our water to 40 fathoms, which gave us much satisfaction.

On the 23rd had a heavy snowstorm, which lasted until the 26th when it cleared up.

On the 29th altered our course to N.N.E. and N.E.

On the 1st of August our lat. was 61 14 long. 191 33. Continued our course along the coast varying as it trended.

On the 5th our lat. was 64 44 long. 192 42. To day we were opposite a small uninhabited island. Hove to and sent our boats on shore. They brought us off some wild cellery, and a kind of chichilling. Mr. Anderson our surgeon died this day of a lingering illness that he had been subject to some years. He was the first person we had lost. His funeral ceremonies were decently performed according to the custom of the sea.

On the 6th stood W. by N. with the American shore a-board carrying from 4 to 6 fathoms soundings.

On the 8th our navigation being critical, and having a violent snow-storm both ships anchored.

On the 10th we had fine weather and opened a large inlet which afterwards proved to be a deep spacious sound, which we called Norton's-Sound after Sir Fletcher, Speaker of the British Commons. It lies in lat. 66 27 long. 188 3. We anchored in this sound. wooded and watered. We saw a few inhabitants of the Equimaux kind, but they seemed to be poor.

On the 11th we weighed, and steering northward; on the 12th passed the eastern and western extremes of Asia and America keeping the American shore a-board.

On the 13th stood to the eastward, with the coast in view until the 17th when the weather of a sudden became piercing cold.

On the 18th we saw ice ahead, broken, detached and low. Lat. 69 46 long. 192. Finding the ice penetrable we advanced into the openings. These loose fields of ice are covered with numerous herds of seahorses who repose themselves upon them, after they have completed their excursions in the water in pursuit of their food, which is fish and such marine productions as they find at the bottom of the water. They are a large unweildly sluggish animal weighing some of them nine hundred and some eleven hundred weight. Their legs are very short and terminate in a webed membrane, with which they swim very swift and are very active in the water though exceeding clumsy out of that element. They are amphibious and between a quadrupede and a fish, their heads are somewhat like those of a dog, without ears, except two large white tusks that project downward from the upper jaw about eighteen inches or two feet; they have a thick skin like that of a horse, and the hair is of a chesnut colour. They are exceeding fat, and will produce more than a barrel of oil.

On the 19th we lay to among the ice, and sent the boats to the ice to hunt the sea-horse. Killed several and brought them on board but it was thought an ill reward for their labor by the people when they understood that the short pittance of European food was to be withheld from them, and this substituted in its room. But Cook was determined upon the point, and set the example himself by making it his constant food while it lasted. The people at first murmered, and at last eat it through mere vexation; and trying to see who would eat most of it in order to consume it the sooner, some of the people rather overdid the matter, which producing some laughable circumstances, the Tars swore they would eat it or any thing else that Cook did, for they were certain that nothing would kill him in the heavens above or the earth beneath or in the waters under the earth.

On the 20th we continued laboring among the ice. Lat. this day 70 9 long. 194 55.

Nothing remarkable until the 25th when we had blowing weather, which rendered our situation among the ice dangerous. This occasioned a council of officers, and it was resolved that as this Passage was impracticable for any purpose of navigation, which was the great object of the voyage to pursue it no further at least that season. The ships too were in bad condition, the weather approaching, and the distance from any known place of refreshment very great.

On the 28th we left the ice and stood S.S.W. Our highest lat. being 71 17 long. 197.

On the 29th stood more to the westward with a view to trace the ice to the Asiatic shore.

On the 1st of September made the Asiatic coast in lat. 58 10 long. 182 2.

On the 2nd we passed again the two capes that form the eastern and western extremes of Asia and America, and as we kept the middle of the channel, which is about 14 leagues over, had the pleasure to see both continents at once. The Asiatic cape is called by the Russians the Ischutka Noss. The American cape, Cape Prince of Wales.

From this we went again to Norton's Sound. Our visit here on our rout to northward being but partial and the supplies we took of wood and water being but small as soon as we could find a road-stead we anchored, determining to supply ourselves well with those articles and to have a thorough survey of this extensive Sound. This detained us until the 17th day of September. We were visited by some of the natives while here, and purchased an agreeable supply of good fish. We also refreshed ourselves much by our exercises on shore in which we were seldom met by the natives and never molested. The country had a tolerable appearance, generally covered with wood and abounded with ducks, bustards, eagles and other fowl, but we saw no animals. We also found an unbounded plenty of whurts, red and black currants. These curiosities were most industriously gathered and eat, and such an excellent effect had they upon us that when we left this place the people (who from long confinement, hard duty, scanty and almost any fare had become pale, languid and poor) were transformed into new beings almost, and were literally grown fat, plump and rosy.

On the 17th the boats that were sent out to explore and survey returned having traced the sound to the head and examined both shores.

On the 18th we weighed and sailed retracing the coasts we had before explored, without any particular discoveries.

On the 25th we had a severe gale of wind, and the *Resolution* again sprung a leak, which was so bad that we were kept pumping and bailing night and day until we again got into Providence-Harbour. We passed several islands during our run to Providence-Harbour, which were barren and uninhabited.

On the 29th were again overtaken with a severe gale rendered doubly so by the embarrassments we were already under from our leak.

On the 2d of October we made the Island of Providence, which we left the 2d of July on our rout to the northward, and the next day entered our old harbour and both ships moored in seven fathoms close in with the shore. Our first care was to examine and repair our leak which we immediately set about. When this matter was completed, we overhauled our rigging, caulked the upper works, and then watered. We had also in the mean time set our armourers and smiths at work to cut up a spare bower anchor and work it into hatchets, spikes, and such other forms as would best answer the purposes of traffic among the tropical islands where we were now going to wait the returns of another season in order to make a second attempt for the Passage, though in fact we were well convinced already of its non-existence. Cook alone seemed bent upon a second trial.

I have before observed that we had noticed many appearances to the eastward of this, as far almost as Sandwich-Sound, of an European intercourse, and that we had at this island in particular met with circumstances that did not only indicate such an intercourse but seemed strongly to intimate that some Europeans were actually somewhere on spot. The appearances that formed these conjectures were such as these: We found among the inhabitants of this island two different kinds of people, the one we knew to be the aborigines of America, while we supposed the others to have come from the opposite coasts of Asia. There were two different dialects also observed, and we found them fond of tobacco, rum, and snuff, tobacco we even found them possessed of, and we observed several blue linen shirts and drawers among them. But the most remarkable circumstance was a cake of rye-meal newly baked with a piece of salmon in it seasoned with pepper and salt, which was brought and presented to Cook by a comely young chief attended by two of those Indians which we supposed to be Asiatics. The chief seemed anxious to explain to Cook the meaning of the present and the purport of his visit, and he was so far succesful as to persuade him that there were some strangers in the country, who were white, and had come over the great waters in a vessel somewhat like ours, and though not so large was yet much larger than theirs.

In consequence of this Cook was determined to explore the island. It was difficult however to fix upon a plan, that would at once answer the purpose of safety and expedition: An armed body would proceed slowly, but if they should be cut off by the Indians, the loss in our present circumstances would be irreparable, and a single person would entirely risk his life though he would be much more expeditious if unmolested, and if he should be killed the loss would be only one. The latter seemed the best, but it seemed extremely hard to single out an individual and command him to go upon such an expedition, and it was therefore thought proper to send a volunteer, or none. I was at this time and indeed ever after an intimate friend of John Gore, Esq; first lieutenant of the *Resolution*, a native of America as well as myself, and superior to me in command, he recommended me to Capt. Cook to undertake the expedition, with which I immediately acquiesced. Capt. Cook assured me that he was happy I had undertaken the rout as he was conscious I should persevere, and after giving me some instructions how to proceed he wished me well and desired I would not be longer absent than a week if possible, at the expiration of which he should expect me to return. If I did not return by that time he should wait another week for me, and no longer. The young chief before-mentioned and his two attendants were to be my guide. I took with me some presents adapted to the taste of the Indians some brandy in bottles and some bread, but no other provisions. I went entirely unarmed by the advice of Capt. Cook. The first day we proceeded about 15 miles into the interior part of the island without any remarkable occurrences until we approached a village just before night. This village consisted of about thirty huts, some of them large and spacious though not very high. The huts are composed of a kind of slight frame erected over a square hole sunk about 4 feet into the ground; the frame is covered at the bottom with turf and upwards it is thatched with coarse grass; the whole village was about to see us and men, women and children crouded about me. I was conducted by the young Chief who was my guide and seemed proud and assiduous to serve me into one of the largest hutts. I was surprized at the behaviour of the Indians, for though they were curious to see me, yet they did not express that extraordinary curiosity that would be expected had they never seen an European before, and I was glad to perceive it, as it was an evidence in favor of what I wished to find true viz. that there were Europeans now among them. The women of the house which were almost the only ones I had seen at this Island were much more tolerable than I expected to have found them, one in particular seemed very busy to please me, to her therefore I made several presents with which she was extremely well pleased. As it was now dark, my young chief intimated to me that we must tarry where we were that night, and proceed further the next day; to which I very readily conceeded, being much fatigued. Our entertainment the subsequent part of the evening did not consist of much delicacy or variety; they had some dryed fish, and I had some bread and some spirits, of which we all participated. Ceremony was not invited to the feast, and nature presided over the entertainment until morning. At day-light Perpheela (which was the name of the young chief that was my guide) let me know he was ready to go on, upon which I flung off the skins I had slept in, put on my shoes and outside vest, and arose to accompany him, after repeating my presents to my friendly guests. We had hitherto travelled in a northerly direction, but now went to the westward and southward. I was now so much relieved from the apprehension of any insult or injury from the Indians, that my journey would have been even agreeable had I not been taken lame, with a swelling in the feet, which rendered it extremely painful to walk; the country was also rough and hilly, and the weather wet and cold. About 3 hours before dark we came to a large bay, which appeared to be 4 leagues over. Here my guide, Perpheela took a canoe and all our baggage, and set off, seemingly to cross the bay. He appeared to leave me in an abrupt manner, and told me to follow the two attendants. This gave me some uneasiness. I now followed Perpheela's two attendants, keeping the bay in view, but we had not gone about six miles before we saw a canoe approaching us from the opposite side of the bay, in which were two Indians, as soon as my guides saw the canoe we ran to the shore from the hills and hailed them, and finding they did not hear us we got some bushes and waved them in the air, which they saw, and stood directly for us. This canoe was sent by Perpheela to bring me across the bay, and shorten the distances of the journey.

It was beginning to be dark when the canoe came to us. It was a skin canoe after the Equimaux plan with two holes to accommodate two setters. The Indians that came in the canoe talked a little with my two guides, and then came to me and desired I would get into the canoe, which I did not very readily agree to, however, as there was no other place for me but to be thrust into the space between the holes extended at length upon my back and wholly excluded from seeing the way I went or the power of extricating myself upon any emergency. But as there was no alternative I submitted thus to be stowed away in bulk, and went head foremost very swift through the water about an hour, when I felt the canoe strike a beach, and afterwards lifted up and carried some distance, then sat down again, after which I was drawn out by the shoulders by three or four men, for it was now so dark I could not tell who they were, though I was conscious I heard a language that was new. I was conducted by two of those persons who appeared to be strangers about 40 rods, when I saw some lights and a number of huts like those I left in the morning. As we approached one of them a door opened, and discovered a lamp, by which to my joy and surprize I discovered that the two men who held me by each arm were two Europeans, fair and comely, and concluded from their appearance they were Russians, which I soon after found to be true. As we entered the hut which was particularly long I saw arranged on each side a platform of plank a number of Indians, who all bowed to me, and as I advanced to the farther end of the hut the arangment was composed of other Russians. When I reached the end of the room I was seated on a bench covered with furr-skins, and as I was much fatigued, wet and cold, I had a change of garments brought me, consisting of a blue silk shirt and drawers, a furr-cap, boots and gown, all which I put on with the same chearfulness they were presented with. Hospitality is a virtue particularly to man, and the obligation is as great to receive as to confer. As soon as I was rendered warm and comfortable a table was set before me with a lamp upon it; all the Russians in the house set down round me, and the bottles of spirits, tobacco, snuff, and whatever Perpheela had was brought and set upon it; these I presented to the company, intimating that they were presents from Commodore Clock, who was an Englishman. One of the company then gave me to understand, that all the white people I saw there were subjects of the Empress Catherine of Russia, and rose and kissed my hand the rest uncovering their heads. I then informed them as well as I could that Commodore Cook wanted to see some of them, and had sent me there to conduct them to our ships. These preliminaries over we had some supper, which consisted of some boiled whale, holybret fried in oil, and some broiled salmon. The latter I eat, and they gave me some rye-bread, but would eat none of it themselves, but they were very fond of the rum, which they drank without any mixture or measure. I had a very comfortable bed composed of different furr-skins both under and over me, and bing harrassed the preceeding day I went soon to rest. After I had lain down the Russians assembled the Indians in a very silent manner, and said prayers after the manner of the Greek Church, which is much like the Roman. I could not but observe with what particular satisfaction the Indians performed their devoirs to God through the medium of their little crucifixes, and with what pleasure they went through the multitude of ceremonies attendant on that sort of worship. I think it a religion the best calculated in the world to gain proselytes when the people are either unwilling or unable to speculate, or where they cannot be made acquainted with the history and principles of christianity without a formal education.

I had a very comfortable nights rest, and did not wake the next morning untill late. As soon as I was up I was conducted to a hutt at a little distance from the one I had slept in, where I saw a number of platforms raised about three feet from the ground, and covered with dry coarse grass and some small green bushes. There were several of the Russians already here besides these that conducted me, and several Indians who were heating some water in a large copper caldron over a furnace, the heat of which, and the steam which evaporated from the hot water rendered the hutt which was very tight extremely hot and suffocating. I soon understood this was a hot bath of which I was asked to make use of in such a friendly manner, and the apparatus being a little curious so that I conceeded to it, but before I had finished undressing myself, I was overcome by the sudden transition of the air, fainted away and fell back upon the platform I was sitting on. I was however soon relieved by having some cold and lukewarm water administered to my face and different parts of my body, I finished undressing myself and proceeded as I saw the rest do, who were now all naked: the Indians who served us brought us as we set or extended ourselves on the platforms water of different temperature from that which was as hot as we could bear to quite cold. The hot water was accompanied with some hard soap and a flesh-brush; it was not however thrown on the body from the dish, but sprinkled on with the green bushes, after this the water made use of was less warm, and by several graduations became at last quite cold which concluded the ceremony, and we again dressed and returned to our lodging, where our breakfast was smoking on the table, but the flavor of our feast as well as its appearance had nearly produced a relapse in my spirits, and no doubt would if I had not had recourse to some of the brandy I had brought which happily saved me. I was a good deal uneasy least the cause of my discomposure should disoblige my friends who meant to treat me in the best manner they could. I therefore attributed my illness to the bath which might possibly have partly occasioned it, for I am not very subject to fainting. I could eat none of the breakfast however, though far from wanting an appetite: it was mostly of whale, sea-horse and bear, which, though smoaked, dryed and boiled, produced a composition of smells very offensive at nine or ten in the morning. I therefore desired I might have a piece of smoaked Salmon broiled dry, which I eat with some of my own biscuit. After breakfast I intended to have set off on my return to the ships though there came on a disagreable snow storm. But my new found friend objected to it, and gave me to understand that I should go the next day, and if I chose three of them would accompany me, this I immediately agreed to as it anticipated a favor I intended to have asked them, though I before much doubted whether they would comply with it. I amused myself within doors while it snowed without, by writing down a few words of the original languages of the American Indians, and the Asiatics who came over to this coast with these Russians from Kamchatka. The Numerals in the two languages are as [f]ollows.

American.	Kamchatka.	English.
Tantuck	Ezuck	One
Auluck	Kaush	Two
Konnoqueet	Choke	Three
Chauung	Chauke	Four

Autung	Komoolke	Five
Ooloong	Kilkoke	Six
Kamichew	Eklunnoko	Seven
Schee	Choketunnoke	Eight
Kaufuck	Chauktunnoke	Nine
Seet	Towoofe	Ten

I shall not make any particular observations on the foregoing specimens, but content myself that I have brought those new and remote languages to the closeness of my countrymen, whose learned ease will better enable them to improve such an object of curiousity in investigating the origin of nations than I might do myself. These languages however are so guttural that it was equally difficult for me to obtain as it is to communicate their true sound by our orthography, and those who speak it properly must do it E Gutture, Per Labia, In Palato, et Per Dentes, as they would the Hebrew which it so much resembles.[8] The word Schee which stands for eight in the list of American numerals, is indeed very nearly like the Hebrew and Sehin. Indeed the guttural is the universal and radical pronunciation of all the aboriginal languages on this continent, from Greenland to the Istmus of Darien, and from Nova Zembla all over the northern parts of Europe and Asia.

In the afternoon the weather cleared up and I went out to see how those Russian adventurers were situated. I found the whole village to contain about 30 huts, all of which were built partly under ground, and covered with turf at the bottom, and coarse grass at the tops.

The only circumstance that can recommend them is their warmth, which is occasioned partly by their manner of construction, and partly by a kind of oven, in which they constantly keep a fire night and day. They sleep on platforms built on each side of the hutt, on which they have a number of Bear and other skins, which renders them comfortable, & as they have been educated in a hardy manner, they need little or no other support than what they procure from the sea, and from hunting. The number of Russians were about 30, and they had with them about 70 Kamchadales, or Indians from Kamchatka, these with some of the American Indians whom they had entered into friendship with occupied the village, enjoyed every benefit in common with the Russians, and were converts to their Religion. Such other of the aborigines of the island as had not become converts to their sentiments in religious and civil matters, were excluded from such privileges and were prohibited to wear certain arms—I also found a small sloop of about 30 tons burthen laying in a cove behind the village, and a hutt near her containing her sails, cordage, and other sea equipage, and one old Iron three-pounder. It is natural to an ingenious mind when it enters a town, a house, or ship that has been rendered famous by any particular events to feel the full force of that pleasure which results from the compleatest satisfaction that can be obtained to gratify a noble curiosity. I was no sooner informed that this sloop was the same in which the famous Bheering had performed those discoveries which did him so much honor, and his country such great services, than I was determined to go on board of her and indulge the generous feelings the occasion required. I intimated my wishes to the man that accompanied me who went back to the village and brought a canoe in which we went on board, where I remained about an hour, and then returned.

Bheering was a Russian by birth, and like his predecessor and Prince, Czar Peter seemed born to render those services to his country which none but the really great and those obstinately bent on doing good can do. There is a history of his life and discoveries extant, but I have never had the happiness to see it. though I was informed Cook had it with him. I am therefore under the necessity of recommending my readers to this history for a more perfect account of his proceedings in general as well as those which concern the present voyage, than what I am now able to furnish them with for the want of it. I am inclined to wish that so great a character as Cook's could not be stained by envy. But it is an absolute fact that Bheering's discoveries upon the coasts of America from the latitudes 59 N. and longitude S 217° E. to the island of Providence, and from thence taking the coast in general to the two famous capes, the Iscutska Noss, and Cape Prince of Wales were antecedant to Cooks, and they not only much facilitated his own navigation, but deprived him of the honor of being the sole discoverer of the N.W. continent of America, though it must be acknowledged that Bheering's knowledge of such parts as he did explore were incorrect, imperfect and infinitely below the consummate accuracy of Cook. Bheering's discoveries were those of an obscure unassisted genius who had every difficulty to surmount that can be thought incident to a man illiberally educated, and to such a vast undertaking, and Cook's those of a person whose fame had already been established, whose genius had all the assistance of it, and whose equipments in other respects were the studied accomodations of the greatest nautical kingdom on earth.

The little bark belonged to Kamchatka, and came from there with the

Asiatics already mentioned to this island (which they call Oonalatchka) in order to establish a pelt and fur factory. They had been here about five years, and go over to Kamchatka in her once a year to deliver their merchandize, and get a recruit of such supplies as they need from the chief factory there, of which I shall take further notice hereafter.

The next day I set off from this village well satisfied with the happy issue of a rout which was now as agreeable as it was at first undesirable. I was accompanied by three of the principle Russians and some attendants. We embarked at the village in a large skin boat much like our large whaleboats rowing with 12 oars, and as we struck directly across the bay we shortened our distance several miles, and the next day passing the same village I had before been at, we arrived by sundown at the bay where the ships lay, and before dark I got on board with our new acquaintance. The satisfaction this discovery gave Cook, and the honor that redounded to me may be easily imagined, and the several conjectures respecting the appearance of a foreign intercourse rectified and confirmed.

Providence Island is about 19 leagues in circumferance, and about 3 miles from the main, hilly and barren as to timber, and such as they make use of is what drifts upon the shores from different parts of the coast on the continent. It produces however several plants and flowers common to the climate, and among others a plenty of whurts.

On the first of November we set sail, and passing through the streights to the southward lost sight of Providence Island steering eastward and southward toward Sandwich Islands. We had now been nine months upon the coast of America, we had seen and suffered a great deal, and we had still more to see no doubt, but I believe nobody thought more to suffer. We had however the agreeable reflection of having explored the greatest part of the unknown coasts of northern and western America, and of having asscertained and fixed the exact limits to the whole of it, as well as the northern and eastern coasts of Asia, and the islands in the intermediate ocean.

★

In November 1778 Ledyard and the crew retreated from the icy north to spend the winter in Hawaii. After a seven-week sail around the archipelago, they landed at Kealakekua Bay on the western side of the

big island of Hawaii. During his three-week stay, Ledyard led an expe-
dition to climb Mauna Loa, a 13,000-foot peak. The two ships left the bay
in early February but returned a week later when the Resolution's mast
broke in a storm. Three days later on February 14, 1779, tensions between
the islanders and the sailors burst into the open, and a melee led to the
death of Cook and four marines, as well as dozens of Hawaiians.

In March the ships left the islands and at the end of April landed
at Petropavlovsk, a small Russian garrison on the Siberian coast. They
stayed more than a month before heading north.

We met with no particular occurrences on our passage from America to Sandwich Islands. Cook was very much inclined to think there were other islands contiguous to those we had already discovered, and distinguished by that appellation on our rout to the northward, and that they lay to the eastward, with this view we sailed eastward until we found ourselves in the lat. of Attowai, and that island 4 degrees west we then run down the longit. This answered Cook's expectation And,

On the 26th of November we discovered land 2 degrees east of Attowai, which we afterwards found to be an island called by the natives Hawyhee or Owyhee.

On the 27th in sailing in with Owyhee we discovered another island, called by the natives Mauwee, which is nearly in sight of Attowai, these with Nehun, Nehow, Maggadoo and some other small islands compose of a group of ten islands mostly in sight of each other, comprehending about of lat. [blank] and [blank] degrees of longitude. Owyhee which is the easternmost and most considerable, lies in lat. 19 28 north, and 204 east longitude from Greenwich, is nearly in a parallel latitude with Cape Lucas, which is the southernmost part of California in South-America, and is about 900 leagues distant from it.

It was immediately and very naturally supposed, that Cook's first object now would be to find a harbour, where our weather beaten ships might be repaired, and our fatigued crews receive the rewards due to their perseverance and toil through so great a piece of navigation as we had performed the last nine or ten months, but it was not so, and we continued laying off and on the north side of Mauwee, and particularly Owyhee until the 7th of December without any other supplies than what was brought off to us by the natives in their canoes some leagues from the shore. This conduct of the commander in chief was highly reprobated and at last remonstrated against by the people on board both ships, as it appeared very manifest that Cook's conduct was wholly influenced by motives of interest, to which he was evidently sacrificing not only the ships, but the healths and happiness of the brave men, who were weaving the laurel that was hereafter to adorn his brows.

On the 8th of December we stretched to the southward and eastward in order to get round to the southern side of Owyhee and get into a harbour, but it was the 16th of January before we found one, owing partly to the predetermined delays of the commander, and partly to bad weather.

On the 17th of January, 1779, we entered our harbour, which was a commodious bay situate nearly in the middle of the south side of Owyhee, and about a mile and a half deep, the extremes of the bay distant about two miles. We entered with both ships, and anchored in 7 fathoms water about the middle of the bay having on one side a town containing about 300 houses called by the inhabitants Kiverua, and on the other side a town containing 1100 houses, and called Kirekakooa. While we were entering the bay which they called Kirekakooa after the town Kirekakooa we were surrounded by so great a number of canoes that Cook ordered two officers into each top to number them with as much exactness as they could, and as they both exceeded 3000 in their amounts I shall with safety say there was 2500 and as there were upon an avarage 6 persons at least in each canoe it will follow that there was at least 15000 men, women and children in the canoes, besides those that were on floats, swimming without floats, and actually on board and hanging round the outside of the ships. The crouds on shore were still more numerous. The beach, the surrounding rocks, the tops of houses, the branches of trees and the adjacent hills were all covered, and the shouts of joy, and admiration proceeding from the sonorous voices of the men confused with the shriller exclamations of the women dancing and clapping their hands, the overseting of canoes, cries of the children, goods on float, and hogs that were brought to market squalling formed one of the most tumultuous and the most curious prospects that can be imagined. God of creation these are thy doings, these are our brethern and our sisters, the works of thy hands, and thou art not without a witness even here where for ages and perhaps since the beginning it has been hid from us, and though the circumstance may be beyond our comprehension let it not lessen the belief of the fact. Among all this immense multitude of people there was not the least appearance of insult. They had heard of our riches by those who had come off to us and traded, and from the people at Attowai, and concluding from our hovering round the island that we should visit them on shore, had prepared to meet us with supplies and give us a welcome. This previous preparation was the reason of this vast assemblage of people and provisions, and every one wanting to make the first bargain occasioned their coming all together. We purchased as many hogs that and the following day or two as we did for two months after, and had besides the advantage of refusing any but such as were of the best kind.

As soon as the *Resolution* was moored capt. Cook went on shore in his Pennace attended only by his barges crew and two of the chiefs, and landed upon a fine beach before the west part of the town of Kirekakooa. His crew were without arms and had himself only his hanger, which he never went without; the chiefs had each two long white poles which they held upright and waved to the people in the canoes, to make room, and as they passed through the throng, the chief cried out in their language that the great Orono was coming, at which they all bowed and covered their faces with their hands until he was passed, but the moment this was done they resumed their clamourous shouts, closed the vacant places astern, and as many as could crouded upon his rear to the shore.

The two chiefs first landed and joined many other of their brother officers who had also white rods in their hands, and observing the transactions of the two chiefs in the Pennace had also made an avenue among the people on shore. Cook in the mean time improving the awful respect he saw paid him among the natives, permitted himself to be carried upon the shoulders of his bargemen from the boat to the summit of the beach: the bargemen uncovered. As soon as he was set down, the multitude on the beach fell prostrate with their faces to the ground, and their arms extended forward. Those upon the adjacent hills, upon the houses, on the stone walls and on the tops of the trees also hid [t]heir faces while he passed along the opening, but he was no sooner past them than they rose and followed him, but if Cook happened to turn his head or look behind him they were down again in an instant and up again as soon, whenever his face was reverted to some other quarter, this punctilious performance of respect in so vast a throng being regulated solely by the accidental turn of one mans head and the transition being sudden and short rendered it very difficult even for an individual to be in proper attitude, if he lay prostate but a second too long he was pretty sure not to rise again until he had been trampled upon by all behind him, and if he dared not to prostrate himself he would stumble over those before him who did. This produced a great many laughable circumstances, and as

Cook walked very fast to get off from the sand into the shades of the town, it rendered the matter still more difficult. At length however they adopted a medium that much better answered a runing compliment and did not displease the chiefs. this was to go upon all fours, which was truly curious among at least ten thousand people. This concourse however did not continue long, for after passing through a finall part of the own only to the Morai, (which I shall describe hereafter.) This being a sanctified spot, and the people in general forbid to approach it, Cook was left much to his satisfaction, attended only by a few chiefs and their domestics, or rather Rikuanas whose characters I shall particularly describe hereafter. The first business Cook wished to accomplish was to obtain a commodious spot to erect his tents upon, particularly the astronomical tents, and observing a square potato patch between the S.E. side of the Morai and the sea that particularly struck his fancy, he addressed the chiefs concerning it. They immediately made him the offer of it which Cook accepted and made the chiefs that were present some valuable presents. Matters thus far had moved with Cook in the old Otaheitte stile, and he did not suppose a greater degree of refinement in negotiating would be required among the chiefs here than there; but he was mistaken, for it was no sooner agreed that Cook should have liberty to possess the before mentioned ground, than the chiefs required that Cook's people should never after sun-set proceed without the limits prescribed, and that their own people should at all times be utterly excluded from entering them, and as a ratification of what they had promised, they directly fixed on the top of the wall that surrounded the ground a number of the white rods before mentioned. The chiefs on our side were made an exception to this agreement, and those among the natives were to be admitted as we pleased. These propositions surprized Cook as they were new and unexpected; and he wished upon the whole that they might not be attended with some of the difficulties they seemed to portend, but when he contemplated the good sense by which they were dictated, and the harmony they were calculated to produce he acquiesed. After this Cook returned on board taking with him several of the chiefs who dined with him upon the fruits of their own country, which they liked boiled and roasted after our manner as well as their own. In the afternoon I was sent with a guard of marines selected for the purpose from both ship to take possession of our intended encampment, and in receiving my orders particular care was taken to mention at large the above mentioned agreement, which I was enjoined carefully to maintain uninfringed. The ardour of curiosity was now somewhat abated, but I had no sooner landed with the marines in compleat uniform, than the town began to pour forth its thousands again, but landing within the limits notified by the white rods, not a single individual approached beyond them, and our tents were pitched and sentries posted before sun-set without anoyance. I could not but reflect in this situation how much I was indebted either to the timidity or real innocence hospitality and generosity of the people whose immense numbers had they all been women would have trampled me to attoms. The intrinsic difference between us and them in every respect was certainly great, but the greatest difference was imaginary respecting them and imputed to us, the moment therefore that this supposed superiority of ours should cease to exist or be diminished, our consequences and importance would be at an end, or at least could only be supported the worst of all aids, an appeal to arms, which in our situation would ruin us though we conquered.

As soon as the sun set I ordered some additional sentries, and though the wondering Indians did not entirely evacuate the surrounding walls until dark, yet they retired in the greatest peace and good order.

The next morning as soon as the sun rose they began again to assemble upon the walls, where they continued untill night in the same manner they had done the preceding day. In this sort matters were conducted at the tents, and peace, plenty and good order prevailed. At length some of those difficulties Cook had foreseen and endeavoured to provide against began to discover themselves. The people at the tents complained that according to orders they were secluded the society of the fair, while the people on board were not, and that it was a just matter of complaint. This was partly true, and to remedy it would be to oppose and argue down the strongest passions; passions which seperately considered were not against the articles of war, and which like hunger would pervade stone walls. Their complaints had never been prefered to Cook in form. Mr. King the 2d Lieut. of the *Resolution* and Astronomer in chief had the command of the tents, accompanied by the Astronomer of the *Discovery* and some other gentlemen. These gentlemen had determined upon giving a tacit consent to the wishes of the people within this sacred jurisdiction upon several principles, they were sensible that should Cook receive their remonstrances from their hands he would resent it, and impute it to the imbecility of their command or to secret wishes in them to abet the demands of the people, and convert them ultimately to answer their own purposes, but were they to suffer the people to admit their mistresses or to go out to meet them without noticeing the matter, should it finally produce any mischief they then would have some colour of excuse—but they hoped this would not be the case, they hoped their sacrifices to Venus would be more propitious and productive of far other circumstances. The people had often attmepted to prosecute the illicit amours when they risqued the resentment of their officers, but they no sooner perceived themselves freed from this restraint by their conduct, than they were determined whenever opportunity favored to improve the hint. For my own part I really foresaw the mischiefs that would ensue, and endeavored to put the matter upon another footing, though without success. The embarrassments our enamouratoes were already under, were still greater from our contiguity to the Morai, which the women of the country never dare approach from religious motives, exclusive of the considerations of being the first to infringe upon the conditions they have subsisting between their chiefs and us of another kind.

There was in short no alternative but for our people to go without the lines and meet their mistresses upon neutral ground. This was at first done by the offices with the utmost secrecy—but what can be hid from jealous love, and the sleepless eyes of enxiety—our soldiers and sailors saw it and practiced it. It was impossible for a number of men upon half an acre of ground to go out and return all upon the same business and not have some rencounter that would lead to a discovery, which was soon the case both between officers and men, and then the covenant was no more. This matter was at last well known among the inhabitants, but as it had never been productive of any misundertandings on either side, it was taken no other notice of by people in general: but the chiefs thought differently, they knew it was a breach of covenant. This might be esteemed trivial on our part and indeed it was, but it was the beginning of our subsequent misfortunes, and acknowledged to be so afterwards when it was too late to revert the consequences. In a few days the white rods were taken down by some of the Inhabitants, and a free egress and regress took place: the inhabitants had access to our tents, viewed our conduct in private and unguarded hours, had every opportunity to form an opinion of our manners and abilities, and contrast them with their own, nay, were even instructed in the nature and use of our firearms, and permited to prove our own personal prowess in wrestling, boxing and other athletic exercises, and in some instances with success on their side. It also flung temptations in their way to theft which they diligently improved and we resented.

It was not however untill some time after our arrival that we saw these appearances, and not till near our final departure that we saw the evils that resulted from them. The third day after our acquaintance Capt. Cook was invited on shore by a number of the chiefs, among whom was a priest, to a kind of entertainment or rather ceremony that he could not understand, as they either could or would not explain it to him, he was obliged to comply at a hazard with their request to come at the knowledge of a circumstance they were more anxious to communicate than he was to receive.

Cook was attended by three of his lieutenants, and a draftsman uniformly dressed. As they passed the tents after landing, I was invited by Lieut. King to make one of the party, our rout led to a romantic silent spot west of the MORAI which was the residence of the priest that conducted the ceremony. It consisted of a circle of large cocoanut and other trees that stood upon the margin of a pond of water in the center of which was a bathing place. Upon the north side of the pond were a row of houses standing among the trees and were most delightfully situated; These houses extended almost to the MORAI, nearest which was that of the priest who was the lord of this beautiful recess. Between the houses and the pond were a number of grass plots intersected by several square holes with water in them which were private baths. On the east side under the wall of the MORAI was a thick arbour of low spreading trees, and a number of ill carved images interspersed throughout; to this retreat we were all conducted and Capt. Cook was placed by one of those images which was hung round with old pieces of their cloths and some viands. When the company were all seated the natives formed a semicircle in front of Cook, who with his lieutenants on each side composed the base. The priest, who had been very busy in forming this arangment now proceeded to the most important part of duty, and began to anoint the head of Cook with cocoanut-oil infused with a milky juce that is obtained from the bread fruit, uttering at the same time with a jargon we knew nothing of some kind of speech, the chiefs at certain periods vociferating with a strong sonorous voice a kind of amen. This part of the ceremony lasted about twenty minutes, and was succeeded by a long uninterrupted, formal oration by the priest, which was run over with the greatest rapidity, and lasted about half an hour. Notwithstanding, the language here is almost verbally the same as at Otaheite and the other islands we could not understand a word this Levite had spoken. At the end of the speech the rest of the natives gave a shout, and this was succeeded by a song of a slow majestic composition and was short. The song ended and was succeeded by a barbigued hog and bread-fruit, but however ceremonious the natives had been in the preceeding part of this exhibition, they now were of a different opinion, and made the most strenuous efforts of dispatch.

It was at this time about ten o'clock in the morning, and we did not partake with our friends, except in a drink of cocoanut-milk; they, however, finished the hog, and then rose to wait upon Cook into town.

We had now been here several days, and had been waiting with anxiety the arrival of their Orono, La Hi or greatest Chief, whose name was Kireeaboo, whom we expected every day, and every hour according to the reports of the natives from the island of Mauwee, where he had been at war with the chief of that island.

On the 22d of January some of the chiefs and other warriors, who had been at Mauwee came into the bay, and the next day several more hundred made their appearance but it was not until the 25th that Kireeaboo came. He was attended by a number of double canoes, the largest we had ever seen, being between 60 and 70 feet in length, and a large retinue of stout, comely bold looking hardy chiefs, besides other attendants and about 30 men with paddles. In the fore and hinder parts of his canoe were placed several ill-formed images of wicker work covered with a variety of feathers, of different colors, but chiefly red and black. These they carry to war with them. They took little notice of the ships as they entered the bay, but landed immediately on the beach near our encampment, which Cook observing, and being anxious to salute Kireeaboo rowed in his pennace directly to the tents from whence he went out to meet him. The interview was worthy Cook and Kireeaboo, and they seemed from that moment to conceive an uncommon attachment to each other. Kireeaboo was an old man and very feeble, about 5 feet 8 inches high, and of a slender make, he had a countenance very expressive of conscious dignity and merit, and conducted himself at all times worthy a ruler of the people.

After the ceremonies of the first salutation were over Cook invited Kireeaboo and led him by the hand to his markee attended by a concourse of his chiefs, who expressed the liveliest sense of the honor done their king. Our astronomers were at this time rectifying their mathematical aparatus in the front of their observations. It was a bright day, and the appearance was even brilliant to us, but much more so to Kireeaboo and his attendants, who even expressed a superstitious fear as they approached it. They had heard what terrible things our guns were, and therefore were particularly apprehensive of danger from our two telescopes that stood elevated above the rest. The quadrants did not appear to be dangerous instruments, but both from their construction and use were a perfect mystery, about which they made endless enquiries, and would have Idolized if one might judge from their extravigant exclamations and gestures. A great part of the forenoon was spent in satisfying the curiosities of these untutored sons of men, and in endeavoring to inform them of our knowledge, and judge of the capability of theirs. But after all the only conclusion they made was that as we had so much to do with the sun and the rest of the planets whose motions we were constantly watching by day and night, and which we had informed them we were guided by on the ocean, we must either have come from thence, or be some other way particularly connected with those objects, and to strengthen this inference they observed that the colour of our skins partook of the red from the sun, and the white from the moon and stars, besides, they said we dealt much with fire that we could kill others with it, but that it would not hurt us though we were close by it, and that we rendered it in all things intirely subservient to us.

When the usual hour of dining arrived Cook invited Kireeaboo and his attendants on board, and his table was no otherwise ornamented than with the productions of Owyhee his guests were the better accommodated.

Kireeaboo made his dinner solely with bread-fruit and a drink of water, but his chiefs who were younger, used both pork and fowls—they made no use of knives or forks, and cramed their mouths as full as they possibly could, but the quantity they eat was very moderate, they also drank only water, refusing wine, porter, rum or any other kind of liquor. After dinner they were conducted upon deck, where they were again highly entertained with a new scene, and one much better adapted to their understanding than that they had lately been at on shore. Some of them were employed in measuring the ship's length, and others her breadth, which they did with a line, and then measured it into fathoms as we do, and some of them ventured as far aloft as the main and fore-tops, but took their rout through lubbers hole rather than by puttock shrouds. None of them would go higher or offer to venture out upon the yards. Others again were in the ship's hold at which they expressed the utmost admiration. Kireeaboo was on the quarter deck with Cook, and had every minute some of the chiefs running to him and relating what they had seen for his in formation. After this the pennace was manned with the crew in black caps and white shirts and rowed uniformly to the *Discovery*, the French horn playing. The evening was spent on board with Capt. Clerke. Kireeaboo was so much pleased with the attention that had been shewn him and his chiefs that he desired Cook and Clerke would spend the next day with him and his chiefs on shore, desiring also that they would bring their chiefs with them, which was readily agreed to, and the next morning both Captains and all the officers that could attend dressed in their uniforms, and went to Kiverua where Kireeaboo generally resided. They all dined together in Kireeaboo's house: The dinner consisted of a hog and potatoes baked after their manner spread on green plantainleaves, round which they all seated themselves cross-legged, there was no ceremony, except that of washing the mouth and hands both before and after dinner with clean water, and the only utensils at the feast were pieces of bamboo, which were used as knives; the natives drank water, and our officers to conform as near as possible to the contour of entertainment drank cocoanut-milk. After dinner they went out to take the air under an adjacent shade, where they were entertained with a dance by the women while they were voluptuously stretched along the grass or reclined against the trees. One of the gentlemen from the *Discovery* brought his violin with him, and one from the *Resolution* a german-flute, and as the company seemed to want a variety, they played upon each in turn. The violin produced the most immoderate laughter among the natives, who seemed to relish it as many do the bagpipes, or much more indifferently, but when we accompanied it by a voluntary dance or cotillion they had a different opinion, the flute they much admired and examined very curiously. The drum and fife (though not present) is the music they most delight in. When the sun was upon the decline Kireeaboo and his suit crossed the bay to Kirakakooa in order to compleat the entertainment of his guests by an exhibition of the gymnastic kind at which a large concourse of people of all denominations were present. The disposition of the assembly was an extensive circle in the midst of which was performed, wrestling, boxing and other athletic exercises which I need not further describe than refering my readers to the accounts of those games at Tongotaboo one of the friendly islands, with which they entirely correspond except in one particular, which was a circumstance we had never before met with, this was a sort of standard or insignia which was brought on and introduced into the circle by one of those who had last excelled in those exercises, and when the sports were over it was taken by the victor or victors, and preserved by them as a testimony of their prowess untill they were excelled in some subsequent rencounter. The loss of this badge of honor never occasioned any uneasiness or repining, and the investment was decisive as the action which won it:

it was the shout of consenting hundreds that closed every feat which declared to whom it was due.

This standard seemed to have a resemblance of the ancient Roman one: The staff was about 13 feet long, on the top there was a truck with some holes in it, through which a line was rove, and to the ends of the line hung a short broad pendant, underneath this about two feet from the truck was suspended by another cord a transverse stick about 4 feet long, to which a large man of war bird was fixed with the tips of the wings spread to each end of the stick, and the whole was ornamented with little tufts of variagated feathers.

This ceremony was very well conducted, but fell short in several respects to those of the same kind at Tongotaboo. At sun-down the sports ended, and after the victors had gone off in triumph with the insignia of victory the assembly dissolved, Kireeaboo went over unattended and without ceremony to Kiverua, and our officers to their several ships.

The next evening Cook invited Kireeaboo and his people to another entertainment, which they afterwards justly called the fiery one. This was the exhibition of some of the fireworks we had brought from Woolwich. The fame of this intended entertainment and the manifest preparations that had been making on the beach at Kireekkakooa by our gunner and yoemen extended the report far and near by which means there was an immense number of spectators. As soon as it was well dark Cook landed at the spot where the preparations were attended by Kireeaboo, and a great number of men and women in their canoes. The natives had been some of them all day waiting, and their expectations were wound up to the last extremity, some of them had begun to jeer at us, and express contempt of our heiva as they called it. Cook expected some laughable circumstances, and was willing to improve it, he therefore took the necessary precautions, and when every thing was ready, and the people as silent as the night he ordered a sky-racket off.

I do think this part of the scene undescribable.—Cook and the officers near him certainly could not do it they were so entirely overcome with laughter: They could hardly hold the old feeble Kireeaboo and some elderly ladies of quality that sat among them, and before they had any ways recovered themselves from this paroxism nearly the whole host that a moment before surrounded them had fled, some towards the town, some to the hills, and some into the water, many they did not know where, and many had been trampled under foot and remained motionless there. It however happened luckily that the object which at first caused their fear did not long continue, and as that expired the terrors of those who fled as well as the few who remained behind subsided, and Kireeaboo rose and called himself to the hindermost of the people to return, and sent after the rest: This had such an effect that many did return, and wait the remaining part of the evening, but there were many who were frightened past recovery, and did not appear any more that night. However when we came to proceed and fire another racket though those that had returned saw their king and the rest of the company safe, and themselves unhurt yet they could not resist the former impulse, and again took to their heels, and though they soon returned they continued to do so occasionally through the whole ceremony, except at the exhibition of the water-rackets, which seemed to reconcile them to the opinion of the entertainment being calculated to please and not hurt them, and when all was over they parted with us highly pleased, shouting our greatness and goodness.

On the 26th of January I sent a billet on board to Cook, desiring his permission to make an excursion into the interior parts of the country proposing if practicable to reach the famous peak that terminated the height of the island. My proposal was not only granted, but promoted by Cook, who very much wanted some informations respecting that part of the island, particularly the peak, the tip of which is generally covered with snow, and had exited great curiosity. He desired the gunner of the *Resolution*, the botanist sent out by Mr. Banks and Mr. Simeon Woodruff to be of the party. He also procured us some attendants among the natives to assist us in carrying our baggage and directing us through the woods. It required some prudence to make a good equipment for this tour, for though we had the full heat of a tropical sun near the margin of the island we knew we should experience a different temparament in the air the higher we advanced towards the peak, and that the transition would be sudden if not extreme, we therefore took each of us a woolen blanket, and in general made some alteration in our dress and we each took a bottle of brandy. Among the natives who were to attend us was a young chief whose name was O'Crany and two youths from among the commonalty. Our course lay eastward and northward from the town, and about two o'clock in the afternoon we set out, when we had got without the town we met an old acquaintance of mine (who ought indeed to have been introduced before.) He was a middle aged man, and belonged to the order of their Mida or priesthood, his name was Kunneava. We saluted each other, and the old man asked with much impatient curiosity where we were going, when we had informed him he disapproved of our intention, told us that we could not go as far as we proposed, and would have persuaded us to return; but finding we were determined in our resolves, he turned and accompanied us; about two miles without the town the land was level, and continued of one plain of little enclosures separated from each other by low broad walls: Whether this circumstance denoted separate property, or was done solely to dispense with the lava that overspread the face of the country, and of which the walls are composed, I cannot say, but probably it denotes a distinct possession. Some of these fields were planted, and others by their appearance were left fallow: In some we saw the natives collecting the coarse grass that had grown upon it during the time it had lain unimproved, and burning it in detached heaps. Their sweet potatoes are mostly raised here, and indeed are the principle object of their agriculture, but it requires an infinite deal of toil on account of the quantity of lava that remains on the land notwithstanding what is used about the walls to come at the soil, and besides they have no implements of husbandry that we could make use of had the ground been free from the lava. If any thing can recompence their labor it must be an exuberant soil, and a benificent climate. We saw a few patches of sugar cane interspersed in moist places, which were but small: But the cane was the largest and as sweet as any we had ever seen, we also passed several groups of plantain-trees.

These enclosed plantations extended about 3 miles from the town, near the back of which they commenced, and were succeeded by what we called the open plantations. Here the land began to rise with a gentle ascent that continued about one mile when it became abruptly steep. These were the plantations that contained the bread-fruit-trees. (What Ceres are thy wheaten sheves, and thy yellow harvests compared with this scene! Have the songs of poets done thee so much honor from a sickly theme, what would they do another deity from beholding this extensive display of spontaneous vexation. Son of——[blank] what are thy fields but the sad testimony of toil, and when thy feeble plants hath passed the thousand dangers that attend its progress to a state of perfection in the field, what is it then, are not the subsequent operations necessary for the use of man still more numerous and complicated. Man eateth it by the sweat of his brow. But behold now these bread-fruit-plains thine eye cannot discern their limits, and the trees are like the cedars of Lebanon in numbers and in stature—can the groveling swine trample them under his feet, or are they destroyed by a gust of rain. Here is neither toil or care man stretcheth forth his hand and eateth without parsimony or anticipated want.)

After leaving the bread-fruit-forests we continued up the ascent to the distance of a mile and an half further, and found the land thick covered with wild fern, among which our botanist found a new species. It was now near sun-down, and being upon the skirts of those woods that so remarkably surrounded this island at a uniform distance of 4 and 5 miles from the shore, we concluded to halt, especially as there was a hut hard by that would afford us a better retreat during night than what we might expect if we proceeded. When we reached the hut we found it inhabited by an elderly man, his wife and daughter the emblem of innocent uninstructed beauty. They were somewhat discomposed at our appearance and equipment, and would have left their house through fear had not the Indians who accompanied us persuaded them otherwise, and at last reconciled them to us. We sat down together before the door, and from the height of the situation we had a complete retrospective view of our rout, of the town, of part of the bay and one of our ships besides an extensive prospect on the ocean, and a distant view of three of the neighbouring islands.

It was exquisitly entertaining. Nature had bestowed her graces with her usual negligent sublimity. The town of Kireekakooa and our ship in the bay created the contrast of art as well as the cultivated ground below, and as every object was partly a novelty it transported as well as convinced.

As we had proposed remaining at this hut the night, and being willing to preserve what provisions we had ready dressed, we purchased a little pig and had him dressed by our host who finding his account in his visitants bestired himself and soon had it ready. After supper we had some of our brandy dilated with the mountain water, and we had so long been confined to the poor brackish water at the bay below that it was a kind of nectar to us. As soon as the sun set we found a considerable difference in the state of the air. At night a heavy dew fell and we felt it very chilly and had recourse to our blankets notwithstanding we were in the hut. The next morning when we came to enter the woods we found there had been a heavy rain though none of it had approached us notwithstanding we were within 200 yards of the skirts of the forest. And it seemed to be a matter of fact both from the informations of the natives and our own observations that neither the rains or the dews descended lower than where the woods terminated, unless at the equinoxes or some periodical conjuncture, by which means the space between the woods and the shores are rendered warm and fit for the purposes of culture, and the sulbimated vegitation of tropical productions. We traversed these woods by a compass keeping a direct course for the peak, and was so happy the first day as to find a footpath that trended nearly our due course by which means we had traveled by estimation about 15 miles, and though it was no extraordinary march had circumstances been different, yet as we found them we thought it a very great one, for it was not only excessive miry and rough but the way was mostly an ascent, and we had been unused to walking, and especially to carrying such loads as we had. Our Indian companions were much more fatigued than we were, though they had nothing to carry, and what displeased us very much would not carry any thing. The occasional delays of our botanical researches delayed us something. The sun had not set when we halted yet meeting with a situation that pleased us, and not being limited as to time we spent the remaining part of the day as humour dictated, some botanizing and those who had fowling pieces with them in shooting, for my part I could not but think the present appearance of our encampment claimed a part of our attention, and therefore set about some alterations and amendments. It was the trunk of a tree that had fell by the side of the path and lay with one end transversly over another tree that had fallen before in an opposite direction, and as it measured 32 feet in circumference and lay 4 feet from the ground, it efforded very good shelter except at the sides which defect I supplied by large pieces of bark and a good quantity of boughs which rendered it very commodious, and we slept the night under it much better than we had done the preceding, notwithstanding there was a heavy dew and the air cold, the next morning we set out in good spirits hoping that day to reach the snowy peak, but we had not gone a mile forward before the path that had hitherto so much facilitated our progress hitherto began not only to take a direction southward of west but had been so little frequented as to be almost effaced. In this situation we consulted our Indian convoy, but to no purpose. We then advised among ourselves and at length concluded to proceed by the nearest rout without any beaten track, and went in this manner about 4 miles further finding the way even more steep and rough than we had yet experienced, but above all impeded by such impenetrable thickets as would render it impossible for us to proceed any further. We therefore abandoned our design and returning in our own track reached the retreat we had improved the last night, having been the whole day in walking only about 10 miles, and had been very assiduous too. We found the country here as well as at the sea shore universally overspread with lava, and also saw several subteranean excavations that had every appearance of past eruption and fire. Our Botanist to day met with great success, and we had also shot a number of fine birds of the liveliest and most variagated plumage that any of us had ever met with, but we heard no melody among them. Except these we saw no other kind of birds except the Screach-Owl, neither did we see any kind of quadrupede, but we caught several curious insects. The woods here are very thick and luxuriant, the largest trees are nearly thirty feet in the girt, and these with the shruberry underneath and the whole intersected with vines renders it very umbrageous.

The next day about two in the afternoon we cleared the woods by our old rout, and by six o'clock reached the tents, having penetrated about 24 miles and we supposed within 11 of the peak. Our Indians were extremely fatigued though they had no baggage, and we were well convinced that though like the Stag and the Lion they appear fit for expedition and toil, yet like those animals they are fit for neither, while the humbly Mule will persevere in both.

According to an attitude of the quadrant, the Peak of Owyhee is 35 miles distant from the surface of the water, and its perpendicular elevation nearly 2 miles. The Island is exactly 90 leagues in circumference, is very nearly of a circular form, and rises on all sides in a moderate and pretty uniform ascent from the water to the Peak, which is sharp and caped as I have before observed with snow, which seems to be a new circumstance among us not altogether accounted for. As a truth, and a Phenomenon in natural philosophy I leave it to the world. Owyhee has every appearance in nature to suppose it once to have been a vulcano. Its height, magnitude, shape and perhaps its situation indicate not only that, but that its original formation was effected by such a cause The eastern side of the island is one continued bed of lava from the summit to the sea, and under the sea in 50 fathom water some distance from the shore; and this side of the Island utterly barren and devoid of even a single shrub. But there is no tradition among the inhabitants of such circumstance.

On the 1st of February one William Watman one of our quarter gunners died. He was an elderly man and having been with Cook in the ship *Endeavour* on a former voyage was much lamented by him—he died with a slow-fever that had partly been hastened if not brought on by intemperance. This was the second person that had died in the *Resolution*. The next day he was carried on shore to be intered, and it seems it was his own request when he found he should not recover, to be intered in the MORAI which Cook promised him should be done. Our old friend Kikinny the priest that anointed Cook, as soon as he heard of Watman's death anticipated Cook's request by making him an offer of a place in the MORAI, and had therefore waited on shore

to attend Watman's body to the grave. When the Pennace landed with
Watman's body we expected the curiosity of the natives would have been
excited to come in crouds to see it and to observe our conduct upon the occasion—but it was quite otherwise, the people all shut themselves up in their
houses and nobody was seen but two or three men who attended Kikinny.

As the circumstance of this mans death was an event that would be
much noticed by the natives as well as this manner in which we should dispose of the corpse, it was determined to render the whole matter as magnificent and respectable as the situation of the affair would permit, the body
was therefore inclosed in a coffin covered with colors and borne by the
bargemen, who walked in the centre. Cook and his officers with some of
the people followed two and two according to their rank. In the front at an
advanced distance preceeding a guard of marines marching to the tune of
a fife that played the funeral march, and with their arms reverted, when we
had asscended the Morai and reached the grave the guard opened their ranks
and performed the usual evolutions on those occassions; Cook and his officers read prayers, and Kikinny and his squat down upon their hams before
them paying great attention, and were ostensibly much affected. When we
began to cover the remains, Kikinny seized a little pig he had under his arm
by his hinder legs, and bearing its head against the stones hove into the grave,
and would have done the same with one or two more hogs they had with
them had not Cook interposed. The ceremony over and the guard marched
off, Cook erected a post with an inscription suitable to the occasion. This
grave was ever after visited by the natives, who strewed it over with viands
and animal flesh. They seemed to pay a greater attention to this mans
grave than to those of their own people. I observed one night a light upon
the MORAI after this affair, and as it was an unusual circumstance, I went up
upon the MORAI to see if I could know the reason of it; when I had asscended
I observed 12 or 13 men sitting in a circle round a fire. I advanced to them
and uncovered my head, not choosing to sit down among them or inter-
rupt their business, nor indeed to stay if I found my company was intru-
sive. The company all looked at me and then spoke to each other: I could
understand some of them: they told some old grey-headed Indians that I
was the Kakakoa Iahi, or chief warrior at the tents, and that I was well known
in the town, & that I was a good man: that Kunneava was my friend, and
that my name was Ourero (a name given me by the Indians) and that I had
saved an old woman from being drowned in the sea by exposing my own
life, all which was true. Upon this representation and more that I did but

imperfectly comprehend, I was called by one of the old Indians to come and sit down by him, which I complied with. I set half an hour there, during which time they killed a pig in the manner Kikinny had done his, opened it while warm and threw the entrails into the fire and left them to consume: the carcase of the pig was thrown upon Watman's grave. When I went away I had several presents of fruit made me, and the next day in consequence of my last nocturnal visit, had several fowls, a pig and other things sent me by the same old men. It seems the sole purpose of this assembly was to sacrifice (if I may so call it) to the manes of Watman, and I related it to shew that their charity to the dead is consistent with the real idea of this virtue, and breaths the purest spirit of philanthropy. It is an example that will put seven eights of Christendom to the blush.

Those readers who have seen the publication of Cook's former voyages will meet with but little that is new in many parts of my history respecting this people, there is so general a conformity in the objects of it to those at Otaheite and the tropical islands throughout. An instance of it is the MORAI at this place, the general structure and the ultimate design of it is the same as at Otaheite. It is a square pile of stones nearly 90 feet long on each side, and is from 7 to 15 feet high according to the elevation of the ground on which it stands: It is composed of different kinds of stone, those that compose the sides are in general large, and many of them square, but do not appear to have been made so by art. The intermediate space seems to have been filled up after the structure of the sides with round stones and some pieces of lava, the surface is even and level all over. On the sides of the wall there is a low paled fence composed of small round sticks rudely put together though at infinite deal of trouble as it was effected without the assistance of any mechanical instruments, but those which we found them possessed of at our first arrival, the best of which was a stone hatchet. On the tops of the pales are fortuitously placed human sculls, and other bones of the human body, which belonged either to their own criminals, who had been there sacrificed to the god of war (called Ehatua) or to those of war, or to both, and they are considered as trophies in either case. The bodies or rather the flesh of those victims are eat, and the entrails burnt as oblations. The Morai is also made a place of interment, but respects only the chiefs, the people inter their dead near their houses, where they erect some ill-formed image over or near the grave, which is also the case with the chiefs that are intered in the Morai with this difference only, that their images are larger and better made. Both the chiefs and commonalty keep up a succession of food near their graves. The particular manner in which they last dispose of the remains of their dead we were never able to learn. There were two deaths at Kireekakooa while were there the first time, but the interments that succeeded were in the night; whether they did this merely to screen the ceremony of their last obsequies from us, or whether it was really the custom we could not tell. Here are however some ceremonies previous to the interment that are curious though I cannot say common since we never knew but one instance of it, and that respected a chief. The circumstance aluded to is this: As soon as the person was dead, and while the body remained flexible it was first placed and supported in a seting posture, then the legs were pressed close to the hams, the body and head bent forward until the chin rested upon the knees, and the arms pressed close to the sides, and bending from the elbows in conformity to the direction of the thighs the hands met at the fore part of each knee under the chin; and in this posture the whole was confined by bandages of cloath, and these were multiplied until the form of the corpse was lost, and could not be known from a bundle of cloath of the same magnitude without any thing contained within it. I think the attitude of this corpse resembles that of some of the postures of the human foetus, and that they mean to have the body left in its last state of existence—and as it is difficult to conceive how they should become possessed of so curious a piece of knowledge as respects the operations in the recesses of the womb of themselves, or that this information should if possible originate from chance: It may be supposed to be a traditionary custom, and the knowledge derived from a source were by the assistance of art and the improvement of the mind: Such a circumstance can only be supposed with propriety to have originated, and that may be from either of the continents remotely or immediately, but it would be a perplex pursuit to enquire from which, or at what period and by what means.

The town of Kireekakooa is about a mile and an half in length, but narrow and of an unequal breadth, and as I have before observed contains about 1100 houses, some reckon 1300 including some detached buildings. It is situate along the shore within a few rods of the water, and is in general very compact, and as the houses in those places stand so as to create a breadth there are a number of little streets that intersect each other very happily though they do not seem to have been the effects of much design, and a very agreeable and uncommon circumstance to be found among these rude sons of nature, was, that these little avenues were generally paved. The houses here differ altogether from those to the southward in their form, though not much in other respects: They are exactly like a tent, the frame is light and for the most part lashed together, except now and then where two large posts met, and there was a kind of a mortice, both the sides and the ends are thatched with coarse grass, and sometimes palm-tree-leaves. They have but one passage which is used both as a door and window: The inside of the house is without partitions above or below, the ground within being hard and dry is covered with thick coarse grass, dryed plantain and palm-tree-leaves, over which they spread large well-wrought mats, which makes the house cleanly, and gives it an air of elegance and comfort, and as they have no chairs, tables, beds and such kind of furniture there is room enough. They are of different magnitudes, but in general they are between 30 and 40 feet square: There are cocoanut and other trees interspersed artificially among the houses all over the town, and in about the middle of it there is a level course for running and other exercises, which is very beautifully skirted with trees from end to end, and is kept very clean. There are also in different places square elevated yards for bleaching and otherwise manufacturing their cloth. The Morai stands in the northwest part of the town opposite that part of the bay where our ships lay. The Town of Kiverua which lies on the opposite side of the bay half a mile distant is about half as large as Kireekakooa. Both the towns contain about 1500 inhabitants, and we were told they were the largest towns on the island. Owyhee is divided into districts or circles, each of which is presided over by a chief or chiefs, who are subordinate to one, which was Kireeaboo, who holding no particular or local possession lived sometimes in one circle, and sometimes in another in a kind of rotation, or as humor dictated or exigencies required. If I have the number right the whole island is contained in 12 circles, and according to their accounts and our own estimation contains almost or quite 100,000 inhabitants. It was difficult for us from a short and imperfect acquaintance with these people, to gain much knowledge of the nature of their government, but the general tenour of it like their other customs, their manners, language, dress, persons and disposition so nearly aproximate to those of the southern tropical islanders, that it certainly does not differ much from theirs, though I think their laws much better administered than at the society islands, especially at Otaheite: there are three orders by which the superior are distinguished from the inferior people, they are called in their language the Orono, the Kakakoa and the Mida, these it seems compose the legislative and executive parts of their police. The Mida are the priests and the Kakakoa are their military men. The Orono is a branch I cannot well define, unless I call it the civil part of the corporation. They are all chieftains, and the Orono go to war as well as the Kakakoa, but the Mida do not act in the field, they stir the people up by oratorical incitements. It was said by some of us that the Orono implied royalty, and that those who had the title were the immediate descendants of the supreme chief. I do not mean by the Kakakoa being a select body of warriors, that they are the only men with the Orono who go to war. The body of the people fight as well as the Kakakoa, but the chiefs are always foremost, and share equally all the honors of victory, and the disgrace of a defeat: this renders them respectable and dear to the people, and makes them proud and valourous themselves—nothing is more disgraceful than for these men or even the commonality to receive a wound in the back, the stigma endures as indelible as the mark, and as they go naked it is constantly exposed.

Whether the investtiture of authority and power are nominal or hereditary is not certain, though I incline to think the latter, which certainly is the best in their system, for two reasons: those who are in power are in no danger of corruption, and the tenures of the chiefs are revocable. This was evident to us from the instance of Kireeaboo's eldest son, who, though heir apparent to his father, was deprived for misdemeanours of his title and authority; he was indeed afterwards forgiven on account of his sincere repentance, and a great many virtues he possessed, and restored to his former privileges. This son was one of the stoutest and most intrepid men I saw among them, was of a complexion so much darker than general that it rendered him singular in that respect, and he always went dressed in black cloth which is an emblem of war among them, which his soul seemed to delight in. He had gone not long before our arrival over to Mauwee where the greatness of his character and the importance of his design soon put him at the head of the whole force of that island, and his activity and enterprizing disposition did not suffer him to stop short of an attack in the very heart of Owyhee, where he fought his father in seven pitched battles before he was entirely subdued, and it was principally owing to this untutored hero that our own quarrels with the Owyheeans subsequent to the death of Cook were so obstinately maintained and protracted by them.

This loose description of the outlines of their government is all we were able to obtain, though no doubt it comprehends a system if thoroughly known that would be much more to their honor in our esteem. It was very evident that their government possessed that energy which is ever the result of economical jurisprudence, and the perfection of government; a proof of it is the cool deliberate deprivation of life when required by their laws, and if this proves the dignity of their authority; the manner in which they execute the decree speaks equally loud in favour of their policy, the chiefs condemn and they make the body of the people execute. The criminal in this case is bound to a stake. The chiefs cast the first stone, and then the spectators at large until the malefactor expires, and there is a particular spot of ground where his body is afterwards disposed of; but I believe this last circumstance respects the chiefs only. A condemned malefactor of an inferior class, we generally understood was preserved as a sacrifice to the god of war, provided they were not then possessed of any prisoners of war. In matters not capital the offender seems to be disregarded as an object not meritorious of public notice, and is generally well threshed or kicked by some of the chiefs, or by all of them whenever they know his demerits or happen to meet him. We could not learn that they had any other method of punishing capital or inferior crimes.

They have marriages among them, but whether they are civil or religiously appointments we cannot tell, but the custom does not seem to be respectable, at least among the chiefs, and we were told that a man could discard his wife at pleasure, and keep all her effects, though I believe this very seldom happens. It is however very manifest among the chiefs that not only marriage, but a commerce with the women in any other respect is in very indifferent estimation, and it is a disagreeable circumstance to the historian that truth obliges him to inform the world of a custom among them contrary to nature, and odious to a delicate mind, yet as such a remarkable incident in the history of a new discovered, a remote and a numerous people, will tend to illucidate the enquiries of the ingenious in such subjects as may transpire from the various accounts of men and manners here or elsewhere given, it would be to omit the most material and useful part of historical narration to omit it; the custom alluded to is that of sodomy, which is very prevalent if not universal among the chiefs, and we believe peculiar to them, as we never saw any appearance of it among the commonalty. As this was the first instance we had ever seen of it in our travels, we were cautious how we credited the first indications of it, and waited untill opportunity gave full proof of the circumstance. The cohabitation is between the chiefs and the most beautiful males they can procure about 17 years old, these they call Kikuana, which in their language signifies a relation. These youths follow them wherever they go, and are as narrowly looked after as the women in those countries where jealousy is so predominant a passion; they are extremely fond of them, and by a shocking inversion of the laws of nature, they bestow all those affections upon them that were intended for the other sex. We did not fully discover this circumstance until near our departure, and indeed lamented we ever had, for though we had no right to attack or ever to disapprove of customs in general that differed from our own, yet this one so apparently infringed and insulted the first and strongest dictate of nature, and we had from education and a diffusive observation of the world, so strong a prejudice against it, that the first instance we saw of it we condemned a man fully reprobated. Our officers indeed did not insult the chiefs by any means, but our soldiers and tars to vindicate their own wonderful modesty, and at the same time oblige the insulted women, and recommend themselves to their favors became severe arbitrators, and the most valourous defenders and supporters of their own tenets.

I have before observed that there is a remarkable conformity in most of the customs and appearances among these islanders and those to the southward, I shall therefore generally confine my observations to those particulars only where there is any remarkable difference. This is in some measure the case with their dress. The people here have indeed the same species of cloath they have to the southward, and it is somewhat manufactured like it, but it is much more variegrated in the conclusive bestowment made upon it; they have a great variety of colours here, and though rudely compounded they look very well at a little distance. These colours they use profusely upon their cloath in a variegated and very fanciful drapery. They wear it in the same manner they do at the southward. But exclusive of this kind of dress they have large cloaks, and caps made of feathers, which are very gay; the plumage of which they are composed is as lively and as varigated as can well be imagined, and is procured from the numerous birds that inhabit the mountains, which they catch with a glutinous matter that resembles our birdlime, but is much better. The cloaks are made nearly square, and are worn over the shoulders with the two upper corners tied under the chin. The form of the cap is a real curiosity being the exact model of the ancient helmet. Many of them have their hair which is coarse and strong cut into the same form.

Both the vegetable and animal productions of Owyhee are like those of the southern islands. The animals are the same not only in their kind, but have that approximation which indicates even the same breed, and what is equally remarkable is that these islands as well as every other of the tropical islands in the south sea have no other animals, and hogs, dogs and rats include the whole of their number, and none of those islands are found without those animals that are inhabited, and those which are uninhabited have none of them except rats. Even New-Zealand hath dogs, and they are of the same kind. It is remarkable too that none of those dogs ever bark, and are equally in 20 deg. north and 40 deg. south the same sluggish, short-legged, little-eared creatures. The bread-fruit here and every where else where it is known is the same, but the yams at Sandwich-Islands are infinitely superior to those of the Island of Nehow, which is the westernmost of Sandiwch-Islands. The potatoes we found here are peculiar to these islands; They are large and sweet, but watery; the eddy-root, or what is known here and at Otaheite by the name of Terra is also much superior to that among the southern islands. Cocoanuts are not so plenty here as at the southward. Another matter peculiar to these islands is salt, but as they have no advantages from nature that would lead to a discovery of the art of making salt, or facilitate the operation afterwards more than they have at the other islands, it is a matter of some curiosity how they became acquainted with it. They make it of sea water, which they leave in the holes of the rocks to evaporate. We procured a quantity of this salt more than sufficient for our succeeding part of the voyage.

On the 3d of February our launch was sent on shore to bring off the *Resolution's* rudder, which had been sent on shore to have the pintles repaired, and the crew not being able of themselves to get it off, the masters mate invited a parcel of the natives that were standing round the encampment to assist them, to which they very readily affected a compliance, and as many as 50 or 60 joined our people, and got hold of a rope that was hitched to the head of the rudder, and pretended to pull and labor very hard, though at the same time they were in fact doing all they could to retard the business, to ridicule and make their pastime of the people. This exasperated the mate, and he struck two or three of them, which being observed by a chief that was present he interposed: The mate haughtily told the chief to order his people to assist him, and the chief as well as the people having no intention, but of shewing their disregard and scorn, which had long been growing towards us laughed at him, hooted him, and hove stones at him and the crew, who taking up some trunnels that were laying by fell upon the Indians, beat many of them much and drove the rest several rods back, but the croud collecting at a little distance, formed and began to use abusive language, challenge our people and throw stones, some of which came into our encampment.

Though I plainly foresaw these things, and was conscious that they originated chiefly from our imprudence as well as the propensity among the
natives to envy, and if they dared to insult our superior merit, yet as an officer and a man who had every consequence to abide in common with my
fellow adventurers I could not justify a passive conduct, and therefore
acquainted the commanding officer at the tents of the disturbance, requesting that I might put the guard under arms, and at least make a shew of resentment, to which he acquiesced and came out of his tent to appease the fray
in person, and it was a pity that so much softness, humanity and goodness
should have been so roughly dealt with as he was, for they pelted him and
the file of men with him with stones back to the encampment. This, however, did not provoke him to fire among them, and after laughingly saying,
they were a set of sad rogues and were spoiled he retired again to this
observatory. At sun-down the natives retired, and the crew got the rudder
off with the assistance of the guard very easily.

Instances of this kind though of less apparent importance had happened several times before this on shore, but on board hardly a day passed
after the first week that did not produce some petty disturbance in one or
both of the ships, and they chiefly proceeded from thefts perpetrated by
the natives in a manner little short of robbery; Cook and Kireeaboo were
fully employed in adjusting and compromizing these differences, and as
there was really a reciprocal disinterested regard between him and this good
old man it tended much to facilitate these amicable negotiations—but in the
midst of these measures Cook was insensible of the daily decline of his greatness and importance in the estimation of the natives, nay, so confident was
he, and so secure in the opposite opinion that on the 4th of February he came
to Kireekakooa with his boats to purchase and carry off the fence round the
Morai, which he wanted to wood the ships with. When he landed he sent
for the Priest Kikinny and some other chiefs, and offered them two iron
hatchets for the fence. The chiefs were astonished not only at the inadequate
price, but at the proposal and refused him.

Cook was much chagrined as they were surprized, and not meeting
with the easy acquiescence he expected to his requisitions gave immediate orders to his people to ascend the Morai, break down the fence and load
the boats with it, leading the way himself to enforce his orders. The poor
dismayed chiefs dreading his displeasure, which they saw approaching
followed him upon the Morai to behold the fence that enclosed the man-
sions of their noble ancestors, and the images of their gods torn to pieces

by a handful of rude strangers without the power, or at least without the resolution of opposing their sacrilegious depredations. When Cook had ascended the Morai he once more offered the hatchets to the chiefs. It was a very unequal price if the honest chiefs would have accepted of the bribe, and Cook offered it only to evade the imputation of taking their property without payment. The chiefs again refused it. Cook then added another hatchet and kindling into resentment told them to take it or nothing—Kikinny, to whom the offer was made turned pale, and trembled as he stood, but still refused. Cook thrust them into his garment that was folded round him, and left him immediately to hasten the execution of his orders. As for Kikinny he turned to some of his menials and made them take the hatchets out of his garment, not touching them himself.

By this time a considerable concourse of the natives had assembled under the walls of the Morai, where we were having the wood down, and were very outrageous, and even hove the wood and images back as we threw them down, and I cannot think what prevented from proceeding to greater lengths, however it so happened that we got the whole into the boats, and safely on board.

There was another accident also that happened about this time on board the *Discovery* that was conducted with equal imprudence by Capt. Clerke: An Indian chief who had from our first arrival been an intimate and a very useful friend of his, finding the ships were preparing to sail had come on board attended by two or three canoes to make him a visit. Clerke knew the value of the man, and had received the strongest proofs not only of his honesty but of his honor and uncommon attachment to his person, and the respect due to him and his people, for this same chief had with his own hands killed one of his men in presence of the ship for striking one of Clerke's boys: And he was equally rigid in his demands upon Clerke when any less abuse happened to be given by those of the chiefs. Clerke as usual invited the chief below to dinner, and as the ship's company were also below at their dinners, and no canoes along side but this chief's, which they never gave themselves any concern about, the deck was without a watch: during this recess from duty the carpenter's mate who had been the forepart of the day at work under the bows came upon deck, and being anxious to finish his work before dark took the jolly boat forward, and went to work before the hands were called.

When the people were turned up the jolly boat was missing, and nobody thinking where she might be, neglected to look further after her than along side, and finding she was not there, the subordinate officers were made acquainted with it, and soon after Clerke who came upon deck, and finding the boat gone gave immediate orders to have the canoes along side seized, and the natives in them brought on board, and was going to punish them. The chief in the mean time knew nothing of the matter, but hearing a noise upon deck, and the voices of his own men, came up and enquired into the matter. Clerke in a base supercilious manner answered him that his people had stolen his boat, and that he would punish them for it. The chief was now highly incensed, ordered his people to come to him, and simply asked them if they knew any thing of our boat, though the manner in which he asked was very striking. The people said they did not. This perfectly satisfied the chief, and turning to Clerke he pointed to his own breast, and desired Clerke to kill him if he would think him so base after all the testimonies of honor and friendship he had made him. This, however, was answered only by a strut across the deck, and a couplet of genteel curses and imprecations, and while the noble chief was standing confounded and dismayed at his situation, behold the jolly boat was found safe under the bows. We shall soon see the consequence of such conduct.

On the evening of the 5th we struck our tents, and every thing was taken on board, and it was very manifestly much to the satisfaction of the natives. A little after dark an old house that stood on a corner of the Morai took fire and burn down; this we supposed was occasioned by our people carelessly leaving their fire near it, but it was not the case, the natives burnt it themselves, to shew us the resentment they entertained towards us, on account of our using it without their consent, and indeed manifestly against it. We had made a sail loft of one part of it, and an hospital for our sick of the other, though it evidently was esteemed by the natives as holy as the rest of the Morai, and ought to have been considered by us.

We had now been 19 days in the bay Kireekakooa, in the Island of Owyhee, we had repaired our ships. had regaled and refreshed our people, and had lain in a supply of pork that would probably support us 6 months; the only article we wanted in particular was water, which was here very brackish and bad, In order therefore to procure a supply of this necessary article, we determined to visit the island of Mauwee, where we were informed by the natives we might get plenty of it, and that there was a good harbour.

On the 6th of February we unmoored and came to sail standing along the south side of Owyhee, intending to visit Mauwee and water our ships.

On the 7th we had a hard gale of wind, and being close in with the southern and western shore of Owyhee, which being high land occasioned the wind that came partly off the land to come in irregular and most terrible gusts, such as we had never seen.

On the 8th the gale became not only more violent but more irregular and embarrassing, and before night was improved into a mere hurricane; we wrenched the head of our foremast, and sprung it about 9 feet below the hounds, and also made a great deal of waste. During the severe night the *Discovery* had lost us.

On the 9th the violence of the gale or rather the tornado ceased, but the excessive mutability of the wind, and the irregular sea, was such as demanded our best skill and unremitted attention to keep the ship under any kind of command.

On the 10th the weather became tolerably settled, and hauling off the land we saw the *Discovery* in the S.E. quarter, and before night spoke her all well. We informed her of our situation, and that in consequence of the misfortune it was determined to return again to our old harbour at Kireekakooa.

On the 11th of February we again entered Kireekakooa bay, and moored both ships in their old births.

On the 12th we got the foremast out and set it on shore with the carpenters, we also sent our two observatories on shore, and a markee for a guard of marines.

Our return to this bay was as disagreeable to us as it was to the inhabitants, for we were reciprocally tired of each other. They had been oppressed and were weary of our prostituted alliance, and we were agrieved by the consideration of wanting the provisions and refreshments of the country, which we had every reason to suppose from their behavior antecedent to our departure would now be withheld from us or brought in such small quantities as to be worse than none. What we anticipated was true. When we entered the bay where before we had the shouts of thousands to welcome our arrival, we had the mortification not to see a single canoe, and hardly any inhabitants in the towns. Cook was chagrined and his people were soured. Towards night however the canoes came in, but the provisions both in quantity and quality plainly informed us that times were altered, and what was very remarkable was the exorbitant price they asked; and the particular fancy they all at once took to iron daggers or dirks, which was the only article that was any ways current, with the chiefs at least. It was also equally evident from the looks of the natives as well as every other appearance that our former friendship was at an end, and that we had nothing to do but to hasten our departure to some different island where our vices were not known, and where our extrinsic virtues might gain us another short space of being wondered at, and doing as we pleased, or as our tars expressed it of being happy by the month.

Nor was their passive appearance of disgust all we had to fear, nor did it continue long: before dark a canoe with a number of armed chiefs came along side of us without provisions and indeed without any perceptable design, after staying a short time only they went to the Discovery where they went on board a part of them. Here they affected great friendship, and unfortunately overacting the dissemblance Clerke was jealous & ordered two centinels on the gangways. These men were purposely sent by the chief who had formerly been so very intimate with Clerke, and afterwards so ill treated by him with the charge of stealing his jolly boat. They came with a determination of mischief, and effected it. After they were returned to the canoe all but one they got their paddles and every thing ready for a start. Those in the canoes observing the sentry to be watchful took off his attention by some conversation that they knew would be pleasing to him, and by this means favored the designs of the man on board, who watching his opportunity snatched two pair of tongs, and other iron tools that then lay close by the armourers at work at the forge, and mounting the gangway-rail, with one leap threw himself and his goods into the canoe, that was then upon the movement, and taking up his paddle joined the others and standing directly for the shore, they were out of our reach almost instantaneously; even before a musket could be had from the armed chest to fire at them. The sentries had only hangers. This was the boldest exploit that had yet been attempted, and had a bad aspect with it. Clerke immediately sent to the commodore who advised to send a boat on shore to endeavor at least to regain the goods if they could not the men who took them, but the errand was illy executed as contrived, and the master of the Discovery was glad to return with a severe drubing from the very chief who had been so maletreated by Clerke: the crew were also pelted with stones and had all their oars broke, and they had not a single weapon in the boat not even a single cutlass to defend themselves. When Cook heard of this he went armed himself in person to the guard on shore, took a file of marines and went through the whole town demanding restitution, and threatening the delinquents and their abettors with the severest punishments, but not being able to effect any thing, came off just at sun-set highly displeased and not a little concerned at the bad appearance of things. But even this was nothing to what followed.

On the 13th at night the Discovery's large cutter which was her usual moorings at the bower buoy was taken away.

On the 14th the captains met to consult what should be done on this alarming occasion, and the issue of their opinions was that one of the two captains should land with armed boats and a guard of marines at Kiverua, and attempt to persuade Kireeaboo who was then at his house in that town to come on board upon a visit, and that when he was on board he should be kept prisoner until his subjects should release him by a restitution of the cutter, and it was afterwards thought proper, he or some of the family who might accompany him should be kept as perpetual hostages for the good behavior of the people, during the remaining part of our continuance at Kireekakooa, and this plan was the more approved of by Cook as he had so repeatedly on former occasions to the southward employed it with success.

Clerke was then in a deep decline in his health, and too feeble to undertake the affair though it naturally devolved upon him as a point of duty not well transferable, he therefore beged Cook to oblige him so much as to take that part of the business of the day upon himself in his stead. This Cook agreed to, but previous to his landing made some additional arrangements respecting the possible event of things, though it is certain from the appearance of the susequent arrangements that he guarded more against the flight of Kireeaboo or those he could wish to see, than from an attack, or even much insult. The disposition of our guards when the movements be an were thus: Cook in his pennace, with six private marines: a corporal, serjeant and two lieutenants of marines went ahead followed by the launch with other marines and seamen on one quarter, and the small cutter on the other with only the crew on board. This part of the guard rowed for Kireekakoa. Our large cutter and two boats from the Discovery had orders to proceed to the mouth of the bay, form at equal distances across, and prevent any communication by water from any other part of the island to the towns within the bay, or from them without. Cook landed at Kiverua about nine o'clock in the morning with the marines in the pennace, and went by a circuitous march to the house of Kireeaboo in order to evade the suspicion of any design. This rout led them through a considerable part of the town which discovered every symptom of mischief, though Cook blinded by some fatal cause could not perceive it, or too self-confident would not regard it.

The town was evacuated by the women and children, who had retired to the circumadjacent hills, and appeared almost destitute of men, but there were at that time 200 chiefs and more than twice that number of other men detached and secreted in different parts of the houses nearest to Kireeaboo exclusive of unknown numbers without the skirts of the town, and those that were seen were dressed many of them in black. When the guard reached Kireeaboo's house, Cook ordered the lieutenant of marines to go in and see if he was at home, and if he was to bring him out; the lieutenant went in and found the old man siting with two or three old women of distinction, and when he gave Kireeaboo to understand that Cook was without and wanted to see him he discovered the greatest marks of uneasiness, but arose and accompanied the lieutenant out, holding his hand; when he came before Cook he squated down upon his hams as a mark of humiliation, and Cook took him by the hand from the lieutenant, and conversed with him.

The appearance of our parade both by water and on shore, though conducted with the utmost silence and with as little ostentation as possible, had alarmed the towns on both sides of the bay, but particularly Kiverua, who were in complete order for an onset otherwise it would have been a matter of surprize, that though Cook did not see 20 men in passing through the town, yet before he had conversed 10 minutes with Kireeaboo he was surrounded by three or four hundred people, and above half of them chiefs. Cook grew uneasy when he observed this, and was the more urgent in his persuasions with Kireeaboo to go on board, and actually persuaded the old man to go at length, and led him within a rod or two of the shore, but the just fears and conjectures of the chiefs at last interposed. They held the old man back, and one of the chiefs threatened Cook when he attempted to make them quit Kireeaboo. Some of the croud now cried out that Cook was going to take their king from them and kill him, and there was one in particular that advanced towards Cook in an attitude that alarmed one of the guard who presented his bayonet and opposed him: Acquainting Cook in the mean time of the danger of his situation, and that the Indians in a few minutes would attack him, that he had overheard the man whom he had just stopped from rushing in upon him say that our boats which were out in the harbour had just killed his brother and he would be revenged. Cook attended to what this man said, and desired him to shew him the Indian that had dared to attempt a combat with him, and as soon as he was pointed out Cook fired at him with a blank. The Indian perceiving he received no damage from the fire rushed from without the croud a second time, and threatened any one that should oppose him. Cook perceiving this fired a ball, which entering the Indian's groin he fell and was drawn off by the rest. Cook perceiving the people determined to oppose his designs, and that he should not succeed without further bloodshed ordered the lieutenant of marines (Mr. Phillips) to withdraw his men and get them into the boats, which were then laying ready to receive them. This was effected by the serjeant; but the instant they began to retreat Cook was hit with a stone, and perceiving the man who hove, shot him dead: The officer in the boats perceiving the guard retreating, and hearing this third discharge ordered the boats to fire, this occasioned the guard to face about and fire, and then the attack became general, Cook and Mr. Phillips were together a few paces in the rear of the guard, and perceiving a general fire without orders quitted Kireeaboo, and ran to the shore to put a stop to it, but not being able to make themselves heard, and being close pressed upon by the chiefs they joined the guard and fired as they retreated. Cook having at length reached the margin of the water between the fire of the boats waved with his hat to cease firing and come in, and while he was doing this a chief from behind stabed him with one of our iron daggers just under the shoulder blade, and passed quite through his body. Cook fell with his face in the water and immediately expired. Mr. Phillips not being able any longer to use his fusee drew his sword and engageing the chief who he saw kill Cook soon dispatched him, his guard in the mean time were all killed but two, and they had plunged into the water and were swimming to the boats, he stood thus for some time the butt of all their force, and being as complete in the use of his sword as he was accomplished: his noble atchievements struck the barbarians with awe, but being wounded and growing faint from loss of blood, and excessive action, he plunged into the sea with his sword in his hand and swam to the boats, where however he was scarcely taken on board before somebody saw one of the marines that had swam from the shore laying flat upon the bottom. Phillips hearing this run aft, threw himself in after him and brought him up with him to the surface of the water and both were taken in.

The boats had hitherto kept up a very hot fire, and laying off without the reach of any weapons but stones had received no damage, and being fully at leisure to keep up an unremitted and uniform action made great havoc among the Indians, particularly among the chiefs who stood foremost in the crowd and were most exposed, but whether from their bravery or ignorance of the real cause that deprived so many of them of fire, they made such a stand, may be questioned since it is certain that they in general if not univerally understood hertofore that it was the fire only of our arms that destroyed them, this seems to be strengthened by the circumstance of the large thick mats they were observed to wear, which were also constantly kept wet and furthermore the Indian that Cook fired at with a blank discovered no fear when he found his mat unburnt, saying in their language when he showed it to the by-stander, that there was no fire he had touched it. This may be supposed at least to have had some influence. It is however certain whether from one or both those causes that the numbers who fell made no apparent impression on those who survived, they were immediately taken off and had their places supplied in a constant determined succession.

Lietenant Gore who commanded as first lietuenant under Cook in the *Resolution*, which lay opposite the place where his attack was made, perceiving with his glass that the guard on shore was cut off, and that Cook had fell, immediately passed a spring upon one of the cables, and bringing the ship's starboard guns to bear, and fired two round shot over the boats into the middle of the croud and both the thunder of the cannon and the effects of the shot, opperated so powerfully, that it produced a most precipitate retreat from the shore to the town. This was done that the boats might land and secure our dead. But the lieutenant who commanded the boats did not chose to improve the hint, though the people in the boats were eager at least to get the bodies of their comrades and their lost commander, if they did no more. Mr. Phillips was so enraged at this palpable instance of apparent pusilanimity, that the altercation he had with this other lieutenant would have ended in the immediate death of one of them had not a signal from the ship that instant hove out put an end to it by orders to return.

When the boats from the shore reached the ships the boats in the mouth of the bay also returned. The conduct of the lieutenant, who commanded the boats at the town, was an object that required an early attention, but from the situation of other matters of more immediate importance it was defected. Our mast that was repairing at Kireekakoa, and our astronomical tents were only protected by a corporeal and six marines exclusive of the carpenters at work upon it, and demanded immediate protection: As soon, therefore, as the people were refreshed with grog and reinforced they were ordered thither. In the mean time the marine who had been taken up by Mr. Phillips discovered returning life and seemed in a way to recover, and we found Mr. Phillip's wound not dangerous, though very bad. We also observed at Kiverua that our dead were drawn of by the Indians, which was a mortifying sight, but after the boats were gone they did it in spite of our cannon, which were firing at them several minutes, but they had no sooner erected this matter than they retired to the hills to avoid our shot. The expedition to Kiverua had taken up about an hour and an half, and we lost besides Cook a corporal and three marines.

Notwithstanding the dispatch that was used in sending a force to Kireekakoa, the small party there were already attacked before their arrival, but by an excellent manoeuvre of taking possession of the Morai they defended themselves without any material damage until the succours came. The natives did not attempt to molest the boats in their debarkation of our people, which we much wondered at, and they soon joined the others upon the Morai amounting in the whole to be about 60. Mr. Phillips notwithstanding his wound, was present, and in conjunction with lieutenant King carried the chief command. The plan was to act only defensively until we could get our mast into the water to tow off, and our tents into the boats; and as soon as that was effected to return on board: This we did in about an hours time, but not without killing a number of the natives, who resolutely attacked us and endeavored to mount the walls of the Morai, where they were lowest, but being opposed with our skill in such modes of attack and the great superiority of our arms they were even repulsed with loss, and at length retreated among the houses adjacent to the Morai, which affording a good opportunity to retreat to our boats we embraced it and got off all well. Our mast was taken on the booms and repaired there though to disadvantage.

About two o'clock Capt. Clerke came on board to take command of the *Resolution*, and the same day Mr. John Gore who had been Cook's first lieutenant, and next in command at Cook's death, went on board to take command of the *Discovery*. About four o'clock Clerke sent three boats well manned and armed to Kiverua with orders to demand the bodies of our dead, and if refused to return without doing any thing to obtain them by force. Mr. King who was now first lieutenant in the *Resolution* took the command in the Pennace carrying a white jack in the stern: the boats formed in a line within stones throw of the shore where they remained about a quarter of an hour conversing with the inhabitants, who upon seeing us approach had assembled again, as numerous and as well appointed as even nothing material happened during this parley: we demanded the bodies and they refused them, on what was robbed, they ridiculed us, and when we moved to return hove stones at us, shewed us Cook's hanger all bloody, and his hat and the cloaths of the other dead.

The people in the boats who supposed they were going to attack them again were much disappointed and at their return vented their complaints, and somewhat more than asked to be revenged upon their savage insulting foes; but they would have taken perhaps an undue advantage had they attacked them from the boats, even supposing them to have had the fairest claim to justice, in a prosecution of the broil, for they were entirely secure even from being wounded in the contest, and in fact it would have looked too much like sporting with the lives of men and turning war which is or ought to be one of the most serious circumstances in life into a cruel farce, not to say any thing worse; besides there really at that time was no necessity for it, for the bodies were gone we did not know where, and had we again strewed the shore with their dead, we never should have obtained the bodys unless we landed and took them. After dark the sentries upon the gangways saw a canoe approaching the ship in a very silent and hasty manner, and when she got within call the officer of the deck hailed her, but the Indians returning no answer the sentry fired at her, and shot one of the Indians through the leg upon which he bawled out tutee, tutee, that is Cook. Clerke was acquainted with the matter and came upon deck and ordered her along side and the Indian on board: there were only three of them, and one had Cook's hat on his head which he gave us to understand he had brought at the hazard of his life; the man that was wounded was taken to the surgeon and his wound dressed. But we were extremely affected and disgusted when the other indian produced from a bundle he had under his arm a part of Cook's thigh wrapped up in clean cloth which he said he saw himself cut from the bone in the manner we saw it, and when we enquired what had become of the remaining part of him, he gnashed his teeth and said it was to be eaten that night. As soon as the wound of the Indian that was shot was dressed, they departed with a promise if they could to bring the remainder of Cook's body the next night.

The prospect of recovering Cook's body though by pieces offered some satisfaction and we therefore suspended the further prosecution of business on shore for the next day. In the evening about the same time he appeared before we saw the same Indian with other parts of Cook's body, to wit the upper part of his head and both his hands, which he said he had been at infinite pains to procure, and that the other parts could not be obtained, especially the flesh which was mostly eat up: the head was scalped and all the brains taken out: the hands were scored and salted: these fragments of the body of the unfortunate Cook were put into a box and preserved in hopes of getting more of them: the Indians who brought them were well satisfied with presents, and returned again to the shore the same night, and though they assured us they could not procure any more of the remains: we yet waited another day but saw no more of the Indian.

On the 17th the *Discovery* having the least draught of water was ordered to remove as near the watering place as possible: moore, and with a spring bring her broadside to bear upon it, in order to protect the watering parties in case of insult. As soon as this was done the boats with a small party landed, and made out to get off one turn of water but no more: the natives had assembled to oppose them behind the houses and the stone walls, from whence they discharged whole clouds of stones, and being in some places within 20 yards of our people; wounded several of them very badly: and at length they began to come out upon the beach upon which a signal was made for the boats to return, and the ship fired two cannon which killed three men, and we afterwards heard took off a woman's arm.

As we had hitherto to act only on the defensive part, and finding we could not succeed we were determined to alter our mode of attack: go to sea without water we could not, and as we made no doubt that our endeavors at any of the other islands who had heard of our situation, would be attended with the same difficulties, we were determined to try the contest here where the broil first originated.

On the 18th we took all the force we could spare from both ships and landed at eight in the morning. We were attacked again in the same manner the small party had been yesterday, upon which we formed such of our seamen as were most expert at small arms into two divisions in conjunction with the marines amounting to about twenty-five each division: Of some of the other seamen we composed two scouting parties armed with pistols, cutlasses, hand-grenades and torches: The waterers had arms and were to act as occasion required. Our first manoeuvre was to draw them from among the houses on to the beach by strategem and expose them to the fire of the ship as well as ours; but failing in this we joined the two divisions and advanced through an avenue that led directly into this part of the town in a solid column: The natives seeing this flung themselves into it to oppose our progress and attacked us at close quarters with their short spears, daggers and stones, but they soon gave way when the front of the column pressed upon them with their bayonets and retired to some houses

about ten rods off where they again rallied: During this little attack we had
several wounded, but none killed; the Indians took the most of their killed,
which were near a hundred: In the mean while our scouting parties improving the opportunity had circumvented that part of the town nearest the
watering place and had just set fire to it, and joining us we retreated to the
beach pretendedly in great disorder, and the natives seeing their town in
flames and supposing we were going off followed us to the water where we
again attacked them, and the ship improving the opportunity made such
use of her cannon that they soon again run and were pursued many of them
into the flames of their own houses, where if they were not instantly killed
they were burnt to death. The fire had now spread universally, and the houses
consisting of light dry materials, burnt with such rapidity that in half an
hour every one north-west of the Morai was leveled, and had this part not
been detached from the southeast part, the whole town of Kireekakooa consisting of above a thousand houses, would have been destroyed: thus ended
this days business.

On the 18th we again landed for water, and as that part of the town was
burnt from whence only we had been annoyed before: we thought ourselves
secure; but we were mistaken, the natives had now assembled upon the top
of a steep hill above the watering place, and rolled down large rocks upon
us: and some of them came down to a house that stood near the bottom of
the hill, where they meant to continue until we should embark and then
attack us: but as the way to this house was obscured by rocks and broken
walls, and favored an approach; as many of our men as could without danger of discovery crept up to it: came by surprize upon those within it and
after a smart dispute killed every one of them: and cutting off two heads
of the natives, fixed them on a pole and exposed them to the view of those
on the hill; one of our men was wounded in the skirmish, and we had two
of our water casks stove by the rocks, but still fortunately no lives were lost.

On the 20th we again landed, and were entirely unmolested, though
great numbers of the natives were still on the hill. In the afternoon we saw
a number of white flags displayed on poles stuck up both on the hill and
on the Morai, and on the tops of the houses in the S.E. part of the town, and
before we went off a number of boys and girls preceeded by a priest came
down the hill with little white flags and green branches, and bringing at
the same time some presents of fruit and provisions: after these arrived, others came from the town in the same manner, and brought a number of hogs,
and bread-fruit enough to supply the ships for two or three days, which was

now highly acceptable: nevertheless we did not accept of it until a boat was sent to the ships to know the pleasure of the commanders: we soon after heard a cannon from the commodore, and saw white colours displayed, which we need not to have informed the natives was a declaration of peace, for they immediately concluded it to be so, and some of them ventured on board with us.

This however on the part of the natives was only a transient overture: a finesse their betters make use of as well as themselves, and are on that account in no danger of being deceived by too much faith in public treaties.

On the 21st having completed the water of both ships and got the Resolution's mast up and rigged, we got everything ready for sea.

On the 22nd finding we were not visited by the natives, and that their declarations of amity were insincere, we unmoored and in the evening got under way, with a light breeze off the land, and as we left the bay we sunk the box that contained the small remains of Cook's body in that Ocean where he had acquired his honor, and in that spot where his exploits terminated: a salute with the cannon was made as usual on such occasions.

Our water on board being bad; after we had passed the Island Mauwee we came to off the Island Wagadoo, in hopes of meeting with better, but being disappointed,

On the 24th we again came to sail, and passing the Island Nehun and two other smaller islands,

On the 25th we anchored in the same road-stead off the islands of Attowai, where we had before been in February, 1778, and which was the first of these islands that we discovered on our first expedition to the northward. As there was a fine rivulet of water here, we were determined if possible to empty all the water we had got at Owyhee, and replace it with this: but it was first necessary to know if this was practicable: we had great reason to suppose it was not, for we had not only more wild uncivilized men to deal with, but an injured and exasperated people: nay more, a people who had heard of our transactions at Owyhee, and knew us to be no more than men like themselves, and therefore no longer in dread of us: we had also at our first visit here spread the venereal disease among them, which had since made the most shocking ravages: though in justice to Cook I must observe that the causes which produced it was such as he would have punished in the severest manner had he known it, as all communication between our people and these were when we were here in 1778 strictly prohibited by him.

The only hopes then that we had of being able to land and water here, were either those that originated from bestowing great presents on all the chiefs at least: and those of mere force, or perhaps a little of each, which indeed was the case. We were on shore three successive days with all the force we could spare from the ships, but had not the chiefs exerted themselves in the most strenuous manner in our favor, they certainly would have attacked us, though they still stood awed when they saw our little intrepid handfull; and so far our force was of service to us: and it was best not put to a further proof, for there were more than 15000 of the natives round us every day, and above half that number fighting men.

On the 28th we had the pleasure to finish our watering business: And as going on shore to trade for provisions would by no means do we remained on board, and though the natives did not come off to us with that plenty they used to do, yet we found it worth our while to continue here several days,

On the 4th of March we again came to sail, and the same day anchored at the Island of Nehow, from which we took our departure on our first passage to the northward in February, 1778.

The greatest part of the produce of this island is yams, and we procured at this visit as well as at the former about two months supply: We did not however at this time as we did before, but sent our boats to the shore which we found answered much better purposes.

The whole group called Sandwich-Islands, make ten in number, they lay in a south-easterly and north-westerly direction.

Owyhee to the S.E. lies in lat. 19.28. north, and longit. 203. east, and Nehow to the north-west lies in lat. 21.49. north, and longit. 198.39. east. Owyhee, Mauwee, Nehun, Wagadoo, Attowai and Nehow are all large islands from 90 to 30 leagues in circumference, and thick inhabited.

In my accounts of the principal one which is Owyhee I have been so particular as to exclude the propriety of adding a distinct and separate account of the rest; but as we are now forever to take our leave of them, and quit the remoter parts of the Pacific-Ocean, it will be natural at least if not requisite to make some reflections on that multitude of islands and immense number of people, who inhabit them throughout this extended and almost boundless world of waters. The islands are a kind of curiosity themselves; in point of situation and formation: But this respects a very learned subject; or rather a speculative curiousity, and is foreign from the more immediate objects of our discoveries. It is a subject only fit for a philosopher: and he must be a very good one too. But I am no philosopher: However as a traveller and a friend to mankind I shall most freely relate any matter of curious fact to be improved by them. It is a fact that every island we visited in the Pacific-Ocean is more or less overspread with lava, marked with fissures, excavations and every indication of subterraneous fire: Many of them shew indoubtable proofs that they have partook of some extraordinary struggle in nature sufficient either to place them in their present situation, or to have destroyed them if their original forms had been what they are now. When, or in what manner these events took place in nature I leave to the ingenious: But as we never could obtain any intelligence of the present inhabitants of any such occurences we cannot suppose it of any late date. But had those people inhabited them originally, either antecedent to the universal deluge, or subsequent to that period, and prior to the eventual convulsions just mentioned, and it had been possible for them to have existed they would have remembered such remarkable events: And again supposing the deluge not to have been universal, and those extraordinary changes never to have taken place in the manner already supposed, but by a less violent and a frequent succession of convulsive alterations, yet the least of such appearances, especially among them would have been noticed let us suppose them to have inhabited these islands at any period whatever: But they knew nothing of any such changes or any thing of the least of those causes which have beyond all doubt existed here, and in some instances according to appearance of the lava and other calcinated matter from the very late eruptions: And these considerations do not only respect the island, but its inhabitants. It argues that if they were created and existed here independent of antecedent derivation from the rest of mankind, that they were very lately made, and have come very imperfect from the latest works of the Creator: And yet I have heard it supposed: Though I confess unworthy confutation.

It argues also that the inhabitants of those islands did not originally exist there, that they are emigrants from some other parts of the earth; and is a presumptive argument that they are not very early emigrants: This is still more evident from anological inferences. We have pretty plain proofs that the Otaheiteans have motions of transmigration, and we know that those sentiments of religion first transpired in India several hundred years since the birth of Christ.

What is more fluctuating and liable to change is their language, and yet the language that pervades even all the islands spoken of in this history (if it may be called such) have many words similar in their orthography, and expressive of the same ideas with those in the present languages of the Malaynese, Javanese, of Prince's Island, and even of Madagascar, and yet it is very probable, that all those different languages were a thousand if not five hundred years ago very different from what they are now.[9]

These considerations respect an emigration, and a late emigration. I esteem an emigration late in this instance that commenced a thousand years back. But I believe those who have read the voyages that respect the islands in this part of the terraqueous world, have before now been fully convinced that the inhabitants of them were derrived from one common origin, and the only difficulty that remained was to fix that common origin, the particular country and people.

It is certainly very remarkable if the inhabitants of these isles did emigrate from the same set of men: The same nation, tribe, horde or sect: And there are the strongest reasons to think so let the local situation of their ancestors be where it might: That must give way to that universal similarity of appearances that supports the prior sentiment. But as providence when we are able to investigate its proceedings ever acts uniformly, and so orders events as to correspond with the causes which produce them, we are not to discredit an extraordinary fact, though we cannot immediately comprehend it, and in endeavoring to account for it we are to judge according to the general operation of things.

I believe it will be thought too curious to suppose that the aborigines of those isles individually considered emigrated from either of the continents: But taking the islands collectively, and supposing them originally peopled from one of the continents is very natural and rational. The case thus situated reduces the enquiry to two questions: From which of the continents America or Asia did the inhabitants of these islands immediately emigrate, and what island or islands did they first emigrate to?

The New-Zealanders say their ancestors came from an island called Hawyjee: Now Owyhee as we have carelessly pronounced it is pronounced by its inhabitants Hawyhee. This is a curious circumstance, and admits of a presumption that the Island Owyhee or Hawyee is the island from which the New-Zealanders originally emigrated: It superceeds anological evidence—but Owyhee is in 20 north, and New-Zealand in 40 south, and not above 300 leagues distant from the southern part of New-Holland, and is besides situated in the latitudes of variable winds, which admit of emigration from any quarter. On the other hand the languages of Owyhee and New-Zealand were originally the same and as much alike as that of Otaheite and New-Zealand: Not to mention other circumstances of the like kind: Whereas the language at New-Zealand and New-Holland have very little or no resemblance to each other: This difference with many others between New-Zealand and New-Holland cannot be reconciled: But the difficulties that may arise from considering the distance between New-Zealand and Owyhee may be as there are clusters of islands that we know of, and may be others unknown that occupy at no great distance from each other the intermediate ocean from Owyhee to New-Zealand. The obvious reasonings that would be used to conclude the New-Zealanders emigrants from Owyhee would be first to suppose them from the Friendly Isles, then the Society-Isles, and then Sandwich-Isles, and the gradation thus formed is very rational and argumentative, because all their manners and customs have the same rout. Suppose then that the islands we have mentioned were peopled from Owyhee, and suppose it to be the first island settled, the second and ultimate question is from which of the continents—America or Asia? Its situation respecting America and the trade winds, strongly infer from that continent, for it is twice the distance from Asia that it is from America; and a ship, fitted for the purpose at China, which is in a parallel latitude, would be more than two months in reaching it, and we must suppose the emigrations that respect these people to have been merely fortuitous: But a canoe drove by stress of weather from the southern part of California, or the coast of New-Galicia, the opposite parallel would reach Owyhee in a direct course in half the time or less: The distance is about 900 leagues, and we saw people at the Island Manganooanooa, who had been driven from Otaheite there, which is 500 leagues.

But if we suppose Owyhee peopled from South-America, we shall be somewhat disappointed in supporting the conjecture by arguments that respect their manners and customs, and those of the Californians, Mexicans, Peruvians, or Chilinese: There is but a faint analogy compared with that which we should find on the southeastern coasts of Asia in these respects. Let us then without attending to the few analogical customs that subsist between the Owyheeans and the South-Ameircans reverse our system of emigration: Suppose the inhabitants of Sandwich-Islands to have come from the Society-Islands, and those from the Friendly Isles, and the New-Zealanders from them, the inhabitants of the Friendly Isles from New-Caledonia, from the Hebrides, New-Guinea, Celebes, Borneo, Java, or Sumatra, and finally from the continent at Malacca.

To give the distinct position of these islands and numberless others of less note all around them would be needless, as a moments adversion to the chart will do it to more advantage. Supposing the emigration we are now speaking of to take this course, the most apparent argument in its favor is the proximity of the several islands to each other from the Friendly Isles to the continent; but its sufficiency will abate if we consider emigrations as I think they are oftener the effects of accident than preintention especially when out of fight of land: Besides it is evident from occular proof that though New-Guinea, and New-Holland are very near to each other, that there has never been any intercourse between them: and yet from many appearances there seems to have been one between New-Guinea and New-Hebrides and the Friendly Isles, although farther distant from each other. There is indeed no remarkable similarity in the people, customs and manners of New-Guinea and the Friendly Isles, but an exact conformity between the domestic animals, and vegetable productions of both countries: Some fruits that we call tropical, are peculiar to all places within the tropics: But bread-fruit is no where known but among these islands and the islands further northward on the coast of Asia: It is not known at New-Holland but it is at New-Guinea. Therefore wherever I can find this bread-fruit in particular, I shall suppose an intercourse to have once subsisted, and the more so when I find a correspondent agreement between the animals of different places: And it ought to be remembered also that there are no other animals throughout those islands unless they are near the continent; those remote islands have no other: It is the same with their vegetables. The remote islands have no water-melons, guavas and such other fruits.

These observations will materially apply to the circumstances of emigration. A canoe in passing along its own coast, or visiting a neighbouring island would take on board a hog, a dog, a fowl and bread-fruit for subsistance in preference to a monkey, a snake, a guava or sour sop: And if she is driven accidentally on to some foreign island they turn to greater advantage still.

On the 15th of March we came to sail steering N.W. from the islands, meaning to fall in with that part of northern and eastern Asia that forms the peninsula generally called Kamptschatka; but according to the pronunciation of the Russian emigrants who inhabit it, and the dialect of the aborigines of the country Kamchatka: This is one of the southern circles of Russian Siberia, called thus from its being a place where malefactors of rank from the Court of Russia are exiled: The word Siberia in Russ signifying a prison: It was formerly called Asiatic Tartary, and was almost wholly unknown until the reign of the present Empress Catherine, who has diffused not only throughout this circle, but nearly all the rest detached companies of European troops, which have lately been encreased by the junction of some of the Cossacks and the Indians themselves: These troops keep the country in awe; and by establishing factories for pelt and fur have of late made great advances toward colonization and added something very important to the revenue of the Empress. At this time we were in want of many European articles that respected not only the comfort of our persons, but the safety of the ships: We had yet an immense tract of ocean to traverse, and re-explore, and after that was finished if we were so fortunate as to escape the dangers that those who best knew them, the most strongly anticipated; other circumstances subsequent to these our best wishes would still add to our embarrassments, and if we were not drowned should be starved to death without some kind of relief. We were besides almost naked for want of clothing of all kinds, particularly shoes, for there was not a new pair in either ship. Indeed it was a certain truth, though not revealed to the people, that should we meet with no recruit of bread, and persevere in our proposed second attempt in the exploration of a North-West Passage: we must have been necessiated to reduce our pittance of bread or flour, which was now at half allowance to a still smaller quantity, and perhaps too small, before we could possibly reach any port where we could be sure of a supply.

These considerations then induced us to bend our course towards Kamchatka, though in fact we had little encouragement to expect relief when we should get there.

I shall not detain my readers with a dull detail of immaterial incidents while at sea on this passage, and only simply observe that it was rendered extremely trying and severe not only from the sudden change of climate in leaving the tropical latitudes, and entering on a winters coast, and a new cost, but from other circumstances: Our clothing as is observed before was really miserable, our food was the same on Monday morning and Sunday evening—pork and yams begun, and pork and yams ended all our bills of fare, and we had besides but half an allowance of the latter of those articles and when pealed, and the rotten and decayed parts defalcated the remainder was oh ye epecures, but scanty I assure ye! Besides, it was the month of March, and to crown the jest our ship was fairly worn out. We pumped and bailed her half the passage.

On the 20th of April in a thick snow-storm accompanied by a severe gale of wind we parted company with the Discovery; our lat. was 48.38.north.

On the 25th we came in sight of the coast of Kamchatka, and the next day we entered a spacious bay, called by the Russians Awatska, and came to an anchor among some loose ice in the chops of the bay.

On the 26th weighed, and run further up towards a village we saw on the north-west side of the bay, but were not able to approach it within three quarters of a mile for the ice that surrounded the shore. The Discovery had been separated from us since the 20th; we were very much concerned for her safety, and were not relieved from our anxiety until the 30th, when to our infinite joy we saw her coming up the bay, all well.

The inhabitants of the village, who consisted at this time only of a Russian guard of 15 or 20 miserable looking men commanded by a serjeant, and about 60 Indians, were very much frightened when they first saw our ships having never before seen any thing of the kind, except two or three little coasting barks of theirs made on that coast, and were therefore drawn up to oppose our landing, which was partly on the ice; but the serjeant understanding a little of the German language made himself intelligible to our draught man who spoke it fluently, and accompanied those who first landed. By this means an eclaircissement soon took place, and the serjeant invited the gentlemen into his house, and regaled them with a dish of fish and some whurts: By him we were informed of several particulars that gave us much satisfaction, and nothing more so than the probability there was of getting some supplies from the commander in chief, who resided at a settlement called Bolchairetskoi or Bolcharecka situate about 50 English miles back in the country towards the Sea Ochotsk: And as the serjeant was going to send off an immediate express to this gentleman to acquaint him of our arrival, it was thought proper to write him by the same opportunity, and as he was a German by birth and education we sent the letter in that language. The courier with these dispatches was drawn by a sledge with 10 or 12 dogs, and returned again with the Governor's secretary, and a letter to Capt. Clerke complimenting him on his arrival, and tendering his best services wherever he was made more fully acquainted with the supplies, and added that after that he would do himself the honor to wait upon him in person. As it was difficult to transmit so perfect an account of such articles as we wanted by letter as if some one who well understood the business could do in person, and for other reasons added to these, Captain Gore (as Captain Clerke himself was very ill) determined to wait on the Governor himself, and to make the visit more agreeable as well as more respectable lieutenant King who spoke the French and Mr. Webber the draughtsman, who spoke the German languages accompanied him, taking the Governor's secretary with them.

In the mean time as the ice broke from the shores we birthed the ships nearer in, and began to water and wood: We also stripped the *Resolution's* bows, and made other necessary repairs and equipments.

On the 5th of May several Russian and Polish traders in fur came to our ships from Bolcharecka, and brought letters to Capt. Clerke from Capt. Gore, who had safe arrived at that place with his fruit.

These traders belonged to others in different parts of Siberia, and were a company comissioned to traffic for furs, for which priviledge they paid the Empress so much annually. They purchased the most of our fur, for which they gave what we then thought a great price, but when we afterwards visited China we found our mistake: They gave us for the glutton-skins each 60 rubles, which are nearly equal to Spanish dollars: For beaver-skins about 15 rubles upon an average.

On the 23rd our gentlemen returned from Belcharecka with the Governor, who was a Major in the Russian army, an agreeable sensible well bred man. He was saluted with eleven guns, and other marks of respect from both ships at his arrival, and when he went away had many very valuable presents made him.

On the 25th the Governor left us, with packets both public and private, which he undertook to transmit to Great-Britain, across the continent by way of Petersburgh: This we found afterwards to be honorably executed.

The supplies we received here were 20 head of poor cattle, 400 weight of tobacco, tar, cordage and canvais, and particularly about 9000 weight of rye-meal which was all they had: This rye-meal we afterwards mixed with our flour, and served it out in equal portions.

The Bay Awatska is large and capacious, being generally 6 and 7 leagues broad: on the south side there is a settlement called Paratanka, containing a few houses, and a church with a Greek priest. On the N.W. side is situate the village opposite which we lay, called Peter and Paul from two lofty mountains behind it, which they have distinguished by those names; it contains about 30 huts, some of which are built with logs, as we do in our new American settlements, and others are erected on posts about 14 feet from the ground, consisting of a slight frame of a conical form and a thatch. Besides the Russians who inhabit it, there are some of the aborigines of the country, who are civilized, and occasionally bear arms: But are generally employed in hunting or fishing. The natives of some of the hordes remote from the Kamchadales are a tolerable people, but the Kamchadales are the reverse, not only of them but of any people I ever saw: They are of a diminutive size, narrow foreheads, high cheek-bones, small eyes sunk into their heads and guamy: Almost no nose, a monsterous mouth and thick lips: their hair is black and strait: They are indolent, ignorant, superstitious, jealous, cowardly, and more filthy and dirty than the imagination can conceive in persons dress and manner of living.

The dress of them and the Russian's consists of a gown tied round the waist with a sash or girdle, and lined with fur, a fur cap and seal-skin boots. The dress of the women is nearly the same. As neither they nor the Russians apply themselves to any kind of agriculture, they have no kind of vegetables but what grow wild, and no bread but what comes either from some of the more southern circles, or from Moscow and Petersburgh: Their principal subsistance there arises from hunting and fishing, but mostly from the latter resource. Among their fish they have plenty of good salmon, which they preserve by drying them, and this forms the principle part of their winters provisions.

The face of the country is high and mountainous, and thick covered with well grown woods, which chiefly consists of birch, pine and beach, and the internal parts of it abounds with a variety of wild animals, among which is the Barran or wild sheep: This is a large, stately formidable animal in its original state, and very unlike the little delicate timid animal that exists in our flocks and folds of that name. As the inhabitants have no horses, they make use of a number of midling sized dogs: And as they travel mostly in winter, they use them mostly for that purpose in light sledges, with which they travel 40 or 50 miles a day very comfortably.

We saw at this place several gentlemen who had been exiled from the court of Russia, particularly a certain Count, who it is said had carried his amours with her Imperial Majesty so far, that to conceal the matter it was ncessary her gallant should spend the remainder of his days in the forests of Siberia—hunt for his own subsistance, and exclusively produce annually so much fur to his mistress as a tribute to her generosity and goodness.

On the 12th of June having received our supplies on board, repaired our ships, wooded and watered, we unmoored and waited a wind.

On the 13th finding no wind, towed to the mouth of the bay and came to.

On the 14th it was calm all day, and in the afternoon we had a slight shock of an earthquake.

On the 15th it continued calm until noon when it clouded up and became very black and dark: the two mountains Peter and Paul were covered with the atmosphere near half way from their summits down, and at two o'clock we had again a small shock of an earthquake, and heard a hollow rumbling noise in the air, and the atmosphere continuing to condense, it became almost as dark as night, and the face of heaven looked very wild: we singled the stops of the sheet-anchor and eased the ship aloft at all these portentous appearances. Between three and four the mountain Paul exploded with a tremendous shock that convulsed every thing around us: The report that attended the explosion was very loud at first, but gradually decreased until it subsided to a sound like that of grumbling distant thunder: About half after four it began to thunder, and the air being surcharged with electrical matter, perhaps from the mountain, the atmosphere was one continued sheet of flame: We put our electrical chains to the mast-head, Soon after it began to thunder there fell showers of small fragments of lava about the size of a walnut: This was succeeded by showers of mud, and by five there followed a fall of dry, white, fine ashes, which produced a very strong sulphureous smell: Our ship was covered with mud and ashes, which lay several inches thick on our decks. About eight in the evening the commotion had pretty well subsided, but the mountains were still covered with a thick cloud and continued to burn. By a mathematical measuration we were 20 miles in a horizontal direction from the summit of the mountain Paul.

On the 16th we had a fair and easy westerly breeze which shot us out to sea: We observed the mountain Paul still emitting columns of smoke as was usual before, it being an old vulcano. We also observed the country all round within 30 miles to be covered with ashes. which being of a light colour looked very much like a new fallen snow: We also found the surface of the sea impregnated with mud and ashes 8 or 9 leagues off the land. There is another vulcano in this bay which some times has its eruptions. The village called Peter and Paul is situate in lat. 53.° 15 N. longt. 158° E.

On the 17th continued our course to the northward.

★

Here Ledyard's journal ends. The voyage lasted 16 more months, with a second passing of Bering Strait and landfalls at Macao on the Chinese coast, Pulo Condor in Indonesia, Cape Town, and Stromness in the Scottish Orkneys, before he and the rest of the crew returned to London in October 1780.

Ann thy spouse, & kiss her for me—& do your will not allow it possible for thy quondam McArthur to receive but two kisses whether immediate or by proxy that can be superior to my own, they will be thine & those of Ben. If Madam Ann thinks to monopolize thy friendship or thou hers—believe me ye are wrongly mounted as might & main will not preserve the hypothesis—or your Ass from the recriminating punctuations of a sharp spandy new pen I have this moment bought from the Palais Royal for the purpose—look well to your way & so ye have my blessing. Hadst thou just arisen satiated from the uniled banquets of love & friendship—"landed property & firms" when thy letter was composed? Quiting thy physical character hath injured society, & is a degradation of genious—and art thou abandoned ingrate, base enough to—Jersey! thy place were witness to far other tales of amity than those which I have seen in France: thy green groves would blush to hear the story told by clad in guilt or in —and so forth—because I amplify a little here.

But after all I swear I love thee & will rail no more—I am sorry for what I have done if it has hurt thy heart but suffer it not—it was an excrescence, & heartily are thou inclined to laugh it off—Josephus cannot wrong Monecca or receive one from him—the gods who formed them would condemn the supposition: I kiss thee friend of my bosom—oh come to my breast thou faithfull companion—on[e] of my earliest & my best Attachements: cause & effect shall cease to be such sooner than I will quit the rich enjoyment—advance benevolent Ben & with thy honst heart compleat the group. That day which permits me to realize the luxury of returning to embraces of my friends, of thought, will compensate for the intermediate toils & danger I see before me & am on that account solicitous to encounter—but my envious fate hath again unhorsed me, & while in full pursuit of glory, left me the jest & riddle of the drama. I am loosing the merit I might obtain by the obligations I am under to pursue good—unless my perseverance will be a consideration sufficient to cancel the objections—but the discussion will become an historian only & I relinquish it. Now said I the devil is in it—soliloquizing. Now calling to mind America & especially my redoubled negotiation at Lorient—with an eye on Bob Morris & one on Berard—the devil is in it said I if *this* negoitation falls through[1]—and yet it did fall through as easy as a needle would pass through the eye of a camel—so very easy that not withstanding my general credulity I could hardly be sure it for a month after—the devil is in it said I if it fails—never once dreaming that it was as possible for the devil to be in it as out of it—especially in european courts where the devil makes at least one character in all negotiations. Now my Ass & I had formed great expectations at Lorient & I also found my affection for the beast so much encreased with my good prospects that I had from time to time given him the fee simple of at least all that part of the NW coast of America that was at present without the pretensions of any European dreamer but myself—& one Island. My Ass was perhaps happeir than he would have been in the actual possessions without the dangerous concomitant of satiety.

From that placid serenity my beast & I were mutualy enjoying & for which we were perhaps mutualy gratefull—any remorse must have been sensibly felt. Therefore this enormous thrust of fate from bliss had no doubt *the devil in it*: it was obviously true to my Ass, & of course the understanding of any other animal is not required to confirm the conclusion or even to reflect upon the premises. The resentments of insulted honesty are keen & the consequent resolutions it adopts are superior to opposition and like finished bravery conquers tho' it dies—

Will you go to Paris said my Ass. I fear I have not money enough said I: I will eat thistles said my Ass but what shall we do when there said I— tho I put the question wrong & so my Ass was silent: I too shall be forced to eat thistles said I answering myself: and will you not also by continuing here, rejoined my Ass—& what is still more disconsonant to your feelings continued the honest indignant Animal—what is still worse will you not discover your nakedness to those who have respect only to the outward appearance & consequently ridicule external poverty—at Paris you will be unknown, & should yo at the worst perish there you will be insured the advantage of dying unknown which many I assure you have wished to do & could not—I am willing also to share your fate in this as such. Thus saying my Ass kneeled down & my heart torn with a thousand desires, I once more mounted. Thus Vasca de Gama & Columbus mounted flying from a positive evil to a possible good, some might imagine I joged on heavily & in melancholly guise: no. the velocity of my journey exceeded the violence of the storm which occasioned it. The mails go it in 4 days: My ass set me down in the Louvre of Louis the 14th in 48 hours: my body indeed fatigued, but the consolations of my gallant life left my mind collected & sedate—even jovial. Ass of Asses! who could abandon so heavenly an Ass. I shewed my Ass the three guineas we had left—it was worse said my Ass—kneeling to receive his back—it was worse when we left new London on our first Journey—worse by two guineas & an half when left New London on our second Journey for Spain—alors—monte[2]—& so I did mount & he set me down at the India House, from whence we shall address thee in a new stile.

Since my first arival in Paris untill very lately my situation has been such as to demand as many virtues as may be imputed to an individual of whatever accomplishments. I cannot impute my present success to the possession of the greatest accomplishments. My affairs stand exactly thus. The celebrated Captain Paul Jones has embarked with me in my expedition: he advances all the outfits himself except the two ships which one or both of which he is now at L'orient endeavouring to procure as lent or chartered by the King of France: he tells me he thinks he shall succeed & his character is to speak & act with great caution: if he should not succeed, he has with the same caution intimated to me that he will reduce the outfits within the limits of his own private fortune & make the whole independantly: two or three weeks will determine the matter & I will inform you whatever depends upon Jones's *stability perseverance & wishes* may be firmly relied upon. he has gone so far as to desire me to procure my Cargoe, send to London for goods &c & advanced me necessary cash. If we succeed our plan is enlarged, we do not risk all on a single voyage but shall establish a factory upon the coast under my direction & under American colours. The first 6 months after our arrival we collect our fur, purchase the sovereignty of our little spot—most probably an Island, & build a small stockade sufficient to keep in safety. my family will consist of a surgeon, my assistant in business & twenty soldiers: one of the ships at the expiration of the six months proceeds to China; when she returns she stays 6 months longer & then both ships leave me & my factory, proceed to China & thence by the way of the Cape of good hope proceed to New York where I wish you may see my friend Paul Jones & read my letters—& perhaps the history of Ben Uncus.[3]

Adieu. Keep me in thy heart my dear Monecca for I have a more tender friendship for thee than any man except our Ben—kiss Ann & Kate for me & her little ones—give half my heart to Ben.

Adieu!

Josephus

★

To Isaac Ledyard
Summer 1785; Paris

From Paris

Bonjour!

I know not when the Messrs. Fitzhughs go nor when I shall close this chaos of nonsense, & not withstanding all this delay my affairs continue much the same.[4] the last letter I recd from Commodore Jones was from Nantes where he is in pursuit of a ship or ships: he sent me a bill to supply me with some cash & told me to be happy for a few days longer when he hoped the pleasure to see me in paris: I am also uneasy of the season: I know too well the southern Ocean to beat it on a [w]rong season even if I should be obliged to persuade & the Commodore to embrace the resolution of sailing at any rate under such a disadvantage. It would be hard and distressing but not so dangerous as to reflect impudence in us to attempt it. Two english ship commanded by an officer of Cooks are sailed 9 days ago from London on the same expedition, but they go East. I wish to be on the coast before then for they are the worst people in the world to follow in commerce or colonization among an uncivilized people. The arrival of paul jones will enable me to write you decisively relative to my affairs: I wish it therefore before I close if he should not I shall write you by some other conveyance. I will not say anything more about my affairs at pursuit because it would be little more than conjecture.

I dined to day with our worthy consul Mr. Barclay if every man in America was as feelingly & as sensibly attracted to that country as he is you would be as singular in virtuous patriotism as you are independent in legislation.[5] permit me to give you a sentiment that every American at table concured in. "May America have no ships of war or any Merchant ship that shall go off its own coast, but like the Chinese command the commerce of all nations that find it their interest to visit her & not suffer by those who do or do not. but what do you intend to do with the Algerians?—it is a question here I assure you—I thought John Lamb of connecticut was appointed to go to that country.[6] You are singular not to have found some kind of treaty with those pirates & you will be still more so to go to war with them—particularly while the english have gibraltar: you know they are as great together as two pick pockets & have both an implacable hatred to you. The english papers here are engrossed with american affairs & are extremely illiberal & false in their accounts of them that they are at length become their own destruction for nobody here but the most bigoted englishmen give any kind of credit to their reports.

good night

bon jour encore

You see what a day brings forth. I took tea with our Minister this morning & while I sat chatting with him, who should be anounced at the door but John Lamb esquire in propria persone with one black eye & a leg broke in a gale of wind off the Isle of Wight with a pair of tarnished black stockings hanging about his heels like monsieur Souffriene, a thick greasy pair of buck skin gloves, a long beard, his hair uncombed, coat waiscoat & breeches full of dust & rumpled all in a heap, one part of his breeches unbuttoned, an old greasy coarse hat in his hand well pinched up in the front cock—and credentials in his hand from Congress as plenipotentiary from yr States of America to the Dey of Algiers & the Emperor of Morocco! It is unfortunate that a man is so well informed of the manners customs, connections, comerce &c of that country should be so ill informed in address or even common politeness: he is shrewed & artfull & yet cannot see that his manners are at constant enmity with the good effects those qualities might produce. I repose entire confidence in your secrecy: I assure you that I am uneasy for him at least about the figure he'll cut: he makes every body so at paris though they know no more of him than a private character, he makes a confidant of me alone. The minister only knows that he is appointed Plenipotentiary to the states of Barbary. Jack Lamb I have this moment 11 o'clock at night put to bed drunk as a lord & nobody will ever know it but you & those he got drunk with. Lamb is honest & well meaning but comes here chagrined about his misfortunes during the war: wants mankind to feel for those things they do not know & could not be supposed to feel much for if they did: he despises the opinions of others & would dogmaticaly impose his own which are singularly unacceptable except when they relate merely to the purposes of his embassy & are then too much degraded by an unhappy vulgarity to be as acceptable as they realy ought to be. We are both lodged in the same hôtel & are very happy together. What I have said of him above respects his public character in which I consider myself interested as a citizen of America. as a private man I owe him a considerable share of friendship: he has always been a neighbour & a friend of my dear dear friends at Groton—has lately parted from them—still more my dear Fanny lives in his house—and more he has made me an immediate offer (if I should want it) of doing me a real & a very essential piece of service A few days and will write you more.

    goodnight

Supplement 1

If my enterprise takes place it is probable that I shall be absent from my family 4 or 5 years perhaps 6 or 7: this is not an exhilirating reflection applied to circumstances of any man that not condemned to the gallows: applied to myself it is as bad as the gallows. I have been cheated of life & hereafter shall be able to live for my friends: altho most avaritious estimate that period cannot be long and may be very short. If I can croud into that small interval of time any thing of worth it will devolve to them, and I hope be received as atonement for the disappointed expectations of that little society allied to me by the ties of consanguinity and all the charms of friendship.

Creator and if Creator Governor of nature—preserve from distress my aged mother—assist my dear sister Fanny—a poor solitary wandering girl. Amen. My brother Tom tho as greviously flagellated with disease as Job himself has nevertheless been so negatively blessed by nature that he can not ever want—especially expectations: he has no more the Idea that he should provide riches than my Ass has that they should be the immediate consequence. He is one of Esope waggoners—not he truly—no more than he is an Esope.[7]

Paris is situated in the center of an extended plain generally rising on all sides into gradual elevation and some little hills happily interspersed on the borders of its horizon. Its extent viewed from the tower of Notre Dame appeared to me less than London: the little muddy shallow meandering never seine divides it into two parts nearly equal by a course nearly east & west: the public buildings are numerous & some of them elegantly magnificent & considering its situation which like all great cities is unfortunate, it is pleasant...[missing] like versailles, both of which are french cities. It is the center of France & its center is the Palais Royal.

Palais Royal

To enter the crouded resort of the greatest virtues & the greatest vice of such a kingdom is to me one of the most momentous visits that a thinking man can make & yet to a mind of another cast I will become the most unimportant object. It is france in miniatures & no friend to france incapable of doing as he would wish should ever see it. It was built by the Present Duc de Chartres & is the only legitimate offspring he has—except his stables. In fact my dear friend the Palais Royal, the resort of the kingdom & the confessed pride of the Ville de Paris, is a vile cinque of polution & contaminated by bawds, pimps & procuresses and not only by such of those who by the glare of dress equipage or assumed titles hide their worst deformities but by the livre strumpets, coarse common street whores: The very appartments of this suberb, rich elegant building are inhabited by coarse bred impudent, abandoned disgusting bawds, women, whores & impoverished young debauches without pretension to family fortune or education but when I reproach them absolute fact that the father, the mother & the daughters are here together for the vile & professed purpose of mutual prostitution you will wish me to say no more tho with equal truth I could enlarge.

Tuilleries
These magnificient gardens are also a resort of the most sickening vices, but I will let them alone. The Tuilleries, no doubt, afford the most consummate display of artificial elegance, and grandeur, to be met with of the kind in Europe—

The Luxembourg
garden, infinitely inferior to Tuilleries & the Palais, is shamefully out of repair.

The Boulvars
Boulevards, original fortifications, is not spelled it right but I mean by it a large broadway that surrounds the City seperating it from the suburbs & is in general lined with fine umbragious elms on each side forming a more beautiful & rational course for coach & horseman: but the farmers general to prevent illicit trade are walking in it, at the expence of a thousand lamentations of the Parisians and several millions of Livres.

The Kings Library
I have been but once to see it & unfortunately was late & saw but the appartments—Papa Franklin as the french here call him, is among a number of other statues I saw. The bust of Paul Jones is also there—did you ever know that Capt. Jones was two or three night successively crowned with laurels in the great Opera house at Paris after the action between the *bon-homme Richard* & the *Saraphis*. Louis the 14th had never so much applause given him as paul jones has had in Paris. The only was on why jones has had the advantage of him in this respect is because he had it not in his power to deprive himself of it by doing just as Louis 14th did—further the jeponant & sayth not.

The People of Paris
I believe the people of paris are the politest people in the world. In Paris

that politeness is said to be prostituted: but so fascinating are the charms of address that they are happy to deceive & be deceived at the expense of their understandings & perhaps I am a fool to be digusted with it. I have even observed that such company as renders a Man easy to himself in polite company: but do not let a rule which I have carefully thrown out to you, see a test for the French politeness: whether it be good or bad let their politeness remain the same: but I swear to you that from the company of Count d'Estaing Marquis la Fayette Count d'artois, duc de Rochefaucault to Feringeries, there is a politeness that generaly excuses that of our people whatever. It true that from a certain point whether above, below, behind or beyond is perfection & imperfection, virtue & vice will unite their extremes & tho at first they commix with so much delicacy as to be imperceptable yet in the end they form a chaos & destroy themselves: the relative mutation takes place in every thing: it is a law of nature if we are pleased with politeness in its innocent infancy & still more enraptured with its meridian charms & if we are even delighted with that in the first symptoms of decline—why should not one be willing to excuse its deformity when just returning to dust, especially when we know that from this dust we shall hail another Phoenix. Now before heaven I see now that I am not certain there is any truth or argumentation or sentiment here. There is undoubtedly prostitution of complaissance [missing]....

Supplement No. 2 The americans in Paris

I find at our Ambassador's table between fifteen and twenty Americans inclusive of two or three ladies. we are very generally a set of poor dogs. I am not worth a sou myself and yet am not the poorest of my brethren. We as generally want the easy elegance of the european manners, tho' we do not want those among us who are determined to be possessed by it. There are some instances of an equal poverty of understanding—but rare and the brightest side of our general character is solid erudition and good sense. It is remarkable we are neither despised nor envied for our love of Liberty but very often caressed. I was yesterday at Versailles. It was the feast of St. Lewis but I never feasted so illy in all my life as at the hotel where I dined and never paid so dear for a dinner. I was too late to see the procession or the King and Queen but I was little disappointed on that account as I had already seen those Baubles.

The King I saw a fortnight before to very great advantage being near him whilst he was shooting partridges in the fields without Paris. He was dressed in a pair of common Musqueto Trousers, a short linen frock and an old laced hat without a Cockade: he had an easy gentlemanly appearance but for a few attendants had he none I should have taken him for a Captain of a Merchant Ship, amusing himself in the fields: he had the lounging swaggering salt-water gait in the greatest perfection though I suppose he never saw salt-water in his life. He is about five feet nine inches in height, well enough made. I could see nothing more than ordinary in his countenance but what the devil must George of England be when I assure you that his personal appearance is much below Lewis. The Palace at Versailles and the gardens do harbour a great and rich kingdom. They are in every respect an ornament to the face of the Globe. It was dirty weather. I wore boots and consequently was prohibited viewing the galleries. I was in company with our Mr Barclay Col Franks of the American Army a young Virginian who will I hope deliver this and an English sea officer.[8] Franks was booted too but honest Barclay was not—he had no bag on—and they were dismissed also—so that boots on and bags off are sad recommendations at the court of Versailles.

    Suppliment 3rd

where I now to St. Genevive the titular St of Paris that your honor may or may not find a full or an empty sheet whether litterally or metaphoricaly understood—it is a matter in future & to fraternity I shall leave it. If the two Fitzhughs remain in town a week longer thou shall have a weeks detail: they dine with me to day in my chamber together with our worthy Counsul Barclay, & that lump of universality Colonel Franks: he has a very great opinion of you & our dear Ben—we have several times taken generousness in vain on such occasions & will to day certainly met your worships with a glass of burgunday—but such a set of moniless rascals have never appeared since the epoch of the happy villian Falstaff: I have but 5 french crowns in the world, franks has not a sol, the Fitzhurghs cant get their tobacco money & the consul tho worth in reality 20,000£ sterling dines here to save ½ a crown. Paris is like a strong whirlpool it collects a parcel of light rubish within its vortex which very seldom returns by the way it entered to the surface of the stream of life, & if I ever do it will not be awarding to the general course of things I assure you for I bid defiance to them when I left America & even bribed the utmost malice of fortune.

    After diner we walked into the Palais royal which is close by the hotel where I lodge our counsul as full of french urbanity soon retired to a worthy wife & a lovely family—I was left as much alone as could be in the Palais royal: I was called by name as I was traversing the walks by a lady who composed a considerable part in a group of married & unmarried whores & who had before seen me at tea in the chamber of an english sea lieutenant a friend of mine who has superb lodgings in the palais royal. External decorum is the greatest & the least requisite here. the lady who called to me had her little old four feet 5 inches husband with her—& a true parisian husband is he—an inch more in his stature, a year less in his age, or a scruple more of virtue or understanding in him would have disqualified him. I took a chair & made use of the words superierement, suberp, magnifique, charmant, beau belle infinement &c. I placed it between the happy pair & seized the hand of the lady the husband found himself deranged & withdrew his chair behind the group where he very complaisantly set while I had entertained his lady with a thousand protestations of eager desire and eternal passion. it will not be her fault if I never see her again, nor will occasion her more than 5 minutes pain or pleasure whether I do or not.

I dined with Mr. Jefferson our Minister to day: we had at table counsul, his lady, & two little daughters, & little Miss Jefferson & a Madam Montgomery from Phila. & her son, & her gallant a young Norris from Phila who came to paris on purpose to embrace the romish religion; Mr. Humphries secretary, Colonel Franks. Fitzhugh & brother, young doctor Preston from Phila, a Carolinian, an Italaian-American. You know the full force of an opinion of mine that Mr. Jefferson is an able minister & his country may repose a confidence in him equal to their best wishes: he is the best representative of his country of all the other representatives of other countries in Paris. Your dukes of Dorset & don Seignors are but the pageantries of old sickly kingdoms—the lacquies of ministers & Kings,— your worthy Virginian whether in public or private is in every word & every action the representative of a young, politic, vigourous & determined State, his only competitors even in political fame are de Vergennes & la Fayette[9]: in other accomplishments he stands alone & I believe from my soul has more erudition than all the embassadors at the court of Versailles tho I do not think his natural genius greater than Doctr Franklins yet he certainly will be a greater Minister. The Marquis la Fayette is one of the most growing characters in this kingdom. he has planted a tree in America & sits under its shade at Versailles. he is now at the court of old frederick his lady the Marquise who is in petticoats when he is in breeches. untill my present connection with Commodore Jones I had business at court & asked the assistance of the Marquiess I am sure that you yourself would not have manifested more alacrity to serve me. We have some folks here that would eat him but for my part I would sooner eat [illegible] to render the Marquis's character more perfect. I have only one fault to find with him which is the manner in which he does business with Americans: it is too formal & in the stile of little majesty: 8 or 10 Americans waiting at his hotel in a morning has more importance with it in paris than he would derive from having an army at his huts among the independent yeomanry of America. The Marquiss is a warm friend to America & would be rendered unhappy in his feelings & his interest should the two countries chance to think differently.

I am verry sorry to inform you that to day Messrs Fitzhughes are undetermined whether they shall go to New York Baltimore or Philadelphia: it deranges my wishes with regard to my letters. if they go to Phila I shall direct them to the care of Andrew Hodge[10]—if to baltimore they must abide their fate. If Jenny or Molly hodge is among ye give them a salute for me & good Nel of the point. Doctr Franklin will be in America (if, neither him or my letters loose their passage the first of the two. I think it will be difficult for any subsequent Plenipotentiary to have as much personal influence in france as Doctr Franklin: it will at least be so untill the cause that created that venerable patriot shall become less recent in the minds of these people; & in the truth a very few years are sufficient to effect that in this country & distinguished virtue & distinguished vice are equally disagreeable after a certain period of duration. I had the pleasure of being at the Doctors house but only once before his departure for which I am very sorry: though under a constant pain from this gravel in the bladder & bent down with age, that excellent old man exhibits all the good cheer of health, the gay philosopher & friendly countryman—I am now reading some of his miscellanious writings & my boosom glows with admiration & pride but alas Franklin thou art as much cursed with blockheads for thy offspring as the roman Cicero—they are indeed illegitimates.

I went yesterday morning & have been this morning to one of the places in the city where they put the dead bodies that are found in the night in the streets murdered: notwithstanding the extraordinary police of the city you may be assured from me that there are upon an average more persons murdered in paris annually than there are days in the year. the laws are severe, no person commits a capital crime according to those laws but murders in order to hide the offence. I have also for a second time been this afternoon to visit the paintings in the Louvre: they are a national exhibition of paintings, a collection of all the celebrated performances in the kingdom of the last year or two or three. I am not only pleased with all the great & lovely passions they inspire me with but am also rendered happy by the proofs they give me of the greatness of the human mind which seems capable of infinite improvement. In the evening I went to the french comedy to see the Cid of Cornel. I have not spelt his name right and am at this moment that I am sensible siting with my pipe in my mouth & a glass of plain burgundy & nothing on but my shirt: it is an indulgence that I have some how happened into to sit naked some two or three hours before I sleep & in the same unconstrained situation I think & occasionally write my friends, which is certainly a poof that I write without disguize & when I tell them of it assured that I keep nothing secreted from them, I think no friend could be pleased with more or less. I am hourly waiting with an anxiety not philosohical for the arrival of Commodore paul jones from L'orient—too much depends on it to leave me be very tranquil, but let to morrow produce its evils—I am determined to possess the pleasure of wishing you good night now and to bon soir—goodnight.

I am again with my pipe, glass & night shirt at your service a successful evening: it has been a holiday today. the nativity of the Virgin Mary[11]—a vile rainy day thank heaven or every public walk would have been so crouded with the holiday saints of this country that an every day christian would have been nore at ease at home than abroad. My friend the Abbey D'aubry tells me that they have but 82 holidays in the year that are publily regarded—we both agree that they have 82 less than they had 82 years ago but there are more than 82 holidays difference between him & me that he will not admit of. however estimated there are certainly 100 days in this city every year whereon all the shops are shut & there is a general suspension of business—for the good policy of which let them look to. You will hear in your papers of an affair between a certain Cardinal & the queen of france: it has been the topic of conversation in paris for 30 days & 40 fools that have expressed themselves too freely in the matter for the police of the country are already in the Bastile, the news of to day is that the King has him tried by the parliament & has wrote to that dying meteor the pope not to intermeddle in the business. the same Cardinal is worth at least 60,000£ sterling per ann[um] & yet has undoubtedly forged a bill by the signature of the queen of france: an hereditary villiany is traced in the Cardinal family or suspected among his political connections & for aught I doubt maybe found among his religious friends: it is by no means an uncommon sentiment in this country at present to think so. the liberality of sentiment in America since the revolution in that country has prevaded all Europe: a remarkable instance of it has lately exhibited itself in one of the fettered provinces of france where there appeared in a Cabel gently decorated, with the following laconic inscription "Liberty or—" goodnight.

Bon Jour

I have been today to take a family dinner with our minister & the Secretary: I was jeering the Secretary about his poetic rage when he up with the anecdote of my trip from Coos to Hartford in a canoe which he had picked up somewhere among ye & been fool enough to preserve.[12] Our Minister laughed most heartily observing that it was no unworthy prelude to my subsequent voyages & that I had observed a great consistancy of character from that moment to this—which is something more than

Sup. 4

some of my friends would have said on such an occasion—particularly my lady betty Westerly & my lord & lady mayoress of hartford.[13] after dinner Mr. Secretary invited me to a seat in his coach & we rode to view the Bicetre. The Biecetre is a large pile of buildings about 1½ miles with the boulvars of Paris: it is a prison for criminals of various discriptions & that unfortunate part of our species who loose their reason & a kind of alms house to the poor of certain descriptions: it includes within its walls a small militia guard a few artificers & above 3000 souls & thos situated eligibly to health 10 & 20 persons very often die in a day. there are about 40 different kinds of madmen confined to cells & about 30 of them in chains, exhibiting a scene too extraordinary to pass unobserved & yet too melancholly to dwell upon. The criminals confined here are of various descriptions & are confined for different lengths of time: the most unfortunate are those who have committed capital crimes & belonged to families who interest enough to send them here in order to evade a public execution which according to an extraordinary law in this country would degrade them even beyond the third & fourth generations: those offenders are let down into a subterraneous receptacle & it is said are never seen or heard of more but the truth is they are taken up after a certain time & assasinated and buried in secracy. Bon soir—

St Clouds & Queens Cardens

I was late home yesterday evening from the feast of St Cloud held at a little town of that name on the banks of the Seine[14]: it is particularly remarkable for its having the queens gardens in it & a house for the queen which is called a palace: the only circumstance that renders the village a place of curiosity to strangers are the waterworks which after the labour of many years & vast expence exhibits a sickly cascade & thru jet d'eaus or fountains that cast water into the air the largest of these has a column of water as big as a mans arm wich rises about 30 yards. In the evening we entered a part of the gardens where some fire works were played off: the tickets were 24 sols. I saw the queen—indeed sat close by her. the fire works were but very few but very good. This little rustic entertainment of the queen in her own gardens was with great propriety attended by very little parade about her person—it was a mere rural revel & never before did I see Majesty & tag rag & bob tail so philosophically blended—a few country fidlers scraping & Kate of the mill triping it with dick of the vineyard.[15] indeed & spouse of Louis thou didst lay aside majesty with a grace that declares thou will never be humiliated with the idea of that indistinction which [a]waits thee. I admire it—thy people adore it.

St. Germains

I have to day been for a second time to St. Germain which is perhaps—indeed I believe decidely is the most beautiful village about Paris—though all are charming. Louis the 14 intended to have built here instead of Versailles: he could at last given but very poor reason why he did not, but he gave a very unkingly one when he said he could not bear to have the Church (St. Dennis) where his body would be interred so constantly in sight, though the church & town of St. Dennis is 3 leagues distant. had Louis built his palace at St. Germains it would have been the most superb situation for a king in all Europe: Versailles which is only bit of it as artificial & has all its water from St. Germains is the admiration of all who see it. St. Germains would have stood unrivaled—but Louis who had madly sought death in the field could not must even the thought of it elsewhere. In pity to us both we will say no more about it.

You see how some few of my days pass away—I see a great deal & think a great deal but derive very little real happiness from either because I am forced into both & am alone in both. oh could I embrace thee my dear Isaac how much greater would my pleasures be! was I among my dear friends the anxieties that now imbitter every hour that passes over me would be almost lost. my dear cousin Kate how very valuable the least trifle becomes in certain situation— one of the sleeve buttons thou gavest me at Middletown point is in my sleeve at the moment: I lost one of them before I left America, but the other I have worn with some different odd ones ever since—like thy dear friendship it abides by me in spite of ill accident. If I should live to shew it thee hereafter me we will talk the matter over. good night my friend, my dear cousin kate: enjoy thy husband & be blest, for by g—d you could not get such a one in france[16]; he is doubly my friend by being yours—take him round the neck & kiss him for me: such embraces are a pleasure to the gods who see them—they are very rare hereabouts; kiss him therefore for the honour of conjugality of human nature, for the few like you can only do it. tell our Nel[17] that among a number of paintings I saw to day in the palace of the duc de Chartres I saw a Miss Elenor Forman the wife of the great painter Reuben done by himself & that I am persuaded it is the same german family from which she descended & that the figures Nel cuts in paper is no doubt a sufficient proof of it. good night.

★

To Thomas Jefferson
7 February 1786; Paris

Saint Germain Feby. 7th 1786
Sir

A gentleman in this town informs me that the Indians who have been asked their opinions about those large bones found in America, say, that tho they had never before seen such bones or an Animal large enough to have them, yet all the indians knew their fathers had seen such bones and the very animal itself but that it had always been found dead. They called it the mole because like the common little animal of that [nam]e it resides in the earth;[illegible] operations and movements we [illegible] mole differing only as the great m[illegible] did from the other in magnitude: that these operations had been but rarely seen and the perfect form of the animal still more rarely, but when seen was found to resemble the little mole in its form.

Perhaps I was wrong, but I observed to Mr. de Carel who gave me this account, that I had frequently observed that when an European queried a savage about a circumstance that perhaps he was totally ignorant of that he was nevertheless unwilling that the European should know it or even think that he was ignorant and to divert his suspicions would make use of the most wily arts and rather than appear to be less informed of the common affairs of his country than the Europeans would say any thing to make the European think favourably of him by thinking otherwise.

But whether the asserted fact exists in nature, or whether it is only the tale of superstition or craft I thought it worth communicating to you; but whether true or false the savage has been more modest than Count Buffon for in accounting for the phenomenon he has not denied its present existance.

I have the honour to be with the warmest esteem & respect [your most o]bliged [s]ervant,

Jn Ledyard

✶

To Isaac Ledyard
February 1786; Paris

February 1786
To Monecca

My last Letters by the Fitzhughes of Virginia left me in the Metropolis of France, the verry football of chance and I have continued so untill within a verry few days of the date of this Letter. All the distresses that you can imagine incident to such a situation, have most faithfully attatched themselves to me: they are now gone, and once more I greet you with a chearful heart: but so curiously wretched have I been, that without any thing but a clean shirt was I invited from a Gloomy garret to the splendid Tables of the first characters in this Kingdom. The medium of our intercourse will only admit of a summary account of things. In about fourteen days I leave Paris for Brussells, Cologne, Vienne, Dresdon, Berlin, Varsovie, Petersburg, Moscow, Kamchatka Sea of Anadivy, Coast of America, from whence if I find any more cities to New York, when I get there I will name them to you in *propria persona*: and so to save time I make another summary!!!!!!!!!!!!!! which I think are exactly Nine marks of admiration more than I ever saw before on any occasion: and which perhaps a reader of hieroglyphics would say denoted that after a tour of that kind had been performed, it was subtracted from the twelve and only a Nine days wander remained Take my heart & after sharing it with B[en] do what you please with the rest. I will write you from Petersburg after I have seen Kate of the North. I embrace thee;

Farewell
Josephus

★

To Isaac Ledyard
8 April 1786; Paris

St. Germains near Paris April 8th 86
To Monecca.

If congress are at New York, this will be delivered by my freind, almost every bodies freind and almost always his own friend—Col Humphreys whom you & my dear B[en].—knew in days of yore. He is Secretary to our Legation at the Court of France: a voluptuos animal, has a good heart and good head. and is devoutly fond of women, wine, & religion; provided they are each of good quality: but the creatures hobby is poetry: and as the English Reviewers allow him merit therein I may venture verry safely to do it. He is a friendly good soul, a sincere Yanky and so affectionately fond of his country, that to be in his Society here is at least as good to me, as a dream of being at home. I imagine he brings dispatches, but as we are Republicans a little more polished than on your side the Water, we never presume to ask impertinent Questions. I imagine you have by this time received my Letters by M' Barrett of Boston.[18] Your hearing from me so often by those who intimately know my Situation, and are so much freinds is a most happy circumstance: but I would freely have relinquished the pleasure, I have in writing this Letter to have been where I supposed I should have been when I wrote you last: but soon after the Departure of Barrett, our minister, the Russian Minister and the American Broker (I mean the marquiss La Fayette) took it into their heads that I should not go directly to St Petersburgh, but wait untill I was sent for which is the occasion of my being here to write you at this time. You see I have so many freinds that I cannot do just as I please. I am verry well in health; a Gracious Providence, & the Indian corn I fed upon in my Infancy, added to the robust Scenes I have since passed thro', have left me at the same age at which my Father died "healthy, active, vigourous & strong." I am a few weeks at the little Town where my Letter is dated, and as I live upon the Skirt of a Royal forest: I am every day in it: and it is usual for me to run Two Miles an End & return: I am like one of Swift's Hughhainums.[19] Ask Humphreys If I did not walk into Paris last Week and return to dine with Mad[ame] Barclay at St Germains the same morning which is at least twenty four of our miles: But this is not the work of Nature: She made me a voluptuous, pensive animal and intended me for the tranquil scenes of domestic life; for ease and contemplation; and a thous'd other fine soft matters that I have thought nothing about since I was in Love with R[ebecca]—E[ells]—of Stonington. What Fate intends further I leave to Fate But it is verry certain that there has ever been a great difference, between the manner of life I have actually led and that which I should have chosen: and this I do not attribute more to the irregular incidents that have alternately caressed and insulted me on my Journey, than to the irregularity of my genius. Tom Barclay our consul who knows mankind & me verry well, tells me that he never saw such a medley as in me. The Virgi[ni]an Gentlemen here call me Oliver Cromwell, and say, that like him I shall be damned to Fame; but however have never dared to prophecy that it would be by a Virginian Poet.—You see what a Budget I have sent you again:[20] you will not receive such another verry soon.—I every hour expect my Summons from the Russian Minister to the Court of his Mistress, where you shall hear from me. I have a delightful Season to pass through Germany, tho it does not suit my tour well I shall loose a Season by it. I am not certain about the result of this Business, and shall not be perfectly at ease, untill I have been introduced to the Empress. Col Humphries is going over with dispatches relative to us and Great Britain.[21] I meant to have said relative to our commercial concerns, but the Ham & mustard in my mouth relish better than my subject. I am hungry, having just been two hours upon the Banks of the River Seine to see the new invented method of walking upon the Water: but the trial failed: The man walked not half over the river before the things on which he floated turned him heels over head & he was taken up by the Boat. It is silly imagined and worse executed: and will not admit of improvement. Your Letter must be in Paris tomorrow mor[n]ing. I go 12 miles on foot to carry it: It is now Nine O'Clock in the Evening and I have other Letters to write. Receive my Embrace: keep me in your mind—Adieu! Adieu my dear B[en].—also Adieu best of cousins best of friends.

Josephus.—

★

To Thomas Jefferson
7 July 1786; Paris
St. Germain en Laye July 7th 86

Sir

It is with great defference that I write you a letter of this kind; and yet was you a king or the minister of a king I should not have wrote it had the access been the same.

Attraction appears to be the first natural cause of motion in all bodies. I suppose the whole system of modern natural philosophy rests upon it whenever it respects *motion*. This being the case that particular motion which respects magnetism becomes a part of this universal cause. As motion is as universal as existance it is as various as universal. To assign reasons therefore for the motion of a part and not the whole is partial.

If the Sun is the center of attractive motion why is it not also the center of that motion we observe in the magnetic needle. If it is, it immediately follows that as the central cause, it is the greatest cause. If it is the greatest cause in what manner as such does it operate on the magnetic needle to produce that motion which we call the variation of the needle.

If the Sun has an effect upon the motion of the magnetic needle, those motions can be made a matter of calculation and reduceable to rule.

I only offer one reason why I can suppose the Sun to operate on the motion of the magnetic needle, which is that the greatest variation of the needle seems to be when at the greatest distance from the Sun and that variation an inclination to the Sun.

This Idea of the sun having the particular influence just mentioned struck me as new, rational and worthy communicating to you. If it should appear so to you I shall be exceedingly honoured.

The letter left for me at your address was from a Gentleman at Edinburgh concerning my affair with the Marquis of Buckingham from whom I expect some intelligence in about a week.[22]

In returning from Paris as I was walking on the skirt of a wood by the side of the high road about ten o'clock I heard a horse stumble and fall and a Person give one groan. I sprang into the road to see what was the matter and found a Man down under his horse and both so entangled together that neither could rise. In making a suden strong effort to disengage the Man I so much strained my loins that I have been ever since Confined to my room—but am better. The Man was much hurt.

I have the honor to be Sr Your much obliged most respectfull & most humble servt.,

J Ledyard

✳

To Isaac Ledyard
8 August 1786; Paris

St. Germains Aug 8th, 1786
To Monecca.

Next to my friendship for you which is very naturally extended to a Degree even romantic by my long separation and misfortunes, I would willingly inform you of the situation of my affairs as the next most important Subject between us, but at this whimsical and uninteresting instant I have not a syllable of the kind for thee. I give you my word that the Strumpet has kissed me as often as she [h]as kick'd me and why she should not smash or kick you all as well as me I know not. Why should I be thus painfully distinguished or by kicks or kisses. If it be for my own sins or the sins of the family. I have been must have been a Devil of a Rake—and rakes capital must you have all been and deeply in debt if it be for you all that I enjoy the painful preeminence.—You will be right to suppose me in a kind of foolish good-natured delirium to write thus and what does it signify how one is if one be happy or even endeavouring to make oneself so: To be foolishly happy is still happiness and to be wiseley so is no more.

For my part I am sick of the little particoloured patches of science I have so long played the harlequin in and of that something that I once was taught to call Philosophy. Those appendages of an illiberal education have sharpened every misfortune, that has attended me since I have been in France. Like Macbeth's Physician not one of them all has been able to administer to a mind diseased. One single thought that has been the offspring of nature only has gone beyond them all: and If I enjoy any happiness this moment I owe it to the exertion of a native sentiment. How often my good departed Ancestors have I had just occasion to damn the Stupidity of the Life they taught me and to damn myself for compleating the deformed thing by my subsequent conduct. but Peace to your faults, and to my own, and peace to my present feelings, for I have unlearnt what you learned me.

I have begun the Letter without knowing I shall ever send it you will therefore treat it as you would a friend who pops in with an undress to take Coffee with you, no Ceremony I beseech you. Having begun to stain a new sheet of paper let me sacrafice the virgin part of it to our friendships. How do you all do? behold me on my knee before ye in all the ardour of esteem when I ask the question: Ye who know me can bear a part with me in these my feelings but none of you all have suffered like me in long and distant separations from those ye loved: so that ye happily have not to sympathise with me in this part of my sensations: in every thing else ye have, and thank Heaven it is not in my power to go beyond you in thinking of friendship or performing its duties; This is one of the few happy circumstance that the malice of fortune will lastly deprive me of if ever, and however foiled by the maloccurrences of Fate while I have the friendship of you and your Brother believe me my dear Monecca I shall always think worth while to live—

It is twelve months since I have heard from you a thousand things contrary to my wishes for your happiness may have happened, or on the contrary a thousand things may have occurred to render you happier than I may reasonably imagine: in either case our friendship is unmoved and beg you will accomodate all my greetings to the Statu quo of things when you read this. Does the dance inspire you or the jocund song "none more blithe than I"—? Is Love the favourite God—the God I love and am his constant votary. Is grief—the theme—I know it well. Ah too well! and can follow you to the very cave of moping melancholy—the bursting of the heart strings—the dark abyss of despair itself—does Ambition fire your Souls?—"Why I'd pluck it from the moon"[23]—The only circumstance wherein I cannot give entire response to your enjoyments and sufferings is your hymenials[24]: there I cry ye mercy. The last letter I wrote you was by Colonel Humphries whom I hope you have seen: I have been at St Germains ever since waiting for the issue of my affairs at St Petersburg. You wonder by what means I exist having brought with me to Paris this time only three Louis d'ors. Ask vice consuls, consuls, plenipotentiaries, ministers and whores of fortune all of whom have had the honor to be tributary to me. At present I have tributized the minister Plenipotentiary of the Duke of Saxe Gotha and have laid plans to subjugate the Chancellor of the British Exchequer.[25] You think I joke—no upon my honor; and however irreconcileable to my temper, genius, disposition or education, it is nevertheless strictly true: Nay more I have even proposed the subsidy to the King of France, he read my Bull after he had eat a *large Poulard* which he does at every meal or something equivalent to it and it is thought would have swallowed my Bull with as much unconcern as he did the *poulard* but for the wary Vergennes,

and so it was not swallowed and the Devil take their Genius for Intrigue—
It is a universal a talent among the French as Basketmaking is among our
American Indians and much resembles it—Every day of my life my dear
Cousin is a day of Expectation and consequently a day of disappointment.
Whether I shall have a morsel of bread to eat at the end of two months
is as much an uncertainty as it was 14 months ago and not more so—If
I had been raised to happiness or plunged in distress twelve months ago
I should not have been surprized: it is the near approach I have so often
made to each extreme without absolutely entering into either, that aston-
ishes, and has eventually rendered me so hardy as to meet either without an extra palpitation. Altho' extraordinary situations naturally imply
some extraordinary occurrence as necessarily incidental to them, Permit
me to relate one which I do not think necessarily incidental to my situation. About a fortnight passed Sir James Hall an English gentlemen on
his [way] from Paris to Cherbourg stopped his Coach at our door and came
up to my Chamber to see me[26]—I was in bed at 6 OClock in the morning & having flung on my Robe de Chambre and met him at the door
of the ante-chamber, I was glad to see him but surprized—he observed
he had to make up his opinion of me with as much exactness as possible and concluded that no kind of visit whatever would surprise me: I
could do no other than observe his Opinion surprised me at least; and
the Conversation took another turn In walking across the Chamber he
laughingly put his hand on a Six Livre piece and a Louis d'or that lay on
my toilet & with a half stifled blush asked me "how I was in the money
way" blushes commonly beget blushes and I blushed partly because he
did, and partly on other accounts: If fifteen Guineas interrupting the
answer he had demanded will be of any service to you, there they are and
put them on the Table—. I am a traveller myself and tho' I have some fortune myself to support my travels. yet I have been so situated as to want
money which you ought not to do.—You have my address in London
&c&c and wished me a good morning and left me This Gentleman was
a total stranger to the situation of my finances and that I had by mere
accident met at an ordinary in Paris. we had conversed together several
times, and he once sent his Carriage for me to dine with him I found him
handsomely lodged in the best fauxbourg in the City, two Members of
the English house of Commons, two Lords Beaumarchais, and several
Members of the Royal Academy at Paris at his Table. He two or three times
after that had seen me and expressed the highest Opinion of the Tour I

had determined to make and said he would as a Citizen of the world, do any thing in his power to promote it. But I had no more Idea of receiving money from him than I have this moment of receiving it from Tippoo Saib.[27] However I took it without any hesitation and told him that I would be as complaisant to him if occasion ever offered. You see what a medley of a life I lead by my Letter.[28] If the Heart by debauch is rendered callous to the severe feelings such reflections would otherwise give, the man who has it should visit those hospitals in large Capitals that are receptacles of Infants thus produced and Women thus neglected. I have once seen them both in Paris, twice I believe I never shall—Not all the morality from Confucius to Addison could give me such feelings. Eighteen Foundlings were brought the day I visited. One was brought in while I was there, and there were about three hundred in all. Dear little Innocents! but ye are happily insensible of your situations—Where are your unfortunate mothers?—perhaps in the adjoining hospital—She has to feel for you and herself too—but where is the wretch—the villain—the monster—I was not six minutes in the House It is customary to leave a few pence—I flung down six Livres and retired. Determined to persevere I continued my visit over the way to the Hospital De Dieu I entered first the apartments of the women, very few of them are here for any other reason than the vener[e]al disease—What havoc does Lust make among mankind Well may there be eighty thousand registered prostitutes in Paris. The number here accounts for it—or that accounts for this.—Why will you my dear Sisters I was going to say as I passed along thro' beds in ranks—why will ye be—But I was interrupted by a melancholy figure, that appeared at its last gasp or already dead. She's dead said I to a German gentleman who was with me—and nobody knows or cares any thing about it—. We approached the Bed-side. I observed a slight undulating motion in one of the jugular arteries. She is not dead said I, and siezed her hand to search her pulse. I hoped to find Life but it was gone: the word dead being again pronounced bro't the Nuns to the Bed. My God! exclaimed the head Nun "she is dead." Jesus Maria exclaimed the other Nuns in their defence she's dead: The head nun scolded the others for their malattendance— "My God" continued she "She's dead without the form! Dieu! said the others she died so silently. "Silence said the elder—perhaps she is not dead—say the form; the form was said and the Sheet flung over her face. I know not how I happened to turn my eye round but while the Benediction was repeated, it struck those of a most beautiful young Nun that was among the rest, and who was as debonair, gay and even lascivious as if She had been in the Palais Royale, and seemed as ready to become a sacrafice to pleasure as the unfortunate victim she had been dismissing with her Benediction had been—. And if she had, said the Gentleman to whom I made the observation— she would not have been the *first* who had, from this very place—I took a walk to Paris this morning, The Marquiss La Fayette has three of the finest Asses I ever saw which he means to send to General Washington. He sent to the Isle of Malta for them, he is a good fellow this same Marquiss: I esteem him and even love him, and so we all do except some few who worship him. I make these Trips to Paris often sometimes to dine with this aimiable Frenchman, sometimes with our minister who is a Brother to me, & sometimes I go buy a fine pair of pumps to walk in. I am too much alive to care and Ambitiou[s] to sit still.

The villanous, unprofitable life I have led goads me I would willingly crowd as much merit as possible into the Autumn & Winter of it. Like Milton's hero in Paradise lost (who happens to be the Devil himself) it behoves me now to use both Oar, & Sail to gain my Port—While in Normandy I was at the seat of Conflans the successor of him that was so unfortunate in a Naval affair with Hawke of England[29]—It is the Lordship of the Manory. The peasants live or die at the smiles or frowns of their Lord, and avaricious of the former they fly to communicate to him any uncommon occurrence in the Village and such they thought our arrival—The place to be sure is very remote and the Gentleman I accompanied an Englishman rode in a superb manner. His Coach, his Servants were in a most elegant Stile, Mr Conflans was informed of it It was my turn that day to cater and the little country taverns in France are such as to oblige [one] to cook for himself if he would eat. I was consequently busy in the Kitchen. The Otaheite marks on my hands were discovered. The Mistress and the maids asked our Servants the History of so strange a sight. they were answered that I was a Gentleman who had been round the *world*

It was enough—. Conflans knew of it and sent a Billet written in good English to know if he could have the honor of seeing us at his Mansion & if he could be thus distinguished, he would come & wait on us there himself.—It was too late; the Englishman & I had begun pell mell upon a joint of roast. If Jove himself had sent a Card by Blanchard inviting us it would have been the same.[30]—We would honor our selves to wait on the Marquis de Conflans in the Evening.—We did so—We could not but be honored with the reception we met. It did honor to a French Nobleman.—Our Minister informs us that New York has at length acceded to the five Per Cent impost—by your Leave, Mr Yorker I think ye have been a little Coquetish in this matter—and—I was going to say something very wise—but your Committee meetings and Oyster Clubs render you so redoubtable in sentimental Politics that I beg to withdraw my motion. The Paris Papers of To-day announces the discovery of some valuable Gold mines in Montgomery County—Virginia which I rejoice to hear but hope they will not yield too much of it, for as Poor Richard says "Too much of one thing is good for nothing" All that I can say is, that if it is as bas as *too little* of it the Lord help ye when it happens to be the case with ye as he has me, who in spite of my Poverty am plump & hearty, and as merry as a fool as appeareth by my Letter. I die with anxiety to be on the back of the American States, after having either come from or penetrated to the Pacific Ocean. There is an extensive field for the acquirement of honest fame. A blush of generous regret sits on my Cheek to hear of any Discovery there that I have not part in, & particularly at this auspicious period: The American Revolution invites to a thourough Discovery of the Continent and the honor of doing it would become a foreigner. But a Native only could feel the pleasure of the Atchievement. It was necessary that an European should discover the Existance of that Continent, but in the name of Amor Patria. Let a Native of it Explore its Boundary. It is my wish to be the Man I will not yet resign that wish nor my pretension to that distinction.

Thus far my new Ass whom I beg leave to introduce to you as an Ass that sprung from the Ashes of my Ass Commerce whom I entered Last January in Paris. Etatis suae[31] thirty months—Peace to its manes.—I shall neither forget the pleasures or the pains it gave me they form too interesting a part of my Existence—But farewell old Ass & welcome new Ass—and farewell to you too for I have just received news which hurries me to London—What fate intends is always a secret—fortitude is the word. I leave this Letter with my Brother & my father our Minister—he will send it the first private conveyance—Adieu!

Josephus

★

In August 1786 Ledyard hastily departed for London in hopes of hitching a lift directly to Nootka Sound in present-day British Columbia.

In December when his ship did not sail, he embarked on his walk around the world, traveling by boat and by foot through Germany, Denmark, and Sweden and then through Lapland and Finland, reaching St. Petersburg in March 1787.

To Thomas Jefferson
16 August 1786; London

London August 16th 1786—
To Thomas Jefferson Esqr
Sir

Whenever I have occasion to write to you I shall not want to say so much on the score of Gratitude, that if I do not tire you with the Repetition of my thanks I shall at least do injustice to the other parts of my Letters unless you will be so good as to accept a single honest heartfelt *Thank You* for the whole in that case I shall always proceed to plain narration

The same Sir James Hall that made me the remarkable visit at St Germains is my friend here. I have arrived most opportunely indeed. An English Ship sails in three days for *Nootka Sound:* I am introduced by Sir James Hall to the Merchants who welcome me to a passage there and as one of them goes himself thank me for my comp[any.] I shall go on board to morrow: An Officer of Capt Cooks goes also. He is hig[h]ly pleased at my accompaning them. Sir J Hall presented me with twenty Guineas Pro Bono Publico—I bought two great Dogs, an Indian pipe and a hatchet My want of time as well as more money, will prevent my going otherwise than indifferently equipped for such an Enterprise: but it is certain I shall be more in want before I see Virginia: why should I repine? You know how much I owe the aimiable La Fayette, will you do me the honor to present my most grateful thanks to him?—If I find in my Travels a mountain as much above the Mountains as he is above ordinary men I will name it La Fayette—I beg the honor also of my compliments to Mr Short who has also been my friend and like the good Widow in S[c]ripture cast in—not only his mite but more than he was able, to my assistance.[32] Adieu

I have the honor to be
Sir your most grateful
and most Obedt humbl Servt
John Ledyard

✳

To Isaac Ledyard
18 August 1786; London

London August 18th 1786
To Monecca—
    Coll Smith secretary to the embassy here will send you this and my other
written in France by the first private conveyance.33 I leave them in his hands
Adieu to Europe! I have but a moment to write you though the last moment
I may ever employ in the tender task. I embark this day on board an English
Merchant Ship that sails by Cape Horne into the Pacific Ocean and to the N.W.
coast of America on a Trading voyage. I land at Nootka Sound which you will
find on the charts & Prints I sent you in Lat. 49° N.—from thence I mean to
make an attempt to cross the continent to Virginia. I go alone except my two
Dogs. If I live to see you it will be in two or three years. Think a little of me
and remember me to all my friends—but I would not wish that all of them or
people in general should know my pursuits. I send you some little matters
within that I ask you to keep for me; it is like parting with life to leave them
but I cannot carry them where I shall go: receive my embrace. Adieu
    Josephus

    I am received with the greatest politeness in London particularly by
the Gentlemen who go the voyage among whom are some of science and
one of Capt Cook's Officers.
    The Sir James Hall mentioned in my other Letter has been the means
of this. Sir Joseph Banks also is my friend, yet I am a deserter in London.
What a world is this ha! ha! ha!
    Adieu—

✳

To Thomas Jefferson
25 November 1786; London

London Novr 25th 1786

My friend, my brother, my Father,—I know not by what title to address you—you are very dear to me. embrace the dear marquis la Fayette for me: he has all the virtues of his country without any of its little foibles. I am indeed a very plain Man, but do not think that mountains or oceans shall oppose my passage to glory while I have such friends in remembrance—I have pledged myself—difficulties have intervened—my heart is on fire—ye stimulate, & I shall gain the victory. Thus I think of you—thus I have thought of you daily—& thus I shall think of you. After all the fair prospects that attended me when I last wrote—I still am persecuted—still the slave of accident & the son of care. The Ship I embarked in was seized by the Custom house & is this day exchequered. If a small subscription now begun in London by Sr Joseph Banks & Doctr Hunter will enable me to proceed you will probably hear from me at Hamburgh:[34] if I arive at Petersbourg you most certainly will. You see the course I was purs[u]ing to fame reverted & I am now going across Siberia as I had once before intended from Paris this time twelve month—what a twelve months! I do defy fortune to be more malicious during another. I fear my subscription will be small: it adds to my anxiety to reach those dominions where I shall not want money—I do not mean the dominions that may be beyond death: I shall never wish to die while you the Marquis & Mr Barclay are alive:—pray Sr if that dear & genuine friend of mine is any where near you do me the honour to present me sur mes genoux devant lui—j'adore son coeur genereux.[35] May I beg to be presented to Mr Short, to Commodore Jones & to Colo Franks if with you: A present je pense comme lui de la gouvernement de cet pays ici—tout est un cabal meme dans leur rues—heureusment pour moi j'entend bien a don[ner] des coups du poins, & have litteraly been obliged to thrash 5 or 6 of those haughty turbulent & very insolent people:[36] one of them at the theatre where I assure you one is still more liable to insult than in the streets even. I have just parted with Colonel Smith: he is well & is trying also to do something for me.

I hear y'o have not been very well lately, tho now better[37]—take care of your health for the sake of our Country & for his sake who begs the honor to subscribe himself with all possible respect & esteem

Sr your very humble
& most obedt servant

Jno Ledyard

★

To Isaac Ledyard
November and December 1786; London

London Nov 1786
To Monecca

I am still the Slave of Fortune and the son of care: you will be surprized that I am yet in London unless you conclude with me that after
what has happened nothing can be surprizing. I think my last Letter
informed you that I was absolutely embarked on board a Ship in the
Thames bound to the N.W. Coast of America from whence I intended to
cross that Continent to New York: this will inform you that I have disembarked from said Ship on account of her having been unfortunately
siezed by the Customhouse & eventually exchequered and that I am
obliged in consequence to alter my route & in short, every thing—all my
little Baggage shield Buckler lance Dogs—Squire & all gone—. I only left—
left to what—to some damned riddle I'll warrant you—or at all events
will not warrant any thing else—My heart is rather too much troubled at
this moment to write you as I ought to do

I am going in a few days to make the Tour of the Globe on foot from
London east, am here without funds or friends sufficient for the purpose—
may in a few days want Bread—or may lie on the road to Fame or may be d—
—d to Fame—am thinking of myself at times—of you am writing my friends
in France brush my own Coat clean my own Boots, am a Deserter in this
Country. dine with Sir this & Sir that on board a Ship one moment in a proud
insolent stiff English Tavern the next—Boxing some Puppy at the Theatre
a la mode d'anglais—in the museum and the Lord knows where. Excuse therefore the manner in which I write—if you cannot call me mad—say I am thus—
but that I love thee do this—& doing it say we love him also. and then what
ever may betide Josephus he will pass it by as the necessary alloy to perfect
happiness, that the Good must meet—but not regard—.

London Decr 1786

I shall Embark in two or three days for Hamburg—have just
receved my passport as an American Citizen to the courts of Petersburg
Moscow Tobolskoi, Jenenskoi Obriskoi Bolcheretskoi, Kamschatka,
Nootka Origon Naudowessie Chippeway &c—farewell.[38]—I shall make

Colonel Smith, Secretary to an Embassy here, the medium of information between us—he desires it. and to be presented to you & your Brother as good old friends I dare not write you any more: to introduce you to the real State of my affairs would confound you. farewell fortitude—Adieu.

Josephus

✷

To William Smith
20 December 1786; Hamburg

Hamburg Decr 20th 1786
To W.S. Smith Esqr
Sir

I am here with ten guineas exactly I am in perfect health, one of my Dogs is no more. I lost him on my passage up the River Elbe in a Snow storm I was out in it forty hours in an open Boat. My other faithful companion is under the Table I write upon. I dined to day (having just come to town) with Madam Parish Lady to the Gentleman I mentioned to you: it is a Scotish house of the first commercial distinction here. The Scotch are very capable of a Refinement in manners, and have by Nature a Majesty of person and dignity of Sentiment that renders them very accomplished. I could go to Heaven with Madam Parish but she had some Englishmen at her Table that I could not go to Heaven with—I cannot submit to a haughty eccentricity of manners so prevalent among the English. They have millions of Virtues but damn their vices, they are enormous. My fate has sent me to the Tavern where Major Langburne was three weeks: he is now at Copenhagen, left his Baggage here to be sent on to him.—by some Mistake he has not Received it and has written the master of the Hotel on the Subject. I shall see his Letter as soon as the Master comes in. I shall write him and give him my address at Petersburgh. I should wish to see him at all events, but to have him accompany me in my voyage would be a Pleasure indeed. I happened to be speaking of going to Petersburg and the Landlord told me a "Gentleman—a very good kind of man and an odd kind of man who had travelled much had lately left him for that Place, took only a Shirt in his Pocket and always

went on foot, had been in America in Paris in London &c &c" It immediately struck me it must be Major Langburne; and upon enquiry I am
sure it is he. He came here from New Castle but the Landlord says he
spells his name Laburne—I have not yet seen his Letter—it is Langburne!
I read his Letter this evening in three days from Copenhagen has not I
am afraid nor ever will see his Baggage again took only one Shirt with
him complains exceedingly of the awkwardness of his situation: he says
it makes People suspicious of him. Whether he left money in his trunk
or Paper necessary to negociate Bills I cannot say, but he intimates a want
of money from the want of his Trunk. I will fly to him with my little all
and some clothes and lay them at his feet at the moment I may be useful to him: he is my Countryman, a Gentleman a Traveller he may go with
me on my voyage. if he does I am blessed if not I merit his attention and
am not much out of my way to Petersburg I dined to day with the ingenious Doct Ross, Physician to the English Hamburg Company and a Stiff
rumped Calvanistical Chaplain and his mummy of a Wife a pair of very
Self Sufficient Stiff Scotch-Germans—but I have happily been compen-
sated by an hour with Madam Parish. You see I take a Sup from the cup
of pleasure on the Road. I wish I had established a little Fame and
Fortune that I might take some larger draught and even be intoxicated
without Danger—to be as happy as Nature intended I should be—I go to
deserve it—Adieu. My compliments to your happy Lady I have the honor
to be—

Ledyard—

✦

To William Smith
5 January 1787; Copenhagen

Copenhgen Janury 5th 1787
To William S. Smith Esqr
Sir I hope this will reach you soon and be some apology for my drawing
on you so soon in favour of Messrs Parrish & Thompson and for adding one
Guinea to the Sum: Charge it to Heaven for by——it was an act of Necessity in
me and one of Charity in you to accept of it that on your part perhaps can never

happen & on mine never shall happen again. Never more will I trouble you.—
if I write you after this it will be to compensate you for your friendship to me
by something in the History of my Travels worthy of your attention. I shall be
at Petersburg before you read this. Thomson's Goodness to me in accepting the
Bill on you relying wholly on my honor has saved me from Perdition and will
enable me to reach Petersburg comfortably tho' a march of a thousand miles
and upwards. I must go higher up the Gulf of Bothnia than Stockholm in order
to cross the ice into the Gulf of Finland. I must inform you that Major
Langburne is here and that the Embarrassments I have laboured under proceeded from my coming here to meet him and from supposing that he would
from what you said to me of him undertake the Tour with me. He will not. We
have lived together here with the Strictest friendship—he was here two Months
without his Trunk and consequently embarrassed for the time in his finances—
We talked of you and I told him of my Draught on you but he would not permit me to say any thing of him to you then and does not know that I do so
now—he will write you when it suits his humor which tho good and like
other peoples when applied to others yet left to himself is very Singular. I see
in him the Soldier (which predominates). the Countryman and the generous
friend but he would hang me if he knew I had written a word to you about him
and so I will say no more than just inform you that he means to wander this
Winter through Norway Swedish Lapland and Sweden and in the Spring to
visit Petersburg. I asked to attend him through his Route to Petersburgh—no—
I esteem you but I can travel in the manner I do with no man on Earth—

Adieu! I have the honor
to be most faithfully your
humble & obedt Servt

Jno Ledyard

★

To Thomas Jefferson
19 March 1787; St. Petersburg

St Petersbourg March 19th 1787[39]
Sir

It will be one of the remaining pleasures of my life to thank you for the many instances of your friendship to me & wherever I am to pursue you incessantly with the tale of my gratitude.

If Mr Barclay should be at Paris let him rank with you as my next friend: I hardly know how to estimate the goodness of the Marquis la Fayette to me—but I think a french nobleman of the first character in his country never did more to serve an obscure citizen of another than the Marquis has done for me: & I am as sure that it is impossible (without some kind of soul made express for the purpose) that an obscure citizen in such a situation can be more gratefull than I am: may he be told so & with my Compliments to his Lady: my Compliments wait on Mr Short, Commodore Jones & Colo Franks if at Paris—with thanks for their favours also. If I was sure Mr Barclay was at Paris I would write him, for no man less acquainted with him esteems him more than I do, believing verily that of such as him consisteth the Kingdom of heaven. I cannot tell you by what means I came to Petersbourg, & hardly know by what means I shall quit it in the further prossecution of my tour round the world by Land: if I have any merit in the affair it is perseverence, for most severely have I been buffeted—& yet still am I even more obstinate than before—& fate as obstinate continues her assaults how the matter will terminate I know not: the most probable Conjecture is that I shall succeed, & be kicked round the world as I have hitherto been from England thro Denmark, thro Sweden, thro Sweedish lapland, Sweedish finland & the most unfrequented parts of Russian finland to this Aurora Borealis of a City. I cannot give you a history of myself since I saw you, or since I wrote you last: however abridged, it would be too long: upon the whole, mankind have used me well, & tho I have as yet reached only the first stage of my journey I feel myself much indebted to that urbanity which I always thought more general than many think it to be, & was it not for the villianous laws & bad examples of some Governments I have passed thro I am persuaded that I should have been able to have given you still better accounts of our fellow creatures.

But I am hastning to those countries where goodness if natural to the human heart will appear independant of example & furnish an Annecdote of the character of man not unworthy the attention of him who wrote the declaration of American Independence.

I did not hear of the death of Monsieur de Vergenes untill I arived here—permit me to express my regret at the loss of so great a man & of so good a Man. Permit me also to congratulate you as the Minister of my Country on account of the additional commercial privileges granted by france to America & to send you my ardent wishes that the friendly spirit which dictated them may last forever: I was extremely pleased at reading this account, & to heighten the satisfaction I felt I found the name of la Fayette there. There was a report a few days ago of which I have heard nothing since, that the french ships under the Command [of] Capt Lapereux had arived at Kamchatka. There is an equipment now on foot here for that ocean & it is first to *visit* the NW Coast of America: it is to consist of four ships. This & the equipment that went from here 12 months since by land to Kamchatka are to cooperate in a design of some sort in the northern pacific Ocean—the lord know what—nor does it matter what with me—nor need it with you, or any other Minister or any Potentate southward of 50° of Latitude. I can only say that you are in no danger of having the luxurious repose of your charming climates disturbed by a second incursion of either Goth Vandal Hun or Scythian. I dined to day with Doctr Pallas Professor of Natural history &c &c—an accomplished Sweed: my friend: has been all thro European & Asiatic Russia: I find the little french I have of infinite service to me: I could not do without it: it is a most extraordinary language: I believe that wolves rocks, woods & snow understand it, for I have addressed them in it & they have all been very complaisant to me: but I dined in a shirt that I had worn *four* days—I have but *two*: & I suppose when I write you next I shall have none.

We had a Scythian at table that belongs to the royal society of Physicians here: the moment the savage knew me & my designs he became my friend & it will be by his generous assistance joined with that of Doctr Pallas that I shall be able to procure a *royal passport* without which I cannot stir: but this must be done th[r]o the application of the *french* Minister (there being no American one here) & to whose secretary I shall apply with Dr Pallas to morrow:[40] & beg liberty to make use of your name & the Marquis la fayettes as to my character. As all my Letters of recommendation have been English & as I have been hitherto used by them with the greatest kindness & respect I first applied to the English Embassy: but witht success: the ostensible apology was that the present political moment between England & Russia would make it disagreeable for the English minister to ask any favour: but I saw the reason—the true reason in the specula of the secretarys eye—& so damn his eyes—which in this case particularly I concieve to be polite language: I hate ill nature & pity a fool.

Sir I have waited on the Secretary of the french embassy who will dispatch my Letter with one of his accompanying it to the Count Segur to morrow morning. I will endeavour to write you again before I leave Petersbourg

& give you some further accounts of myself—In the meantime I wish you health. I have wrote a very short Letter to the Marquis. Adieu!

    I have the honor to be with respect & friendship
    Sr Your most obliged
    & most obt
    & most hbl Servt
    Ledyard

✹

To William Smith
15 May 1787; St. Petersburg

Petersburg May 15—1787.
Sir
    You & I had both concieved wrong notions about traveling in this Country, & there is only a possibility of doing it as either of us supposed: there is no country in Europe or Asia (leaving out of consideration the extent of a tour) so difficult to pass through as this & the difficulty arises from the manners & dispositions of the inhabitants: excuse me if I explain myself to you only by saying that if the inhabitants were all Sweeds (for instance) I could eat drink sleep & travel at my *ease,* or if you please in the manner we each concieved of when I saw you in London—.
    but they are not Sweeds. I shall *ride* full 4000 english miles in company with a young Scotish physician, & after I leave him 7 or 800 miles on the river Lena & then the lord knows how for about 300 miles more to Ohotsk in Kamchatka—I write you this because it goes by water to London & because I am determined you shall hear from me *to the last.* I would be circumstantial in this Letter, but my spirits are bad: my heart is ill:—it is oppressed: I think too severely: my designs are generous—why is my fate otherwise: the Comte de Segur has not yet sent my passport: but this shall not stop me. I shall surmount all things, & at least deserve success. There are 4 American Ships here & 4 more expected: you see by this that I am not the only American of enterprize
    There is no particular news here & I am too angry with the Country to write any thing of its political affairs I had however a visit this afternoon from a Russian officer a great favourite in the family of the Grand Duke:[41] a friend of mine/ & will tell you a little of our chat—that is exactly 10

words "Sir we pay no attention to any thing but *eclat*." He was in the Country with the Grand Duke when he recd a billet of mine—about 25 miles from town & came on purpose to see me—this was polite & friendly—he is more, he is a *thinking* Russian.

The best of all is that I am likely to obtain a passport by his means of the Chancellor: if so I set out immediately.

I know not what kind of a winter I shall have of it in Kamchatka—but if able shall write you. My Compliments to your Lady—

farewell Yours always

J. Ledyard

Part iii

The Siberian Journal and Letters
June 1787–May 1788

*

In June 1787 Ledyard left St. Petersburg. Joined by a Scottish physician who was returning to his post in Barnaul, Ledyard traveled by kibitka (a horse-drawn coach) along the Russian postal roads. Even with extended stays in Kazan, Tobolsk, Barnaul, Tomsk, and Irkutsk (the capital of eastern Siberia), Ledyard managed to travel 5,500 miles in two and a half months. After a three-week boat journey down the Lena River, he reached Yakutsk, the last frontier outpost in eastern Siberia, just 500 miles from the Pacific Ocean.

JOURNAL OF HIS TRAVELS thro' Siberia, to Pacific Ocean, in his attempt to circumnambulate the Globe—

June 1st 1787} After having been three months in Petersburg, I left it in company with Mr William Brown physician, who was going as far as the Province of Kolyvan to reside.—From Petersburgh to Moscow, we rode post, and arrived there the 6th.

The last day's ride, overtook the Grand Duke & his Retinue: who were going to Moscow to meet the Empress, on her arrival from Cherson.

Habitka travelling is the remains of the Caravan travelling—it is your only home—it is like a Ship at Sea. On the 8th we left Moscow with hired horses and a driver, who is to carry us to Kazan and drive three horses for 34 Roubles—The distance from Moscow to Kazan is 735 versts about 550

English miles.[1] We arrived all well at Kazan—began here first to feel the want of houses of entertainment.

Description of Kazan.[2]

The interior parts of Continents, as well as of Islands, are the highest. Their *Lakes* give rise, & their height, force to Rivers. Having staid about a week at Kazan, we set off for Tobolsk.

On the 11th of July arrived at Tobolsk. The country between this and Tobolsk, about 50 versts and which formerly belonged to the Poles, must be poor indeed, if judged of by the wretched appearance of its inhabitants: this, in a greater or less degree, is observable generally of those places which are so unhappy as to be the frontiers between nations.—

Like step-children are they. The practice of burying among trees is hitherto uniform through the Country I have passed. Having staid at Tobolsk three days we set off for the town of Barnowl, the capital of Kolyvan, where we arrived the 23d of July.

General Observations, and most remarkable Occurrences, before arriving at *Barnowl.*

The face of the Country from Petersburgh to Kolivan, is one continued plain. The country before arriving at Kazan, is very well cultivated, afterwards cultivation gradually decreases. Before arriving at Kazan in many places, and particularly near a town called Waldivia, we saw large mounds of earth of 10, 20, 30, 40 feet elevation: which I conjectured, and on enquiry found to be ancient Sepulchres. There is Analogy between those, our own graves, and egyptian pyramids: but an exact similarity with those piles, supposed to be of monumental earth, found among some of the Tribes of North America.

The first Tartars we saw was before our arrival at Kazan. Their dress, the large cap &c—

See little Journal, Saw a woman with her nails painted, like the Co[c]hin Chinese, red. Notwithstanding the modern introduction of Linen into Russia, the garments of the peasantry still retain not only the form, but manner of ornamenting them when they wore skins. This resembles the Ornamenting of the Tartars: & this is but a modification of the *Wampum* ornamenting, that is still discernable westward from Russia to Denmark thro' the Finlands, Laplands, and Swedes. The nice Gradation by which I pass from Civilization to Incivilization appears in every thing: their manners, their dress, their Language, and particularly that remarkable & important circumstance of *Colour* which I am now fully convinced originates from natural Causes; and is the effect of external and local circumstances. I think the same of

Feature. I see here the large mouth, the thick lip, and broad flat nose as well as in Africa—and the same village of Tartars. I see also in the same village as great a difference of Complexion—from the fair hair, fair skin, and white eyes, to the olive, the black jetty hair and eyes: and these all of the same Language, same dress, and I suppose same tribe. I have frequently observed in Russian villages—obscured, and dirty, mean and poor, that the women of the peasantry paint their faces profusely both red and white. I have had occasion from this, and many other circumstances I shall mention to suppose that the Russians are a People, who have been very early attached to *Luxury*. They are every where fond of *Eclat*. The Contour of their manners is Asiatic and not European I ascribe also their disposition to thieving to the Same cause. The Tartars universally neater than the Russians, particularly in their houses.

The Tartar however situated is a voluptuary: and it is an Original and striking trait in their Character from the Grand Signor to him who pitches his tent, on the wild frontiers of Russia & China, that they deviate less from the pursuit & enjoyment of real sensual pleasure, than any other people. The Emperor of Germany—the Kings of England and of France have pursuits that give an entire different turn to their enjoyments—& so have their respective Subjects—Would a Tartar live on *Vive le Roi?* would he spend ten years in constructing a Watch? or twenty in forming a Telescope? In the United States of America as in Russia we have made our efforts to convert our Tartars to think and act like us, but to what effect? Among us Sampson Occum was pushed the farthest within the pales:[3] but just as the Sanguine Divine who brot. him there was about to canonize him—he fled and sought his own heaven in the Bosom of his native forests: In Russia they have had none so distinguished. They are generally footmen or lacquies of some other kind.

The Marquis de la Fayette had a young American Tartar of the Onandaga Tribe who came to see him, and the Marquis at great expense equipped him in rich Indian dresses—After staying some time he did as Occum did.[4] When I was at School at Mount Ida there were many Indians there: most of whom gave some hopes of Civilizing: and some were sent forth to preach, but as far as I observed myself and have been since informed they all, like the ungained Sow returned to the mire

Diary from Barnowl, and from thence towards Ohotsk. Arrived at Barnowl on Friday the 23rd of July and billetted at the House of the Treasurer—Treated with great Hospitality: but obliged to sleep in my Cloak on the Floor, as I have done ever since I left Petersburgh. On Saturday dined

with the Governor. (See the other Journal) On Monday Tuseday and
Wednesday dined with two old discharged officers (Colonels) who at their
own request have quitted the Service, and constituted Judges and Justices
of the *Law*. On Tuseday evening we quitted the house where we billeted and
went to hired rooms—miserable they are: But it was fortunate for us: for the
same night the house we left, with twenty four others, in the same Street
were burnt to the ground. Our Host was a good hospitable creature; and sent
word to us next morning of the disaster. Doctr B went—found him very
merry—Three hours after I met him in the Street bawling out Ivan! Ivan!
without a hat & very drunk—I had no body to give consolation to

> Distances according to the Russian Almanac,
> from Petersburg to Barnowl—Versts 4359
> Barnowl to Irkutsk   —do 1732
> Irkutsk to Yakutsk   —do 2266
> Yakutsk to Ohotsk   —do 952
> Total distance from Petersburg to Ohotsk—9489
>
> From Ohotsk to the Bay Awatka in Kamschatka
> 1065+9489=10554—
> Distance to come—4539   10,554 Versts equal
> Do—to—go   —4950   7916 miles English

Thursday 29th. dined with the Governor. Saw the Armorial Bearings
of forty two Provinces in this Empire—informed that the Salt produced by
the Salt Lakes in this province affords some what more to the Revenue than
the mines: the Governor says also that this province sends more to the
Revenue than any other: estimate the value of 650 poods (36 English
pounds to each pood) of Silver Bullion.

Suppose the produce of the Salt-works equal to that sum: tho' the
Governor says more—then allow for the Gold extracted from the Bullion
about——poods and you have pretty nearly the Sum total of the Revenue of
this province. This without filling up the Blank for the gold extracted in the
process of fining the Silver would be a very large Sum even for so vast a
province as Kolivan: The Governor must therefore mean it for the whole prod-
uct of the province. With respect to Longitudinal distance I want only 100
English Miles easting to be in the Centre of this part of the Continent reckoning from Petersburg to Ohotsk. And if I count from the Western Coast

of Norway to the Eastern Coast of Kamschatka somewhat more In this Central situation between the Atlantic and Pacific Oceans. I find the Climate is very hot. and must at times be subject to furious gales of wind: which in many places (some I have passed) tears up by the roots, or breaks down the trees for nine or ten miles in extent I am told here that if a fall of Snow is accompanied by one of those Gales of Wind nothing can oppose its fury— And that it often buries the Traveller in drifts of Snow: and where often he is lost. This town is situated on the Banks of the Oby: and by the Russian Charts in Lat 52 and odd Long 100 east from the Russ Meridian (which is the Island of Ferro). The mornings here are exceedingly hot: a serene cloudless sky—and a dead Calm.—After the Meridian, have a little air which increases by gentle degrees, towards evening, and continues thro' the night until Sunrise the next morning—I am told that it seldom rains here—

30th July dined with the Governors son in Law—saw his little Cabinet— a piece of curiosity petrified wood and a great variety of minerals. Doctr Pallas says this piece of petrified wood is a Tropical production.—

31st At home preparing to recommence my journey this evening. At nine Oclock waited on the Governor with my passport.—He was well pleased with it, gave me a Co[r]poral to conduct the affairs of the Mail; told me I had nothing to do but sit in my Kabitka; and mustered up French enough to say "Monsieur, Je vous souhaite un bon voyage"⁵ I took an affectionate farewell of the worthy Dr Brown, and left Barnowl.

*

To Thomas Jefferson
29 July 1787; Barnaul

Town of Barnowl in Siberia July 29th 1787
Sir
        you will find this town by the Russian charts situated in about the Latd 52°: & Longd 100: it is near the town of Kolyvan & in the province of Kolyvan: the residence of the Governor of the province: it is near the silver mines & has a foundery in it wc produces anualy 650 poods of silver bullion besides some gold—a pood is 36 pounds english: it is also situated near the salt lakes wc produces more to the revenue than the mines: I am

4539 versts from petersburg & have 4950 versts to go before I arive at Ohotsk, & if I go to Peter & Paul in Kamchatka I have 1065 versts more to go before I see that Ocean which I hope will bear me on its boosom to the coast of America; how I have come thus far & how I am still to go farther is an enigma that I must disclose to you on some happier occasion. I shall never be able without seeing you in person & perhaps not even then to inform you how universaly & circumstantialy the Tartars resemble the aborigines of America: they are the same people—the most antient, & most numerous of any other, & had not a small sea divided them, they would all have still been known by the *same name*. The cloak of civilization sits as ill upon them as our American tartars—they have been a long time Tartars & it will be a long time before they are any other kind of people. I shall send this Letter to Petersburg to the care of Doctor Pallas Professor, of the royal Academy president, & historyographer to the Admirality: I hope he will transmit it to you together with one to the Marquis in the Mail of the count de Segur. I hope yo & your friends & mine enjoy as much good health as I do which is of the purest kind—but notwithstanding all the vigour of my body—my mind keeps the start of me & anticipates my future fate with the most sublimated ardour [[It is certainly Pity it is that in such a career one should be subjugated like a horse to the beggarly impediments of sleep & hunger]]—

The Banks of the large Rivers in this country every where abound with some thing curious in the fossil world. I have found the leg-bone of a very large animal on the banks of the Oby & have sent it to Dr Pallas & told him to render me an acct of it hereafter—it is either the Elephant or Rinoceros bone, for the latter Animal has also been in this Country: there is a compleat head of one in a high state of preservation at Petersburg. I am a curiosity myself in this country: those who have heard of America flock round me to see me: unfortunately the marks on my hands procures me & my Countrymen the appelation of wild men. Among the better sort we are somewhat more known: the Governor & his family get a peep at the history of our existance thro the medium of a Septennial pamphlet of some kind. We have however two Stars that shine even in the Galaxy of Barnowl, & the healths of Dr Franklin & of Genl Washington have been drank in compliment to me at the Governors table: I am treated with great hospitality here—hitherto I have fared comfortably when I could make a port any where—but when totaly in the Country I have been a little incommoded: hospitality however I have found as universal as the face of Man

When you read this—perhaps 2 mo[n]ths before you do If I do well I shall be at Ohotsk where I will do myself the honour to trouble you again & if possible will write more at large

If Mr Barclay should be with you I pray you present me to him—my compliments wait on all my Parisian friends—remember that I am & always shall be with the highest esteem & gratitude

Sr yr much obliged

most obt hbl Servt

Ledyard.

✳

On Tuesday the 3d of August, I arrived at the town of Tomsk. at 6 in the morning, 407 versts from Barnowl: this is upwards of 300 English miles, & was travelled in two days, and three nights. Tomsk, stands near the banks of a good river, to which it gives name: This river is about the size of the Irtis where I crossed it; and is the first river I have met with since leaving Petersburg which had a gravelly bottom or shore. Its appearance in other respects is like the other large rivers in this Country: It has many times changed its bed—formed Islands and left them. and formed banks and left them. I find near its banks those little mounds of earth, which I at first supposed, but now know to have been the dwelling places of those who inhabited it before the time of the Russians: these were the Bratskoi or the Calmucs. Some of these hillocks have been dug into and laid open—I suppose by some former traveller. I find the nights very cold: I have not felt the like in any Country I have yet seen where it was as hot by day. From Barnowl here those hard winds I have before mentioned have done still greater damage—and must have blown with greater violence: since they have not only blown down trees but have broken down & destroyed whole fields of Corn also—Since leaving—*Barnowl* a sudden alteration has taken place in the manners of the peasantry—They are like the people at Barnowl very hospitable; and it is very rare that I can prevail on them to take anything for what I eat and drink, and when they do it is inconceivably trifling. I had yesterday as much good barley soup, onions, quass, bread & milk, as served me and the co[r]poral for *one Kopeek* and the women would not take more. Elephants Teeth do not seem very rare here or regarded much as curiosities. I saw two to-day lying in the Streets—

Wednesday 4th of August} Went last evening to see the Commandant of the Town who kept me to sup with him, and kept me drinking strong Liquors until 1. OClock and departed quite fuddled: but did not think myself so much so as I really was. I never was so ill after a debauch as I have been to-day. The Commandant is 73 years; add to this that he is a Frenchman, and I never saw any of that nation drink like him. He has been 25 years in Siberia 30 odd in Russia: and from France—and is now a healthy man. He has forgotten a great deal of his native language, speaks it very imperfectly, and writes it still worse. Saw the Shoulder Blade of an Elephant at his house—. His name is Tomas, born in the Rue de Grennel in Paris—spoke much of his birth and family.—I asked him if the town or its environs afforded any thing curious in natural History: his answer was that there were in it,—thieves, liars, rascals, whores, rogues, and villains of every discription. W[h]ether he meant these as natural curiosities I did not ask him—I was convinced however that he was one himself. He lives expensively and has a considerable fortune. Took a walk towards evening and bathed in the fine river Tomsk,—feel better after it—.

Thursday, 5th of August. It seems that I am detain[ed] for the arrival of the *mail* from Tobolsk. I find the Russians very charitable to their poor.

In the house where I lodge, who are pretty wealthy people: their is every morning 10, or 12 farthing pieces of money laid in the window for the charitable purposes of the day. Early in the morning the Beggars begin their rounds and go formally from house to house, and very rarely go away without something. Those who do not give money give bread. First come the Slave in Irons, and then others: if the money first deposited in the window is gone they put more there. They never ask any questions of the Beggars but give indiscriminately and without grudging. The demand is uniformly made "pour L'amour de Dieu"—for which one may have more in this Country than any I have seen.

Irkutsk August 15th 1786—I arrived here Sunday the 15th and presented myself and the Corporal at the Levee of the Govr &c&c.

Observations on the Road from Tomsk—

General face of the Country. open and pretty well cultivated. Approaching the river Yennessee at the town of Krastnyack, and on the banks of the Yinnessee I first find the real craggy peaked high hill or mountain. Krastnyack is beautifully situated on the Banks of the

Yennessy, is about the size of Tomsk Tobolsk and Barnowl. The Commandant is a Prussian. I eat and drank with him, he was drunk. By information here the Yennessy is 260 feet deep, and 3000 and some perches wide.

It is a fine stream runs opposite the town 5 knots—gravelly bottom. From this river all the rest to Irkutsk run swifter by 2, 3, and 4 knots than the western ones. From Barnowl here I have ferried over 10 good navigable rivers, and some smaller ones From Petersburgh here 25 rivers all running north

I am now just about two-thirds of my distance from Petersburgh to Ohotsk. I shall have [crossed] 37 large navigable rivers, every one of which except the Wolga discharge themselves in the northern Ocean—Allowing the rivers between here and Ohotsk to be as wide as those I have passed: and those average half a mile in breadth, and eight fathoms in depth: and there will be a column of Water 18½ miles breadth, and 296 fathoms deep, constantly flowing into the Northern Ocean—Allow that where those rivers disembogue themselves into the Ocean they are only as wide, and as deep again: then I have a column of Water 37 miles in breadth, and 592 fathoms in depth. But considering the difference of distance from the Sea, where these rivers were crossed; all of them a great way from it, and some of them near their sources:—this ground of calculation is too vague to be much relied on. Taking the account of the Officer at Krastniack as a leading data of computation, it would very much enlarge the idea of these rivers: tho he could not make me understand him, what part of the Yennessy he meant, as being 3000 Archuns (about 3 miles english) wide and above 80 fathoms deep: but even suppose he meant at its arrival at Ocean (which is not at all probable) yet considering that many other rivers, as the Oby, Kolyma, Tobolsk, Kama, &c are nearly of the same size; and the Lena and some others larger than the Yennessy: and the unusual depth of their beds generally here: and then allowing 37 [miles of column] in all, supposes a vast quantity of water indeed moving in this direction: and must be the cause of the great quantity of Ice about the Pole. An estimate on this data, reducing the whole to one body as above would make it about a hundred miles broad and about 3000 fathoms deep. Tho' this ground for calculation must be allowed to be as vague as the other: yet both together, enable the reader to conceive of a very great flux to the Ocean, and the ingenious *observer* to form his opinion on the above hypothesis.—Passing on east from the Yennessy to Irkutsk the Country is thinly peopled. A very few and those, miserable houses are to be seen on the road, and none at all from it. The

Country is hilly, rough, and mountainious and covered with thick forests, and that which I have passed on the road now disappears.

Yennessy is the first stony road I have yet met with. The rivers here also have rocky beds and are rapid in a degree from 3 to 5 miles per hour.

The autumnal rains are now begun, and they set in severely. I have passed some of the Calmucs, who are married with the Russians—I staid at quarters all day, and took some rest after a very fatiguing route—rendered so by several very disagreeable circumstances—going with the Courier, and driving with wild tartar horses at a most rapid rate over a wild and ragged Country.—breaking and upsetting Kabitkas—beswarmed by Musquetoes—all the way hard rains and when I arrived at Irkutsk I was, and had been the last 48 hours wet thro' and thro'—and one complete mass of mud—delivered my letter to Mr Directeur of the Banque, who waits on me to morrow.—

Monday 16th August. I have not been out this morning, but I shrewdly suspect by what I see from my poor little talc window that I shall *even here* find all the fashionable follies—the cruel ridiculous extravagance, and ruinous *eclat* of Petersburg.—

I have been out, and find my suspicions well founded—Dined with a Brigadier, Colonel, and Major, a little out of town—Germans—had at the table a French Exile who had been an Adjutant. Not a day passes scarcely but an exile of some sort arrives here There are in this town at present 150. The most of the Inhabitants, and particularly of this remote part of Siberia, are convicts. I find that the worst idea I had formed of the Country, and its Inhabitants does not require correction. This Country originally inhabited by the great Mongul or Calmuc Tartars who are I conclude the same people. No fruit will grow here any more than at Tobolsk—Cold by Reaumers Therr sometimes at 30 degrees—[6] Find no account about the Calumet. The French Exile had been at Quebec and thinks the Tartars here much inferior to the American Indians both in their understandings and persons. I find the Tonguse to be the Tribe who have not the Mongul and Calmuc faces: but moderately long, and considerably like the European face. These form the second class of Tartars; so apparently distinguished by their feautures from other Tartars and from Europeans What I call the third class, are the lighteyed and fair complexioned Tartars which I believe include the Cossacs

The Ischutskoi are the only northern Tartars that remain unsubjugated to the Government. The Lake Baikal 60 versts from here is 800 versts long and 400 wide surrounded by high cragged mountains: has a ragged bottom: and among its few fish, is the Chien de la Mer.[7] Town of Irkutsk is the residence of a Viceroy (Jacobi) a General, and has in it two Battalions of infantry—has 2000 poor Log houses and 10 Churches.—to think of the rascality of this place.—10 kopeeks for shaving me. Jacobi commands from here to the Pacific Ocean—an immense Country. There are no volcanoes in this Country. Waited this morning on the Director of the Bank Mr: Karamyscherff—find he was a pupil of Linnaeus—He is very assiduous to oblige me in everything: Sent for three Calmucs in the dress of their Country—nothing particularly curious about them: but their pipes which are coarsley made of copper, by themselves *the form altogether Chinese.* Information from Karamyscherff, the Mongul and Calmuc Tartars the *same people* From his house I went with the Consillier d'etat, who introduced me to Monsieur Jacobi the Viceroy; he is an old venerable man; and tho I believe like Pallas he is "an homme de Bois," yet he received me standing and uncovered.[8] Our conversation was merely respecting my going with the Post, which he granted me and besides that told me I should [be] particularly well accomodated—wished me a good and successful voyage,—and that my travels might be productive of information to mankind. Spoke to him in french thro the interpretation of the Consellor who informed [me] as follows "The white Tartars you saw about Kazan are natives of that country, and we call them Kazan Tartars. Kazan was once a kingdom of theirs. From here to Yakutsk you pass among the Calmucs At Yakutsk you see the Yakutsk and also the Tonguse who are more personable than the Calmucs or Monguls and more sensible: but the Yakutsk are more sensible than either They are indeed a people of good natural parts and genius: and by experience are found capable of any kind of learning. From Yakutsk to Ohotsk you pass through the Tonguse all the way to Ohotsk. In the time of Zinghis Khan the Tergiss and Thibet Tartars—viz—Calmucs or Moguls made incursions into this Country—We have 200:000 Russians: and as near as we can estimate, half the number of Indians of all discriptions in this Province. Marriages, in and near the villages take place between the Russians and the Tartars—but they are not frequent I believe the extreme cold and want of snow here during winter, and the sudden change of weather in the summer season to be the reason, why we cant have any fruit here. We have often here in the months of May and June ice, three and four inches thick: Besides this Country as you have observed is subject to terrible gales of wind, which blows away both bud & blossom. We have nevertheless a few little Apples about the size of a Buck-shot, which we eat at our tables, and they are not without flavour"—thus much the Counseller. Trees of all kinds in this Country are generally rotten in the heart: they are almost altogether Birch.—No Lava about the Baikal—But some of it scattered about in different parts of the Country. Mr Karamyscherff tells me there are many bones of the Rhinocersous in this country: and also the same large bones that are found on the banks of the Ohio in America. It seems that the places to find those and other curious fossils is at the mouths of the great rivers yennesy Lena &c among Islands that are formed in their different mouths. Here they all are lodged that are washed from undeground thro' the different Countries which those Rivers traverse. Irkutsk situated on the River Angam which is a Mongul World.

16th—To day it seems the Jubilee (on account of the Empress having reigned 25 years) is observed.—In coming from Karamyscherff's I met the Governor and his suit of Officers.

The Brigadier I dined with yesterday &c to the amount of 200 Officers all going to dine with the Viceroy who on the Occasion *keeps open house*. The Governor and all saluted me as they [passed]: those who did not know me wondering what could procure me such attention to one so poorly and oddly attired. I was pressed by some of the company to go and dine. If I had good clothes I would have gone—but I will dine with Karamyscherff—Dined with Mr Karamyscherff, it is a Tartar name and he is of tartarian extraction: Saw in his Garden an Apple tree, and he gave me specimens of the fruit, and the size is that of a full sized pea in France and England. It is the true and real apple and their Naturalists distinguish it by the name of Pyrus Ranata. These are the only apples in Siberia those are found only in the environs of Irkutsk. Karamyscherff says that the Yakutsky tartars are the *veritable tartars*, by which I understand a people less mixed with other tartars than any other—their language he says is the *oldest langu[a]ge* and that all the other Tartars understand it. They in this respect resemble the Cherokees in America. The Yakutsky formerly possessed this Country but were dispossessed by the Calmucs, who attacked them by *surprise* and by a succession of surprises drove them to the Lena on which they fled and settled at Yakutsk. After rising from table the Russians first cross themselves and bow to their images and then to each other. Karamyscherff has in his house four children descended of a Calmuc man and a Russian woman: The first resembled its father, and is entirely Calmuc; the other its mother with fair hair and eyes and &c and is entire Russian and the other two alternately Calmuc and Russian: they are all likely healthy Children and I saw three of them myself with him. I find that Karamyscheff knows not among what nation to rank the Khamchadales. He acknowledges with me that their faces are entirely Calmuc: but says they come from America, which controverts of the natural opinion that America was peopled after Asia. He is bedevil'd with the wild system of the french naturalist Buffon. I find universally that the Tartars have their beards. The ears of Calmuc and Mongul Tartars, project uniformly and universally farther from their heads than those of Europeans. I measured those of three Calmucs at Karmyscheff's to-day and on a medium they projected 1½ inches and they were by no means extraordinary examples.—the ears of the Chinese are the same.—Informed that Ischutskoi are tatowed. People here are subject to frequent disease: especially a very active and putrid fever, which often proves suddenly fatal. Many die here also of apoplectic disorders. The fevers by what I could learn are not of the intermitting kind. I find French & Spanish wines here: but so mutilated that I was told of it before I knew it to be wine Karamyscherff is fully sensible of the Luxury & vanity I complain of in this Country, that is but *begining to begin*, as I told him to day—and laments it, and declared to me frankly that Patriotism and the true solid virtues of a Citizen were hardly known. The Geographical termination of Russia and commencement of Siberia is at the city of Perm: The natural boundary is the river Yennessy. I observe that the face of the country is very different, and Karamyscherff being a Botanist observes that the vegetable produc[ts] are as different. Archangel Dress the true Russian Dress and is derived from Greece and Egypt. Mongul and Calmuc are Thibet Indians—Counted Sitxy Streams that empty themselves into the Baikal (there are more see fo[r]ward).

Tuesday 17 August. Went this morning to see Some Curiosities from different parts of Siberia. Saw some Sandwich Island Cloth at the same place. This was obtained from Capt Cook's Ship at Kamschatka when he was there. Saw the Skin of a Chinese Goat. the hair of which was the whitest, longest and most delicate I ever saw. I also saw some excellent Sea Otter Skins: the best valued at 200 Roubles. Saw likewise the Bow, quiver, and all the military apparatus of a Calmuc, which was very heavy. The Calmuc and Mongul are here called the Burett or in Latin Buretti. Went to the Archbishop's to see a young Savage of the Ischutskoi: The good Bishop to whom I related the story, like Dr Wheelock with Sampson Occum, had taken great pains to humanize him—but informed me he had lately taken to drink and *died drunk:* or in the Conclusion of the Bishops own words "Somebody had given him a present of ½ a Rouble and he went out with it but never returned, and was found dead by the Side of a Kabai"9 Dined with my

friend K— who presented me in lieu of a domestic, a young Lieutentant
to go with me to buy a few things, "but" says he "don't put any money in his
hands, he will not return it." We had at the table the wife of a Clerk to Mr
Karamyscherff whose mother was a Savage near Ischutskoi and her father
a Russian. She is a fine Creature and her Complexion of a good middling
colour: It strengtheneth my opinion that the difference of Colour in Man
is not the effect of any design in the Creator; but of causes simple in themselves, and will perhaps soon be well ascertained—It is an extraordinary circumstance but I think I ought not on that account to conclude that it is not
a Work of Nature—

Wednesday August 18th—For the second time I have observed that in
the Wells about 12 feet down there is a great deal of Ice adhering to the Sides.
I am told that in [latitudes] 58 and 60, it never thaws above two or three feet
down. Went this morning to see a Merchant owner of a Vessel that had
passed from Kamschatka to different parts of the Coast of America. Shewed
some Charts rudely discriptive of his voyages. He says there are on different parts of the Coast of America 2000 Russians: and that as near as he can
judge the number of skins produced by them in that Country amount to
12.000: has a Vessel of his own at Ohotsk. which leaves that Country for
America next Summer, and offers me a passage in her. Dined with a German
Colonel, and after dinner went to the Lake—Baikal which in the Calmuc
Language (the original inhabitants of its environs to the Thibet) signifies
the *North Sea*. After a good and friendly dinner with the Colonel, the
Chevalier and I mounted his drosky, with post horses and set out for the
Lake—. After 7 hours ride over a miserable road. we arrived at the little ham-
let of Nicolskoi where formerly the Russian Embassadors resided before
they embarked to cross the Lake to China—After crossing the Lake they go
south about 300 versts to the town of Kiatka, which is now the frontier town,
and where they meet the Ambassadors from Pekin. This village has a
Church in it dedicated to the Russian Neptune St Nicholas & all the
Sailors on the Lake resort to it. We lodged here during the night, and next
morning early renewed our Journey and reached the little village. Here is
a Galliot that plies as packet in the Summer across the Lake and 6 or 7 houses
among which the largest is a house ordered to be built by the Empress for
the accomodation of all Strangers that should pass this way. We hailed the
Galliot which was at anchor in the Lake the Capt. came to see us, and we
went off with him in a small Boat with a line and Lead to take soundings,
but having only 50 fathoms line, and it raining very hard we could not make

much progress; 100 feet from the shore took all my line viz 50 fathoms: we retired to the house, breakfasted and waited an hour for the rain to abate, but finding it to continue, we requested of the Captain to send us in his boat to Irkutsk, he complied with our request and made us a canopy of hides to defend us from the rain, we sent our d[r]ochky back by the Post-Boy and embarked with two Sailors to row us.—we passed from there along the shore to the mouth or outlet and down the river to Irkutsk. This Lake is 769 versts in its longest and 60 versts in its broadest part, its depth said to be unfathomable: it has an annual ebb and flux: The one is caused by the autumnal rains, and the other by the dry Springs It has emptying into it 169 small streams from 20 to 80 yards wide and 3 larger ones from $\frac{1}{4}$ to $\frac{1}{2}$ mile It is supplied with but one outlet by which to dispose of this redundancy from all these influxes. The one mentioned, called by the Calmucs or Monguls—Angara and this which is but $\frac{1}{4}$ of a mile is very shallow at its Offset from the Lake and far from being rapid. Dined with a Gentleman at his Glass manufactory and returned in the evening to Irkutsk—

Saturday 20th August} The Government of Irkutsk has four Districts, three north and one South of it viz. Its own Province Irkutsk, 2d Yakutsk 3d Ohotsk and 4th Narchintsk. Each of these provinces are sub-divided into smaller districts. Irkutsk has 4 viz. Irkutsk, Verchna Oodintsk, Kerensk, and Noshnayoodintsk. In these Districts, the Inhabitants are Russ Burett (or Calmuc) Tonguse, Yakoot, Lamootkee, and Ukagee. Province of Ohotsk has 4 Districts viz Gesheginsk Aklansk and Nashknay. Kamschatsk—(called by us Kamchatka) the inhabitants are Russ. Tonguse Yakoot. Koriakhee Kamchadales. Alutore, Kuriles Ischutskoi and other Indians yet unsubjugated. Province of Narchintsk has 4 districts: viz Narchintsk, Barguzin, Straytinsk and Doroninsk, The inhabitants are Russ. Burett and Tonguse. Mr Karamyscherff says that they suppose here that those extraordinary large bones were the Behemoth. Houses here guarded by great Dogs—every yard full of them. The Russ proper are descended of the Polanders, Sclavonians, Bohemians, and Hungarians, those of the Greeks and they of the Egyptians, and they of the Chaldeans. The present Russ Dress is Egyptian

Monday 22d August—Informed by the Viceroy that the post will not be ready until Wednesday He sent a Surveyor with the latest Chart of the Province to give me the dimensions of the province or Government of Irkutsk as I had requested and by exact measurement I found its Latitudinal extent from its Southern extremity in Lat. 49° 10' N to the Icy Ocean N. to be 2700 versts: and is Longitudinal extent from the Longitude 113° 30' to

the Iskutskoi Nos its eastern extremity on the Strait that divides the
Continent from America opposite the Cape Prince of Wales of the Coast—
to be 3.900 versts. I find that I have lost some of my linen between a servant and the washerwoman: the universal propensity to thieving in this
Country from people of some condition to the lowest orders is a severe tax
on the budget of so poor a traveller as I am.

Tuesday 23d August I find that the commerce of Irkutsk is very little with
Europe and consequently at present is at a very low ebb, since there is no open
trade with the Chinese who are their nearest neighbours of a commercial
Character. The frontiers between this Country and that are pincipally defended
by an army of the Burett or Calmuc Tartars. They are mostly horsemen like
the Cossacs in the western dominions and amount to 5273 men, there are two
Convents near the town, one of men and one of women separated by a river—
I observe in Siberia that in all their Cities their is one great burying place and
that wherever that is (and it is commonly out of town) there is a Church and
the best Church of the place—this is but another kind of *Pyramid*, a *large
mound* or a mound modified. The averaged population of the Russian Empire
is 274 men to each square-german-mile total amount twenty millions and a
half—the same estimate has not yet been made of Siberia: Of this province it
may be made easily by the table I have of it. England Ireland & Scotland is said
to have to each German-square mile 2942 total twelve millions & a half—

★

To William Smith
20 August 1787; Irkutsk

To William S Smith Esqr
Sir.

Pray receive my compliments of friendship & present them to your Lady
also. I am on the wings and can only say how d'ye to any of my friends at
the present, the principal reason of this extreme haste is that I fear being overtaken by the winter before my arrival on the Borders of the Pacific Ocean,
for I have 1000 versts to go where there is no road at the best season of the
year, but in Autumn impassible, unless on foot, and without a guide which
is an inconvenience too great not to be avoided when in my power. You and

I were extremely uninformed, in Our conversation together at London of this Country. With my finances I never should have been able to have passed through it on foot. Yet as I have travelled it I am here and shall arrive at Kamskatka comfortably situated in that respect. At this place I am in a circle as gay, rich, polite, and as scientific, as if at Petersburg I drink my French and Spanish wines: and have Majors Colonels, and Brigadiers, by Brigades, to wait on me in the town, and disciples of Linnaeus to accompany me in my philosophic walks. In Russia I am treated as an American with politeness & respect and on my account the healths of Dr Franklin and General Washington have been drunk at the tables of two Governors: and at Irkutsk the name of Adams has found its Way. Among the middling Class of People, I am a kind of Phenomenon, among the peasantry a right down wizard. The first characters know very little of our History, except the military part of it and that they have had thro the medium of some Septennial English Gazette

I am now about two-thirds of my Asiatic voyage; 6271 versts from Petersburgh or 4704½ miles English. You will find the City I write from near the South part of the great Lake Baikal on the banks of the great River Angam which has its Source from the Baikal. From here I shall go 200 Versts by land and then embark in a Batteau on the Rive Lena—the largest in this vast Empire

I continue my voyage on the Lena 2266 versts to the City of Yakutsk which you will find situated on its banks to the northward: from thence if I am not too late, I shall ride "a la mode des Tatars["] thro' a wilderness of about 1000 versts to Ohotsk, which is the end of my journey here: If I am too late I know not how I Shall go—as no post goes after Snow falls—at least very seldom: I suppose either on a Sledge drawn by dogs or rein-deer I am told so; here As for going on foot, it is ridiculous in this Country. It has been to this moment a source of misfortunes to me that I did not begin to ride post from Hamburg. I have footed it at a great expence besides the Loss of my Baggage, which I severely feel this instant Never did I adopt an Idea so fatal to my happiness, it is I hope nearly past however.

If you have opportunity to remember me to Dr Ledyard at New York, and he will inform my other friends where I am—Farewell

I am with esteem & friendship. Your much Obliged
and most Obedt humble Servt
Ledyard—

✳

Wednesday 25th August. This morning leave town: find the Country well cultivated between here and the river and a good Country Among the Burett or Calmucs find the American mockasin— the common mockasin like the finland mockasin. The houses have octagonal sides covered with turf, fire-place in the centre; an aperture above for the Smoke. The true American Wigwam and like the first calmuc tartar house I saw in this Country which was near Kazan. Mr Karamyscherff says they have the wild horse on their Chinese frontiers. The people here (the Burett) ride and work the horned cattle; they pe[r]forate the cartilage and put a cord thro' it to guide them by. This is to be wondered at as this Country is so level and they have such vast droves of horses.

Thursday 26th. Had last night a hard white frost and it was very cold: my feet suffered. run away with by these cursed unbroke tartar horses and saved myself each time by jumping out of the Kabitka—Thank heaven! 90 versts more will probably put an end to my Kabitka Journeying for ever.

Friday 27th August Arrived 10 Oclock at the Lena Autumn must have made its appearance 10 or 14 days ago, the trees have most of them dropt their foliage. The river here twenty yards wide surrounded by high steep mountains. a number of little falls—river in general 234 feet water—

Saturday Aug. 28th The prevailing wood on the borders of the Lena is small pines. The environs of Irkutsk well cultivated: there are fine fields of wheat, rye and barley a good breed of cattle: and the mutton particularly is of a good size: and have the fat tail like the sheep at the Cape of Good-Hope. it however not particularly well flavoured.

Monday 30 August. Mountains decrease, and the country opens with the increase of the river which is yet small. Very cold with fogs all night until 11 Oclock in the morning.

Tuesday 31st August. River widens, but does not alter its depth much. Mountains are come to hills and horizon enlarges: my ink frose in the Boat last night tho' we were covered overhead: we stopped at the Stage an hour this morning to get a little stores: They killed us a sheep gave us three quarts of milk, two loaves of Bread and some cakes with carrots and radishes baked in them Onions 1 doz fresh and 2 doz salt fish, Straw also and bark to mend the covering of our Boat for only 40 kopeeks about 14 pence sterling! They complained (so Lieut Laxman a young Swedish Officer who travels with me said)[10] of a scarcity of bread, and the poor creatures brot us their straw to shew us their grain blasted by the frost: and it had been reaped 10 days past which makes it the 21st of August. The borders of this river have a few poor houses as Stages for Boats, for those who go by water: and horses for those who go by land. The peasants say those mountains are full of bears and wolves Plenty of wild fowl which we shoot as we please. I have seen no fish but ca[r]p and salmon—trout.—they fish with Seins and also with spears and a torch: this last custom is a very universal one for they fish with the torch in Otaheite. The Burett inhabit all the borders of the Lake Bailkal: they have tents or wigwams covered with matting bark or Skins, and are the genuine American wigwam form thus. I find we go about 110 or 20 versts a day. The double headed paddle or Esquimaux is here.—

September 1st Wednesday. Yakootsk is the last place where you will be able to make any *enquiries.* therefore let them be extensive. If Mercury was the God of theft among the Ancients the Russians ought to enroll him in their mythology I find the Chinese Pipe universally among the Siberian Tartars and think it therefore probable that the custom of Smoking migrated with them to America and thence by Sir Walter Raleigh made its way east to England—if so customs travel in a singular manner for why did it not come W. to England.—One English book in the Library of Chevalier Karamyscherff printed London 1621 Sir John Denham's works.[11]

Thursday Sept 2d Stopped this morning at a Little village to complete the hospitable invitation of a Merchant and a priest with them: My rascal of a Soldier stole our brandy got drunk and impertinent. I was obliged to handle him roughly to preserve order fixed a little sail to our boat. Mr Karamyscherff and I were both of opinion that *wampum* is of Grecian origin some how like that.

Saturday 4th September arrived at the village or town of Keringa at daylight and staid with the Commandant until noon and was treated very hospitably by him and some Merchants sent us some stores. It is the custom here if they hear of the arrival of a foreignor to load him with their little services. It is almost impossible to pass a town of any kind without being arrested by them, and their hospitality is of the natural kind, or that which has not Civilization for is cause. They have the earnestness of hospitality. They fill their tables with *every thing* they have to eat and drink, and not content with that they fill their wallet. I wish I could think them as honest as they are hospitable. Keringa situated between the rivers Lena and Keringa has 700 inhabitants, of those 300 are women, 6 merchants 15 Officers, a few soldiers 12 superranuated among which there are those of 70, 80, and 92 years, 5 privates and 50 men in a *Convent*. The reason why this Commandant at Keringa did not shew his wife, was because he was jealous of her. I have observed this to be a prevailing passion here.

NB. The word Chamant signifies Priest—

Monday 6th September.

At Keringa	R[ubles]	K[opeks]
beef p Pood		90
Sugar	15	0
Tea	10	0
poor Bread		60
best do		90

The stones I send to Irkutsk were taken at the foot of the highest cliff of rocky mountains between Ischastinskoi and Doubroua. They are the highest mass of rocks I ever saw I suppose that among the Stones there is part of the leg of an Elephant—The river here bounded on each side by those vast stony cliffs. Birch and pine share pretty equally the soil.

Tuesday 7th September. For the first time I have had any horizon at all. I have one appearing a head 30 english miles, we are within a few versts [of] half our distance to Yakootskoi.

September 13th Monday. Have had for several days hard head winds and rain—went ashore to day to dress our provisions. saw the hide of a bullock fixed on the top of a tree; supposed to be put there by the Shamant as a sacrifice.

Wednesday 15th Sept. Snow squalls with fresh gales, up all night at the helm myself.

Friday 17th Sept Had squally weather till now—am 90 versts from Yakootsk. Passed yesterday a very odd arrangement of rocks which form the margin of the river for about 60 versts—they are of *Talc* and appear to have formerly been covered with earth but are now entirely naked. they are all of a pyramidyical form, extending to about 150 feet height—detached from their bases & disposed with extraordinary regularity. Those rocky banks at present appear to terminate the long mountainous South and east bank of the Lena that have uniformly continued from Katchuga here. I am now in upwards of 60° N.L. and which as it applies here might be called Latitude of Low-land: 90 versts from hence (viz) at Yakutsk it takes it[s] long northern and north-western direction.

✴

Unbeknownst to Ledyard, the governor of Irkutsk, Ivan Iakobi, suspected the American traveler was a spy for British fur-trading interests. He sent a secret message to the commandant of Yakutsk, Grigorii Marklovskii, asking him to quietly prevent Ledyard from traveling beyond Yakutsk, and he wrote of his concerns to the Russian foreign minister in St. Petersburg, requesting Ledyard's arrest and deportation. As per Iakobi's order, Marklovskii persuaded Ledyard to winter out in Yakutsk. In November Joseph Billings, an old shipmate of Ledyard's from the Cook voyage, appeared in Yakutsk and Ledyard joined his expedition. After Christmas, Ledyard and Billings went by sledge up the frozen Lena to Irkutsk where they planned to spend the balance of the winter.

Saturday Sept 18th Arrived at Yakutsk after a very fatiguing voyage on the Lena of 22 days—delivered my letters to the Commandant of the town, who very politely procured me quarters and waited on me there: but in our first conversation received the dejecting intelligence that it is impossible to proceed to Ohotsk this winter. What alas! shall I do for I am miserably provided for this unlooked for delay. By tarrying the winter I cannot expect to resume my march until May, which is 8 months. My funds! I have but two long frozen Stages more and I shall be beyond the want or aid of money, until emerging from her deep deserts I gain the American Atlantic States and then thy glow[i]ng Climates. Africa explored, I lay me down and claim a little portion of the Globe I've viewed—may it not be before. How many of the noble minded have been subsidiary to me or to my eterprizes: and yet that meagre devil POVERTY who hand in hand has travelled with me o'r half the globe—and witnessed what Oh ye feeling Souls!—the tale I'll not unfold—'twould break the fibrils of your gentle hearts. Ye Sons of ener[v]ating Luxury ye Children of wealth and idleness! what profitable Commerce might be made between us, had you the will, and I the power to enter on the trade. A little of my toil might better brace your nerves. give spring to mind, and zest to your enjoyments and a very little of that wealth you scatter round you, would [put it] beyond the powers of any thing but death to oppose my kindred greetings with all on earth that bear the stamp of man. This is the third time I have been overtaken and arrested by winter and in both the others by giving time for my *evil genius* to rally her hosts about me have defeated the Enterprize. Fortune thou hast humbled me at

length, for I am at this moment the slave of cowardly solicitude, least in the
womb of this dread winter, there lurks the seeds of disappointment to my
ardent desire of gaining the opposite Continent. I submit and proceed
with my remarks. At Kazan there is abundance of snow, at Irkutsk which
is in about the same latitude there is very little snow to fall. Irkutsk is in a
higher situation is much colder and the snow cannot so readily descend—
Here at Yakutsk the Atmosphere is constantly charged with Snow: it sometimes falls but very sparingly and that in the day rarely if ever at night. The
air is much like that we experienced with Capt Cook in *Mare Glaciale* in Lat.
70° to 72° seldom a serene sky or detached Clouds, the upper region is a dark
still expanded vapour with few openings in it, in the lower Atmosphere there
is a constant succession of Snow. Clouds floating over head resembling Fog-
Banks. In general the motion of every thing above and below is languid.
The Summers are dry days very hot, the nights cold. The weather exceedingly changeable, subject to high winds, generally from the North, and sometimes heavy Snows in August. I have seen but one Aurora Borealis, and that
not an extraordinary one. The first settlers in the time of Ivan Ivanitch, which
was about 250 years ago came round by the North Sea The present Viceroy
has per annum 6000 Roubles and is allowed 6000 more for his Table. As
nearly as I can estimate the whole Amount of Government expenditure is
about 156000 Roubles. There is a large mine of pure transparent salt formed
into large crystals in a mountain near the Lena It runs in veins like other
mines it affects meat like Saltpetre There is also a blue and red sort. Here
are many instances of Longevity. There is a man of 110 years in perfect health
and labours daily. The images in the Russian houses, which I should take
for a kind of Household Gods: are very expensive: the principal ones have
a great deal of silver lavished on them.

   To furnish out a house properly with these *Dii Minores* would cost 8
or 1000 Roubles:[12] when burnt out which I have witnessed several times,
they have appeared more anxious for these than any thing else. The warm
bath is used here by the peasantry early in life from which it is common
to plunge themselves into the river: and if there happens to be a new-
fallen snow, they come naked reeking from the bath and wallow therin. Their
Dance is accompanied or rather performed by the same odd twisting and
wreathing of the hips as at Otaheite. In their marriages among the
Kamchdales the woman draws on several pairs of breeches the man is
naked, of all the other grades or divisions of man the Savage is the most formal and ceremonious and these among a people whose wants and

occupations are but few whose minds necessity has [not] tortured almost to disstraction for the means of preservation on account of difficulties which the Luxury of Civilization hath created even for its ordinary members, he who with a happy indifference can endure a State of privation whose apprehensions are not racked with the Legends of future purgations, and whose heaven is peace and leisure, these are ceremonials with him like the uninterrupted tenor of his mind may be supposed to be transmitted unchanged thro' many generations: hence many things which marked the earliest period of history & which have left no vestige among civilized men show themselves at this day among Savages and testify for record, Their Luxury if such it may be called is of that kind which nature intimates. Dress which in hot climates is an inconvenience further than for the concealment of modesty does not become so much the object of delight. here therefore the Savage is more nice and scrupulous in the indulgence of his appetites. On the other hand in cold climates bodily covering being of all importance, ingenuity is directed to that point: a feeble kind of infant fancy grows out of the efforts of necessity, and displays its little arts about the persons of such regions in awkward and fantastic decorations. But here the appetites are less lively and distinguished with respect to food the vilest and that totally unprepared does not come amiss, and the most delicate is not siezed with ardour. Voracity does not exist near the 60th Degree of Lat not even with the animals. Give a cake to a Swedish Finlander or northern Tartar and he eats it leisurely: do the same to an Otaheitan, and Italian peasant or a Spanish fisherman and he will put the whole Cake into his mouth if he can. The Empress has caused houses to be built at the expense of the Government in the Russian manner and ordered them to be offered to Yakuttee upon the single condition of their dwelling in them, but they have universally refused: prefering their apparently more uncomfortable Yoorts or Wigwaums. Dogs are esteemed there nearly in the same degree that horses are in England for besides answering the same purpose in their way [of] travelling. they aid them in the Chace and after toiling for them the whole day become their safe-guard at night. They therefore command their greatest attention. They have Dog-Farriers to attend them in sickness, who are no despicable rivals in art, at least in pretension to the Horse-Doctors of civilized Europe. They command also a high price. What they called a leading dog of prime character will sell for 3 or 400 Roubles. It is true that Volcanoes are almost universally where there is water—but it is salt water for I know of none near the largest Lakes or rivers. The compact part of a Continent approaches the Ocean by a regular descent from the highland in the centre. To be travelling into the interior parts of a continent you will pass first an extent of low-land proportioned to the extent of the Continent in the direction in which you travel. if contrary wise you first encounter ragged mountains; you may generally conclude that your march will be intercepted by Gulfs &c. when this is not the Case you will perhaps find those mountains to be, or you may conclude they have been volcanoes—Tonguse tatowed— Samoiede have the doubl-headed paddle Manner of fishing with nets under the ice. Buretti have the Mahometan lock of hair, The Russians half (22 in all) of the Islands under their Government. Kuriles are tatwood. A Journal from a Russs Officer says that the Kuriles are very hairy: Mostly where we have it. but the arms, legs and thighs are altogether covered with hair. Their traffic with the Japanese. Feathers and fish. The Islands have little vegetation. Kuriles reserved and sentimental in conversation: They are a comely people: have their materials for boat or house building from the Continent or Japanese They are very wild and receive all strangers with the most threatening and formidable appearances—but afterwards they are kind and hospitable. The Coast of the frozen Ocean full of trees and drift wood for 5 versts out. It is remarked by the Russians that since their knowledge of that Country the land has increased towards the Sea and drove it northward: 100 versts. a circumstance perhaps attributable to the large Rivers that empty themselves there. The Yakuttee is the mother language of all the Tartars and they all know something of it tho' they do not speak it From the following short specimen the reader may form some little idea of this (no doubt) very antient language—To a girl to go with me. Will you go and live with me at Kamschatka? Nay eezwalishlay yayhut somenoyoo e jeet ev Kamschatkay— I want a woman to go and live with me at Kamschatka—Ya hoctchoo eemayt de efkoo ektobooy soglasshalass jeet somenoyoo ev Kamchatka.

People at Yakutsk have no wells, they have tried them 50 & 60 feet deep;[13] but they freeze: the consequence is that they have all their water from the River Lena. This in Summer is very well but in Winter they cannot bring Water from thence, it freezes in the Cisterns in which they bring it, so that in the Winter they bring large Cakes of Ice to their Houses & pile them up in their yards & as they want them bring them into their warm rooms where they thaw & become fit for use.

The Yakutee bring milk to market in Winter in frozen Cakes. a Yakut came into our house to day with a Bag full of Ice—What the Devil said I to Laxman has the Man brought Ice to sell—it was Milk.

Tonguse are a wandering People, who solely live by the Chase. They have Tents or Yoorts made of Bark which they leave on he spot where they have encamped: They never stay above 2 or 3 days in a place, & the day they march they tell their Women that they go to such a Mountain, River, Lake, Plain, or Forest, & leave them to bring the Baggage.—They are extremely active in the Chace—They have no Letters, & do not write their Language. The Tents or Yoorts are universally of the same form & that is that of the American Wigwaum. Tonguse are often found dead, having pursued the Chace down some precipice.

The *Calmuc or Buretti* write their Language in Columns like the Chinese. The *Cossacs or Kazan Tartars* like the Hebrews from the right to left.

The Calmucs live mostly by their Flocks & Herds which consist of Horses, sheep, Goats & Cows. In the Summer they dwell in the plains—In the Winter they retreat to the Mountains for Shelter & where their Flocks feed on Buds Moss &c—They have much Milk which they eat, & of which they also make Brandy—They hunt also. If they have any of their Flock Sick or lame they eat them.

I observe that there is one continued flow of Good nature & Chearfulness among the Tartars—They never call names & abuse each other by words, but when angry look for revenge either secret or open.

The Tonguse fight Duels with their Bows or Knives. They & the other roving Tartars have their hunting grounds marked, ascertained, & limited like the Americans. A Sentiment I observe that those Nations who like the Tartars & Negroes from time immemorial have not commixed, and &c and intermarried with other Nations are not so handsome (admitting our Ideas of Beauty) so strong, nor have so much Genius as us.

The Reason why the Buretti write is that they are last migrated from Thibet.

There is not another Asiatic Tribe in all Siberia that write their Language or have any remains of writing or orthography among them. a Proof, if there were no other, of their latest migration—perhaps of something else.

It is almost an universal Custom among the Russian Women to make their Teeth black, it is consequently considered as a great Ornament. This Custom prevails now in Persia, India, & I think in China.

The *Sound* of the Yakutee language is exactly like the Chinese, & so indeed are the languages of all the Asiatic Tartars.

People in this Country that are born half Russ, half Tartar are very different & much superior in their Persons to either the Tartars or Russ.—The

European Nations that commix and intermarry most with other nations are the handsomest.—How far might this Cause be supposed to have made the Negro & Tartar so different from the European—or might not this commixing have originally made the European different from the Tartar or the Negro—might not this circumstance have been the greatest Cause of that difference among Mankind which exists.

A Gentleman showed me to day a copy of a Marriage [contract] done at Moscow 205 years ago. It is a folio page in length; & there are only 16 words intelligible to an ordinary reader or that correspond with the orthography of the present day: This rapid alteration in the Russ language leaves a proportion to the alteration in their manners since that period.

Their practice of bathing is once a week—their Baths are very hot.

The Empress gives three Ranks to Officers that come into Siberia & serve six years—2 while out from Petersburg & one on their return. It has two important effects; it civilizes Siberia, & is a prostitution of Rank & Honour, which in a Government like this is a prostitution of every thing-This is not Hypothesis, I have before my eyes the most consummate Scoundrels in the Universe of a Rank that in any other civilized Country would insure the best virtues of the heart & head, or at least common honesty & common decency. The Empress of Russia will be a Bankrupt at this rate to her own Ambition. Siberia is more than half of her Dominions, & it is professedly a Nursery of the most infamous Characters in her Dominions. The Succession of those characters is every 6 years, & the number annually increasing. at present there are 6,000 of those Officers in this province only, without estimating the extra annual increase this in 6 years furnish 36,000 Scoundrels—of full proof.

The Yakutee here take their children out in the Evening & teach them the names of the principal Stars—how direct a march by them—how to judge of the weather. Astronomy is an early Science.

The Russ & Yakutee appear to live together here in harmony& peace, & without any difference as to national Distinction, or of Superiority and Inferiority. I know but of one Circumstance (but alas it is a great one) wherein the Yakutee are not on an equal footing with the Russ—They have no Office civil or military.

The Russians have been here 250 years & the Yakutee Tartars under the Russian Government since that time; yet have the Yakutee made no alteration in his manners or Dress in general: The Russians have conformed themselves to the Dress of the Yakutee. There are but very few of the Yakutee who have embraced the Christian Religion & those who have perform its duties with a species of sarcastic Indifference that is very curious. In this respect particularly, the Tartar whether in Asia or America acts up to that Excentricity & singularity of Character which distinguishes them from any other people—Religion of any kind, & professed by any other people than the Tartars is always a matter of a serious contemplative & important nature & forms at least as strong a Trait in their several Characters as any circumstance of Art or Science—But it forms no part of the character of a Tartar—I have not in my mind the Christian System particularly; its Doctrine are indeed a Mystery to the greatest minds & the best hearts—to a Tartar they must surely be more so, & the surprize is less why it forms no part of his Character. But the Mahometan System, for example, which courts the Senses & fascinates the passions of Man, it has operated on the Tartar no otherwise than to induce him to shave his Head—there it stops—it does not enter it—nor the heart.

The Tartar is a Man of Nature—not of Art—his Philosophy therefore is very simple—but sometimes very sublime—let us enumerate some of its virtues—He is a lover of Peace. No Lawyer here perplexing natural rights of property—no Helen, & no System of Religion has ever yet disturbed it. He is contented to be what he is. never did a Tartar I believe speak ill of the Deity, or envy his Fellow Creatures. He is hospitable & humane—He is constantly tranquil & cheerful—He is Laconic in Thoughts Word & action—They do not prostitute even a Smile or a Frown any more than an European Monarch.

This is one reason (& I think the greatest) why they have been constantly persecuted by nations of another Disposition & why they have always fled from before them & been content to live any where if they could only live in Peace. Some have attributed this conduct solely to a Love of Liberty: I can only observe that I believe their Ideas both of Peace & Liberty to be very different from ours, & that a Tartar if he has his dear Otium would be as likely to call it Liberty as Otium.[14] There is much liberty in England, for Example, but I think it would be less agreable to a Tartar to live there than in Russian Siberia where there is less Liberty. They indeed think differently in most things from the people of Europe & indeed of Africa.

If the planters in the state of Virginia were to give their Negroes large commodious houses to inhabit instead of poor huts & encourage them otherwise to do so, I believe the African would think like the Virginian Planter & very gladly accept the proposals. The same thing exactly has been offered the Yakutee here by the Crown, & they have besides much greater Inducements to accept the proposals than the African, but they have not

& they will not; & there is no expence attending the acceptance; but rather contrary wise. they will inhabit the Yoort.

The Yoort or Hut as we generally call it, or as the American Tartars call it pretty generally Wigwaum is in this Country a Substitute for a Tent: in milder Climates it is made either with Skins, Canvass, or Bark of Trees, of Sedge or some other kind of Grass: & in cold Climates it is made also of Skins if they are sufficiently plenty; and in any of those cases it is always of a conical form, not divided into apartments: an Aperture in the Top & in the Center & the fire made in the Center: round the side of the Yoort if they are only temporary ones are placed their Baggage & Furniture; if not temporary then are round the Sides Seats to sit or sleep on.

Here [in the neighbourhood of Russian Settlements] the Yoorts are made a little different; they are sunk two or three feet in the Ground; square; divided into apartments—the frame of wood—the Sides plaistered with Mud—a flat Top & covered with Earth. They have the fire in the Center & a slight little Chimney—They have 2 or 3 little Windows, in Summer of Talc, in Winter of Ice, & like the Scotch Highlanders one Apartment of the Yoort is for the Cow, Ox, or Horse, if they have them—these resemble not a Tent—but remote from Towns all the Tartars have Tents either of Skins Bark or Grass.

The Commandant shewed me to day a Man descended of a Yakutee Father & Russian Mother & the Son of this Man. I remark that the Colour of the first descendant is as fair as that of the second, & that this Colour is as fair as the Russian Mother. I conclude therefore that after the first descent, the Operations of Nature by Generation have little or no effect upon the Colour, & I remark also that whenever this change in the Colour by generation takes place that the alteration is from the darker to the lighter Colour much oftener than the Reverse. The Colour of the Hair & the Eyes also incline to be light, but do not always accompany the change in the colour of the Skin. My general remark is that Nature with respect to the colour of Man, inclines to a colour fairer than the Negro & the Indian—(Nature is so inclinable to the fair Colour that she does her Business at once) I have caught her sporting in this as in other cases. I have in my Memoranda at Irkutsk mentioned an instance of it, wherein 4 Children descended of a Tartar & Russian Parents were alternately fair & dark complexioned—it was the most curious Circumstance of the kind I ever saw. Upon the whole with respect to the difference of the Colour of the Indian and the European they appear to me to be the effects of natural Causes. I have given much attention to the Subject on this Continent: its great, its vast extent, & variety of Inhabitants affords the best field in the World in which to examine it, & I again remark that by the same gentle gradation in which I passed from the height of civilized Society at Petersburg to incivilization in Siberia, I passed from the Colour of the fair European to the Copper-coloured Tartar. I say the Copper-coloured Tartar, but there is the same variety of colour among the Tartars in Siberia as among the other Nations of Earth. The Journal of a Russian Officer which I have seen here informs me that the Samoiede (amongst whom he lived 2 years) are fairer than the Yakutee who are of a light Olive & fairer than the Tonguse or Buretti who are Copper coloured; & yet the three last mentioned Tribes are all Mongul Tartars.—General Remark is that far the greatest part of mankind compared with European Civilization are uncultivated & that this part of Mankind are darker Coloured than the other part *viz* European. There are no white Savages & few uncivilized people that are not brown or black.

Among other remarkable circumstances that distinguish the Tartars is the form & features of the Face. It is perhaps the most remarkable circumstance. It invites me to a field of observation that I am not able to set bounds to. neither my Travels nor my knowledge of their history are sufficient for the purpose, & indeed to do justice to the Subject I should be able to describe the face anatomically. I cannot do it—I remark that it is not an European Face but very remote from it; it is more an African Countenance. The Nose is the most remarkable Feature in the human Face. I have seen some Instances among the Calmucs where the Nose, between the Eyes, has been much flatter & broader than the negroes, & some few instances where ut has been as flat & broad over the Nostrils, but the Nostrils in any case are much smaller than the Africans. Where I have seen those Noses they were accompanied with a large Mouth & thick Lips, & these people were genuine Calmuc Tartars. Universally the Nose protuberates but little from the face & is shorter than that of the European. The Eyes universally are at a great distance from each other & very small, & over each Corner of the Eye the Skin projects over the Ball—the part appears swelled. The eyelids go in nearly a strait line from corner to corner. In the act of closing the eye, the two corners draw in from the centres by which the lids are enabled to meet. When opened the eye appears as in a square frame. The Mouth in general is of a middling size, & the Lips thin. The next remarkable Features are the Cheek Bones; These like the Eyes are very remote from each other, high & broad, & project a little forward. The Face is flat. When I regard a Tartar en profile, I can hardly see the Nose between the Eyes, & if he blows a Coal of fire when I view him in profile I cannot see the Nose at all. The face is then like an inflated bladder—Their Eye is straiter: the Lid has not the European Curve—The Forehead is narrow & low. They have a fresh Colour & on the two Cheek bones there is a good rurddy hue. There is not a variety of expression in their Faces. With but few objects to contemplate the mind must be supposed to be generally without employment of course the face without expression. I think the predominating one is Pride: but whenever I have viewed them they have seen a Stranger.

The generating cause does not operate so completely in producing a change of Features as of Complexion between the Tartar & the European. I have seen the third Descent lineally & the Features of the Tartar predominated over the European Features.

General Remark is that the Tartars from time immemorial (I mean the Asiatic Tartars) have been a people of a roving, wandering disposition—That they have ever been more among the Beasts of the forest than among men, & when among men it has been only those of their own Nation. That they have ever been Savages averse to Civilization, & have therefore never until very lately & now rarely have commixed with other Nations That whatever cause might originally have given them those remarkable Features the cause why they still continue is that they have not commixed with any other People, but I doubt the originality of their Features because by commixing with Europeans they have changed into those of Europeans. I am also ignorant how far a people constantly living with Beasts may operate in changing the features of the Face. But am persuaded that this circumstance together with an uncultivated state of mind if we consider a long and uninterrupted succession of ages must account in some degree for this melancholy singularity. I have thought that even in Europe medical employments having been continued among the same people for a length of time has had a considerable influence in uninforming their faces. I am not insensible how far a cultivation & non-cultivation of the Mind alters the Features. I even observe in Europe that Mechanics of different professions have different Faces.—I know of no Nation, no people on Earth among whom there is such an uniformity of features except the Chinese, the Negroes & the Jews as there is among the Asiatic Tartars. They are distinguished by different Tribes, but this indeed is only nominal—Nature has set a Barrier to this Distinction & to all Distinction among them that marks them wherever found with the indisputable signature of Tartar: No matter if in Nova Zembla, Mongul in Greenland, or on the banks of the Mississippi they are the same, & form the most numerous, & if we except the Chinese the most ancient Nation in History—& I myself do not except the Chinese because I have no doubt of their being of the same Family.

So strong is propensity of the Russians to Jealousy that they are guilty of the lowest faults on that account; the observation may appear trivial to an European: but an ordinary Russian will be displeased if one endeavours to gain the good will of his Dog. I affronted the commandant of this Town very highly by permitting his Dog to walk with me one afternoon—He expostulated with me so seriously about it that I could not believe him in earnest; I told him so, & I told him that whatever declaration he might make to the contrary I *would not* believe it—This is not the only Instance. I live with a young Russian Officer with whom I came from Irkutsk; no circumstance has ever interrupted a constant harmony between us but his Dogs, & they have done it twice & I have been obliged to tell him positively that they shall not do it a third time. A pretty little Puppy has come to me one day & jumped upon my knee; I patted his head & gave him some bread; he flew at the Dog in the utmost rage & gave him a blow that broke his Leg; the Lesson I gave him on the occasion has almost cured him—but I have told him to beware how he disturbs my peace a third time by his rascally passion, & he has done it. I remarked that this observation may appear trivial to an European. I observe also that I am not fond of trivial Observations.

I have observed from Petersburg to this place & here more than any where that the Russians in general have very few moral Virtues, the body of the people are almost totally without. the Laws of the Country are mostly penal Laws; but all civil Laws are but negative instructors; they inform people what they must not do and affix no reward to the Virtue: the penalty to the transgression. but they do not inform people what they should do and affix the reward to virtue. Untaught in the sublime of morality the Russian has not that glourious basis on which to exalt his nature. This in some Countries is made the business of Religion & in a few instances of the civil Law. In this unfortunate Country it is a business of neither civil nor ecclesiastical Concern. A Citizen here fulfills his duty to the Laws if like a base Asiatic he licks the feet of his superior in Rank; & his duty to his God if he adorns his house with a set of ill looking brass or silver Saints & worships them.—Sherlock! Tillotson! Sterne! what a Revolution would your Sermons produce among such a people.[15] They have never heard that sweet Truth that virtue is its own Reward & know no more of such an Idea than a New Zealander. It is for this Reason that their Peasantry, in particular are indubitably the most unprincipled in Christendom. I looked for certain Virtues of the heart that are called natural. I find them mo[s]t in the most remote & obscure Villages in the Empire but on the contrary I find the rankest vices to abound as much as in their Capital.

The Tonguse are Tatowed—The Ischutskoi are tatowed—The Kuriles, the Alutore, & the Nova Zemblans are also tatowed The Mohegan Tribe in America are tatowed.

I find as yet nothing analogous to the American Calumut except that the Tartars here when they smoke the Pipe give it all round to every one in the Company. The form of the Pipe here is universally the identical form of the Chinese Pipe. I expect to find it the same in America since the Pipe they have on the Tomohawk resembles it. This form intimates Economy & that the original Custom of smoaking the Pipe was a mere Luxury: it holds but a very little. The manner in which the Chinese & the Tartars here use it corresponds with that Idea. They make but one or two draughts from the pipe & these they swallow or discharge thro' the Nose & then put the Pipe by. They say that the Smoke thus taken exhilarates.

I observe that among all nations the Women ornament themselves more than the men: I observe too that the Woman wherever found is the same kind, civil, obliging, humane, tender, being; that she is ever inclined to be gay & cheerful; timorous & modest; that she does not hesitate like Man to do a generous action of any kind. (And yet nature has bestowed more beauty on the Male of every Species of Animal)—The Woman is never haughty, arrogant or supercilious; full of courtesy & fond of Society; economical, ingenious; more liable, in general, to err than man, & in general have more virtue & perform more good actions than him: they have not so great a variety of character as Man & few are above or below this Description. I do not think the Character of Woman so well ascertained in that Society which is highly civilized & polished as in the obscure & plain walks of Life; it assumes an importance here unknown to higher Life.

My general Remark is that Climate & Education makes a greater difference in the Character of Men than Women. That I never addressed myself in the Language of Decency & Friendship to a Woman whether civilized or savage without receiving a decent & friendly answer—even in english Billingsgate.[16] With Man it has often been otherwise.

In wandering over the barren plains of inhospitable Denmark; thro'
honest Sweden & frozen Lapland; rude & churlish Finland, unprincipled
Russia & with the Wandering Tartar, If hungry, dry cold, wet, or sick Woman
has ever been friendly to me and uniformly so. and to add to this Virtue so
worthy the appellation of Benevolence; those actions have been performed
with so free & kind a manner that if I was dry I drank the sweetest draught
& if hungry eat the coarse Morsel with double Goût. Those who have been
used to contemplate the female character only in Societies highly civilized
and polished may think differently from me but having viewed in almost
every parcel of the Globe, in the uttermost obscurity in unadorned Simplicity
where nature only dictates, and where her page is clear and legible they would
agree with me that with less variety of character than man the number is
not great that is above or below this discription.

Every body at Yakutsk has two sorts of Windows; the one for Summer
the other for Winter. Those for Winter are of many different forms and materials—those made of the outside skin of the paunch of the beef are the best,
but none of them keep out the Frost. This however is of no consequence
with respect to the warmth of the Room. The inconvenience is that they
are so covered with Frost on the inside that they are not transparent & consequently so far useless. A large Glass Window is covered with 1 ½ & 2
Inches of Frost, so that it is but a little more luminous than an Ice Window,
but you can see nothing without not even the body of the Sun at Noon. The
most common is Ice in winter and talc in summer: these afford a gloomy
kind of light within which serves for ordinary purposes.

The Asiatic like the American Tartars never change their Dress. They
are the same on all occasions, in the field, in the house, on a Visit, at the most
dirty work, on a holyday, It is all the same they have never but one Dress,
& that is as fine as they can make it.

Those Tartars that live with the Russians in their villages are seldom above
mediocrity as to Riches, and discover the same indifference about accum-
mulating more & for the concerns of to morrow that an American Indian doth.
They stroll about the Village, & if they can, get drunk, smoak their Pipe or go
to sleep. The Gardens of the Russians are cultivated more or less, but theirs lie
unmolested. The House of the Russian is a scene of rural occupations filled
with Furniture, Women Children, Provisions, dirt & noise: That of the Tartars
is as silent & as clean as a Mosque. If the Season admits they are all abroad except
an old Woman or Man. Very little Furniture & that rolled up and bound in
parcels in a corner of the house, & no appearance of Provisions; If it happens

that the[y] profess the Russ religion they treat it with the same indifference, not thinkingly but because they do not think at all about it.

I have not as yet taken any Vocabularies of the Tartarian Languages & if I take any they will be very short ones. Vocabularies are very delicate things when taken by a perfect stranger. they constitute a part of the history of the people & men of scientific Curiosity make use of them in investigating questions in philosophy as well as History, & I think too often with too much confidence since nothing of the kind is more difficult than to take a Vocabulary that shall answer such a purpose. The difference in the orthography of the Languages of Europe is an insurmountable difficulty. The different manner in which two persons of the same language would write a Vocabulary of a new Language would make the Vocabularies thus wrote different the one from the other, so that a Stranger to either of the languages might suppose them to be two different Languages.

Most uncultivated Languages are more difficult to orthographize than the cultivated. They are generally guttural but when not so the inflection of the voice in either case cannot soon enough accommodate itself to the modified Ear of the European to catch the true sound. That must be done in a moment which among ourselves we are not able to do in several years. I catch the accidental moment when I observe a Savage inclined to give me the names of things. I write & he speaks until we both understand that he speaks what I write, & that I write what he speaks. The medium of this conversation are only signs.

The Savage would wish to say head to me & lays his hand on the top of his head; I am not certain whether he says—the head, my head, the top of the head or perhaps the hair of the head—he may also wish to say leg and put his hand to the Calf I am not certain that he means the leg or the calf or flesh.

There are other difficulties—The Island of Oonalashka is on the coast of N. America opposite Asia; there are a few Russian Traders on it; I was there with Captain Cook. I was walking one day on Shore with a Native who spoke the Russ Language. I did not know it. I was writing the names of several things. I pointed to the Ship supposing he would understand that I wanted the name of it: he answered me with the Words Ya Snaiu which in Russ is I know I wrote a Ship. I gave him some snuff which he took & held out his hand to me for more making use of the Word Malinko which signifies in Russ little, I wrote more.

I think therefore that to judge the analogy of Languages it is best to form an opinion from the tone & inflexion of the voice, from sound only

& to give an opinion accordingly without risking a thousand dangers & difficulties that attend the reduction of it to orthography. I think it better for many reasons. It is the surest way because the sound does not vary like the Orthography. Sound was before Orthography: that is nature, the other art. Two persons of different Languages would think more in unison of a third from the *Sound* of it than its *orthography*. There is always more difference in the Sound or pronunciation of different Languages than their Orthography. Living Languages in general are first learnt from their Sound, & are always better spoken when thus learnt than otherwise. The Chinese Language can be learnt much easier from its sound than from its own orthography. Europeans cannot reduce it to their orthography. The sound of any Language is more characteristic of it than it[s] orthography.

Captain Billing's Command from the River Kovyma arrived here the beginning of this month (Novr 1787) & I went to live with him a few days after at his Lodgings as one of his Family & his Friend.

Captain Billings Mistress ill, partly occasioned by a bad air that the Peet gives when the top of it is too soon shut down; it gives violent Head aches & Vomitings. This is the case also when a house is newly heated & inhabited. She has also an illness about the Navel. This I am informed by Captain Billings is frequent among Women in this Country, & he supposes proceeds from some imperfect conduct of the Midwife at the time of Delivery—*NB.* The Husband delivers the Wife.

The action of Theft arises from Want either real or imaginary. In savage Society there are no imaginary Wants & I cannot say indeed if there be any real wants unless they affect the whole community & in that case there can be no theft for a Community cannot steal from itself. If in such a Society there are any real wants which affect individuals they must be *few & temporary* & that lessens the inducement to steal; but if I consider the principles of hospitality that so generally prevails in such Societies I cannot suppose that there is ever room for want; besides no persons would be at the Trouble to steal if they could have their wants relieved without that trouble. In Savage Societies *theft* when known is not considered a Crime. Want is not considered a Crime. the manner of Life they lead subjects the Community as well as Individuals to temporary wants, but it is only temporary, if it was otherwise the Savage would be more anxious about the approaching inconvenience than he is & he cannot be less so & is almost as indifferent about every other future event.—

Captain Billings has a drawing of this which he showed me; it was taken among the Ukagere Tartars. In a few words it is thus.—The Woman when supposed near the Moment of Delivery is alone except the Husband & one more Woman. a Place like a Gallows is erected in the Room as high as the Breast. The Woman leans herself forward upon it pressingly below her Breasts. The Husband stands behind her & applies his two hands to her Belly pressing the Feetus downward. The Wife stands strideling & before her sits the other Woman with a Skin in her hand waiting the appearance of the Feetus. In the room is hung up near at hand a Bow for the Boy if it prove to be such, & for the Girl a piece of Embroidery.

Novr 24 1787} The arrival of Captain Billings at Yakutsk is a circumstance that gives a turn to my affairs. I have before had no occasion to write Journialment.[17] I now commence.

Captain Billings is last from the Kovyma River where he has some small Cutter built vessels in which he last Summer made an attempt to pass the Shalatskoi Noss. The Event of this Undertaking & other circumstances relative to the Tour both by Land & Water I am yet uninformed of, perhaps some accounts will be kept secret from me, but as others will naturally transpire in the course of my acquaintance with him I shall write them as they occur. Went out in the Evening to a Birth Day Feast which the Russians in these parts commemorate with the utmost extravagance & debauch. At all these places there is a melange of Character I have seen in no other Society, but this peculiar difference that there is no particle of honesty or honour in the mixture.

Thermom: 34

Novr 25} More of the Command arrived belonging to Captain Billings. we have lately had a Church burned to the Ground in this Town. The time was very favourable or the fire would have burnt the whole quarter where it stood. The Images form almost the whole decoration of the Russian Churches & those melted on this occasion are estimated to have been worth at least 30,000 Roubles. Superstition how long wilt thou continue to debase & to curse my Brethren & my Sisters.

Clean Mercury exposed to the air is now constantly frozen.[18] Captain B—has not yet made any experiments on the Coldness of the Air but judges it to be 38 Degrees.

Pennant in his Introduction to his Natural History makes mention of a Disease he calls the *Black Death* which he says once spread itself all over this Country among others.[19] Captain Billings informs me of a horrid disease at this day among the Tartars N.E. of this Place, that well deserves that name. he says it is a kind of Rotteness of If I may so say a Mortification of the whole Frame. The Flesh putrifies & falls off from the Bones &c. I have not as yet had a particular Description of it, if I get one will insert it. He once ordered a Physician to endeavour to cure one of the Tartars thus afflicted. The Physician began a Salivation: The Tartar from the operation of the Mercury supposed the Remedy worse than the Disease & run away in that condition without affording the Physician an Opportunity of continuing his Experiment.

Novr 29} The Witch of Injeginsk is a tale yet untold & for which I leave a Blank

I find that Mr Pennant does not take notice of the Rocks in his description of Coasts—They are a naked, detached, high, craggy rock & situated inland, in the form of Towers, Pyramids &c The most remarkable I ever say [sic] or heard of are on the banks of the Lena

The Asiatic Tartars have different methods of hunting the Moose & such kind of Game, but the most prevalent is that used by the Americans in forming an Ambuscade. They even hunt Ducks in that manner at the mouth of the River Kovyma. The Otaheitans catch Fish sometimes in the same Manner. It is simple, universal & antient. The uncivilized part of Mankind war against each other in the same way.

Question—Is the Light-coloured or the dark-coloured Eye the most predominant among white coloured people? It strikes me that in drawing the line between the Fair, the brown, & the black of the human species that this Feature considered would be of particular Service.

No Sea Otter Skins have ever been seen in either Hudsons or Baffins Bay, or any of the Eastern Coasts of America. How far is this a proof that no Commercial Intercourse has ever subsisted (tho' supposed by Captain Cook) either with the Hudsons Bay Company or Indians or with the eastern Indians of America. Does not this Circumstance tend to invalidate the Authenticity of several pretended Voyages & Discoveries on the N.W. Coast of America? Why should Captain Cook & the Russian Voyagers be the only ones who found them; others have not even made mention of them, & yet they are not only very plenty with the Natives, but we with Captain Cook also saw them frequently in the Waters of the Coast alive.—

I understand from Captain Billings Journal that the universal Method among the Tartars N.E. of this, in the Ceremony of Marriage, is for the Man to purchase the Woman that he demands in Marriage or make presents to her Parents which I consider as the same thing. It is also customary for the young Man, the Groom, to come & serve a stipulated time with the Parents of the Bride. In case of disunion afterwards which is done without passion, the presents made are returned. In case of death either party marries as soon as convenient & the sooner the better they say because the Loss ought not to be lamented if it can be repaired. This sentiment is peculiar to the Tartar both here & in America (& so indeed are the above mentioned Ceremonies) & demands Reflection. I suppose myself that Love in this case is infinitely below that which existed in the Bosoms of Eloisa & Abelard;[20] & I suppose the Philosophy as infinitely superior to that which Eloisa & Abelard discovered, as the Love is below it.—Speak of a medium between the two—if they are extremes—I confess I cannot oppose the Tartar Sentiment at all, if I make my appeal to Reason; its Logick alone is invulnerable. If I appeal to my passions I should love like Abelard. The Feast on the occasion like all the Feasts among the Children of Men is a Sacrifice to the Passions, which among all Savages is carried to a greater degree of Extravagance than elsewhere. In the number of the lesser Ceremonies which form parts of the Ceremony I find nothing that appears remarkable indistinct from being the Customs of a strange People. Formality I have already observed takes place in every transaction in Life among every savage people & is more or less minute & complicated in proportion to their incivilization; there are therefore numberless Ceremonies on this occasion. The best that can be said of them is that they are succedaneous to pleasure which among these people have too little of intrinsic Virtue to exist with them & that they are therefore justifiable in making use of them by our own mode of thinking They reflect no analogical Light on any historical or any other Subject that I recollect.—Religion forms a part of the Ceremony—A Priest with a Male attendant is present. They are exactly like those described by the unfortunate Carver in the interior parts of N America indeed like most or all other priests from him who taught the Magic Art in Egypt to the one I speak of, the most accomplished Jugglers.[21] Captain Billings who was, with all his Officers, present on this occasion, & who had read Carver told me he had from a [sic] determined if possible not to be deceived like Carver in the Story of the Bean flung into an Indians Mouth, placed himself & his Officer in such a manner as could best detect any of the Arts of the Priest on this Occasion; but the Priest deceived them all. The Circumstance in which he thus triumphed was plunging a Knife into his Bosom & vomiting Blood: I cannot dwell in detail on such a Subject. It answers my purpose as it did the Priests—that *every body present were deceived.* The Priest gives his *Benediction*

& receives his Reward. It is remarkable that he was the *first* served & the *best* served on every occasion.

I remark that all the Tartars like the Americans coincide in this Sentiment of Religion *viz* "that there [is] a great God, & that he is so good as that they have no occasion to address him for the bestowment of any Favours, & that being they good he will not do them any injury. But as they say they certainly meet with Calamities, so they say there is another God the source of evil and that he must be a God distinct from the other; that he must be very powerful because they have many Calamities; to this Deity they therefore sacrifice; not affirmatively to bestow good, but negatively not to do harm." Their Priests (Shamants) have therefore nothing to do with the good God: their Business is solely with the other whom they divid[e] into a plurality of Character having a Subordinate evil Spirit presiding over each Evil; this affords the *Shamant* an opportunity of playing the Devil in the extraordinary manner they do, with the same success that the introduction of *Saints & Images & Angels* have afforded to Priests of ——I leave this Blank for him to fill up that can do it without blushing: & the following vacant Page I leave a blank for the animadversions of an honest Man on the religious Sentiment above-mentioned informing such at the same time that the sentiment affects immediately all the Religions of Savage America & savage Asia, & col-laterally that of every untutored human being.

The more I reflect on the Circumstance the more it appears to demand Reflection & of course attention, even to others. I declare frankly that appearances have alone given birth to the Sentiment. I have already made some observations with regard to the difference of Colour in the human Species. The Result is that I think this difference is the mere effect of nat-ural Causes, & of the most [powerful] of these, that of Generation.

But my other Sentiment is that which respects the still more remark-able Circumstance in the Human Species, viz, the Anatomy of the Face?—I have not time nor even abilities to amplify. I humbly ask. To what a degree can exterior objects operate on the Feetus or any other Circumstance? Mr John Hunter has made or is making some Anatomical Strictures on the Head of a Negro which it is said exteriorly at least resembles that of a *Monkey*. If I could, I would send him the Head of a Tartar who lives by the Chace and is constantly in the Society of Animals who have high Cheek Bones; & perhaps in his Strictures on this he would also find an Anatomical likeness to the Fox, the Wolf, the Dog, the Bear &c.

I began a Thermometrical Diary at Yakutsk & continued untill the latter end of November. I had a Mercurial Thermometer, & found according to the observations made by others that the Mercury froze at 32 ½ degrees below o by Reaumur. Captain Billings has also found the same in his N. East expedition—He has there had frequently 42 ½ Degrees by a Spirit Thermometer the coldest 43¾ [22]—Strong French Brandy in well corked Phials thickened like coagulated Blood but did not become hard. We have here no Spirit Thermometers. Two ounces of pure Quicksilver freezes here every Day in December quite hard so as to be cut with a Knife like lead. This quantity has froze by a Watch here in fifteen Minutes. Good French Brandy exposed openly coagulates; I suppose therefore that at Yakutsk we have 40 Degrees of Cold. These severe Frosts are uniformly attended by a thick Mist over the surface of the Earth about the height of a common Fog & almost of an equal Density with the thickest Fogs. It is dangerous to be much abroad at such times on account of the quick & subtle operation of the Frost The Houses & Rivers keep a continual Cracking & all Nature groans beneath its Rigour.

Mr Pennant observes that the Scythians scalped their Enemies.

Pray is there not an analogy between the custom of scalping & that of taking the Foreskins of the Enemy as among the Philistines.[23] I have ever thought since my Voyage with Captain Cook that the same Custom under different Forms existed throughout the Islands in the Pacific Ocean. It is worthy remark that though the Indians at Owhyhee brought a part of Captain Cook's head, yet they had cut off all the Hair, which they did not return to us. I have also frequently observed the Islanders to wear great quantities of false Human Hair. All savage Nations however have ever been fond of preserving some badge or testimony of their Victory over their Enemies of *this kind*. In the time of Sampson, *Foreskins* were in Repute. Whether this means the *Prepuce* or the skin of the *Forehead* I know not.

Among the antient Scythians the *Scalp*, & so among the Aborigines of America. Among the Islanders in the Pacific Ocean Teeth & Hair are in Repute—They have all given the Preference to some part of the head—except the Izraelites

✦

To Peter Simon Pallas
18 October 1787; Yakutsk

Yakutsk October 18th 1787
My dear friend
    I have the misfortune to be obliged to winter at this place having arrived too late in the season to pass to Ohotzk: my heart is quite dejected: there are a thousand lessons why it should be so: the consolations it requires are when I am among a people that have pretensions to sociality are of the nicest kind—my mind is equaly an epicure, & when I am among those who ought to be good nothing will satisfy it but the feast of reason & the flow of soul, but it has still more reason to complain than my heart: it affords me however some relief to my misery that I can write to you & that I can complain to you of my misfortunes because you can judge of them & still more have so good a heart that you can feel for me. I have already wrote you from Irkutsk of the civilities I need from Mr. Karamyschev but said nothing in particular of those I need from y'r governor general: those I suppose were principals given in consequence of the letters from my generous Doctr Reiniggs. I know not how Reiniggs procured them, but they were from some source that has procured me more services from Mr. Jacobi than I had any idea of receiving and I wish as do honour to him & to me. I shall remember them. I am also somewhat compensated for my unfortunate detention here, by being among two great tartar nations the Yakutee & Tongyese—& I wish all here were Tonguse or Yakutee—I shall be able to examine their manners at leisure, & it is well I have leisure to do it: I might as well look for figgs & grapes here as information. I expect that this will be delivered to you by a Captain Espravrek—who has been some time in this country & now retires from service: his phisiognomy will tell you that he is a good thinking creature: I know no more of him: but he is so kind as to promise to take this letter & the packet that accompanies it to you: it will be some time before he sees you but the opportunity was so direct & apparently so safe yet I could not but embrace it & particularly my dear dear Pallas when it was to you that I should write: you do not know how much I love you: your friendship to me had not half its relish with me at Petersbourg: a deprivation of it has brot me to my senses, and the farther I go from you the more I love you: this is a kind of paradox, but it is a truth & I think a very curious one in the human character: it is a weakness too in theory, but I never heard of any one any more able than myself by prac-

tice to overcome it & love at all times with equal ardour: pray tell Madam Pallas yt my love for her increases in the same proportion: you may think if you please that the *passion* I had for my charming little blue eyed german lass is no more, but you will be decieved—it keeps pace with my other passions: kiss her for me you or doctor Reiniggs: I wish I could die to night at her feet, or higher up—kiss her for me & assure her of my esteem. I sent you from Irkutsk a terrible budget & almost as bad a one now I send you

I am already bankrupt to you, but what can one do when one has debts of honour to pay among the Antipodes—or the Antoeci at least: I most humbly beseech you once more to take charge of my letters pray deliver those like my others to Mr. Browne & give yourself no farther trouble about them[24] I also sent two little letters of friendships to the American Ambassador at Paris & to my old acquaintance the Marquis de la Fayette which if you can, send by the courier de Mons. le counte de Segur with my best compliments to his excellency on the occasion or to the secretary if he is absent: if you cannot set them lay in your window untill some private conveyance offers

I hear no where of any news from Mr. Billings. Young Bheering of his party is here & seems very contented: the manes of his intrepid & enterprizing grandfather will I believe not be a very strong inducement to call him far thro stward: I know not why he is here[25]

I cannot ask you to write me here: but I hope to find a tiny morsel of something from you to comfort me at Ohotzk where I hope to be next May. Remember me to all those you think would wish to hear from me: I shall always remember any instance of politeness that I have received at Petersbourg: it is one source of happiness to me to reflect on past actions of friendships & politeness; both philosophy & my native temper have made me gratefull, & all mankind would oblige me if they could have as much pleasure in doing it as I should have in acknowledging it: you will see doctr Suthere: he is a cunning artfull man but a very good one & his lady has the same character: they will both be as glad to recive my friendly compliments as I am to give them: I give the right hand with all my heart to the candid & friendly doctor Rogers: if it is 24 times in a day that you see Mr. Lleyscheff remember me to him: certainly his politeness & civility do honour to his country. Sr since writing the above I have concluded. as it would save you trouble to desire the Captain to deliver my other letters to Browne & Porter himself, which he will do. I must also inform you that the Bearer (the Captain) is well acquainted with this country & therefore beg liberty to introduce him to your conversation supposing that from the plain matter of fact he is acquainted with you may possibly & very probably meet with some information that may please you. He has been several years in Siberia: has made his fortune & comes to live in Petersbourg. We have a remarkable fine season here To day is the coldest day we have had & Reaumers Thermometer has only 13¾ degrees of cold: the Commandant tells me that last winter they had 42 degrees of cold.

Ledyard

✳

To William Smith
22 October 1787; Yakutsk

Yakutsk October 22 1787
Sir
I left letter for you last july at Barnowl in the Province of Kolyvan in the care of Dr Brown with whom I traveled as far as there: at Irkuts[k] in August I again wrote you & sent you a little present; these Letters were left with the Chevalier Karamyschev of that City: those & these Letters go under cover to doctor Pallas at Petersburg who delivers them in a packet directed to Browne & Porter. You will now find me situated on the Banks of the great river Lena in Latd 62°: 30" Longd 145° east from Ferro. After leaving Irkutsk I rode 200 versts by land & embarked on board a small batteaux on the Lena near its source at the village of Katchuga which is 2266 versts from Yakutsk. I was 22 days on the voyage & arived here on the 18th of Septr—when I left Irkutsk (the 25th of August) the environs of wc produce good crops of corn, it was just harvest time & the reapers were in the fields & when I arived here the boys were whip[p]ing their tops on the ice & there was about 6 inches of snow & a good path so yt for the sake of riding on a sledge on the 18th of Septr, I disembarked from my boat 2 miles above the town & came by land, leaving the batteaux with the Soldier ye Viceroy sent to conduct me to bring here to town. the sledge was drawn by an Ox & a Yakootee Indian on his back: the Ox was guided by a cord fastened to the cartalige of the nose wc is perforated for the purpose. I waited on the Commandt of the town with my Letters from General Jacobi the Viceroy at Irkutsk & dined with him: he said he had orders from the Viceroy to

shew me all possible kindness & service; and Sr continued he the first service I am bound to render you is to beseech you not to attempt to reach
Ohotzk this winter: he spoke to me in french. I almost rudely insisted on
being permitted to depart immediately & was surprized that a Yakutee
Indian & a tartar horse should be thot incapable to follow a Man educated
in the Latd of 40:[26] he declared upon his honour that the journey was
impracticable; & the contest lasted 2 or 3 days, in wc interval I was (being
still fixed in my opinion) preparing for the journey by taking some rest after
a *very* fatiging passage on the Lena in w'c I took the severest cold I ever had.
The Commandant at length waited on me & brot with him a Trader (a very
good respectable looking Man of 50) who had for 9 or 12 years uniformly
passed from & to Ohotzk here as a witness of the truth & propriety of his
advice to me: I was obliged however severely I lamented the misfortune to
surrender to two such advocates for my happiness: the Trader held out to
me all the horrors of the winter here & of the severity of y'e journey in the
best season, & ye Commandt the goodness of his house & the society
here all of which would be at my service.

The difficulty of the journey I was aware of: when I consented to the
impracticability of it, it was a compliment for I do not believe it so to a
European & hardly any thing else—it is certainly bad in theory to suppose
that the seasons can triumph over the efforts of an honest man.

The proffered hospitality of the Commandant I had a good opinion
of because in Russia in general & particularly in Siberia it is the fashion
to be hospitable: it is brobable [sic] also that it is a natural principle. I should
however have said less to them about the matter if I had not been naked
for want of cloaths & with only a guinea & ¼ in my purse—& in a place
where every necessary of life is dearer than in Europe & clothing of any
kind still dearer by the same comparison: and besides the people here of
all descriptions as far as they are able live in all the excess of asiatic luxury joined also with such european excesses as have migrated hither: add
to all this that they are universaly & extremely ignorant & averse to every
species of sentimental enjoyment, & I will declare that I never was so totaly
at loss how to accommodate myself to my situation. The only consolation
I have of the argumentative kind is to reflect that him who travels for information must be supposed to want it, & tho a little enigmatical it is I think
equaly true that to be traveling is to be in error: that this must more or less
necessarily anticede the other, and that an error in judgement only, is
always to be forgiven. I shall be able by being here 8 months to make my

observations much more extensive with respect to the Country & its inhabitants than if I had passed immediately thro it & that also is a satisfaction. I have already made myself tolerably acquainted with that of the Buretti, Bratskoi, Calmuc or Mongul tartars who are & have been since the time of Zingis-Chan the most warlike & most numerous of any no[r]thern tartars: those in the province of Irkutsk that pay tribute (Men only) am't to 49764 & 5000 horsemen who pay no tax. I am now among the Yakutee & Tonguse nations, the next most considerable Tribes: the Yakutee am't to 42956, & the Tonguse to 13264: these were driven hither from the fronteirs of China by the Calmucs & have more of the Chinese manners, particularly the Yakutee than any other tribe. The tout en semble is a feast to me at all times. I cannot say that my voyage on the Lena has furnished me with any thing new—& yet no traveller ever passed by scenes that more constantly engage the heart & the imagination & yet I suppose yt no two disinterested philosophers would think alike about them: two painters & two poets would be much more likely to act in unison. There are however some circumstances that are not unworthy of philosophical enquiry & when I am by the side of a philosopher I will talk with him about it: the River Lena at Katchuga is forty yards wide: here it is 5 english miles over but not so wide by 2 miles above & I believe not below Yakutsk: it is but very ind[i]fferent for navigation from here towards Irkutsk. There is in some mountains near the Lena large salt mines that constantly afford a supply to all the adjacent country: it is a pure solid transparent mineral salt found in veins: the peicies that I have seen here with the Commandant are 6 & 9 inches square: when pulverized for the table it is much the most delicate salt I ever saw: of a perfict white: & an agreeable taste: but I imagine not so strong by ⅓ as our West Indian salt. there are also upon the banks of this river & indeed all over this country great quantities of elephant bones: there are here with the Commandant some teeth of yt animal larger than any that I saw in the royal Museum at Petersburg & are as sound as they ever were—The Comd't has the hafts of knives, spoons & a variety of other things made from them & they equal any ivory I ever saw from Africa: if I can I will send you a specimen of this fine bone, & the salt also. Indeed I want to send you many things: but it is an embarrassing circumstance when one has correspondents among the antipodes, & tho no man could shew more kindness or render more service to a traveller than doctor Pallas has to me yet I am reserved in asking them upon all occasions. poor Brown & Porter too: I wonder their patience is

him a long letter with some circumstances in it that I wish you to know also & have not time to recapitulate I have begged of him to grant you the perusal of this, if you please. You will also receive by this conveyance letters from Capt Billings with a collection of subjects in natural history both for yourself & for the college: but the best collection he has is unfortunately at Ochotsk which you cannot receive he tells me untill next winter & you cannot regret the circumstance more than he does: he also send Madame Pallas some beautiful sables for a cloak, & I am jealous on the occasion because I cannot on my part send an equal number, & what is worse I am so devlish poor that I cannot send one: I am afraid that this present will make her love him more than she will me which I will not suffer: I am willing she should love us both alike, because we both love her alike, & you also, & that is exactly like Brother & Sister. Capt Billings is from the Kovyma pray my dear Pallas how far can one go in professions of friendship & esteem? you will understand what I mean by the question: I want to tell you the real truth: but I am afraid you would think of me as Besborodka would of a bow from a new fledged lieutenant. I bow most humbly to the superiority of your genius: it is your heart only that I count an acquaintance with & therefore cannot bow to it: I am charmed with that because I am able to judge of it, & want to join mine with it because I think they were both formed for generous purposes. Moloffsky has sailed. I have some reason to suppose that my friend Doctor Reineggs is with him: but if he is still with you, I beg of you to say everything to him in my behalf towards thanking him for his civilities to me that you will suppose I should say to him personaly, & as occasion offers I beg to be remembered to those you think would receive my compliments

I have wrote in the letter that accompanies this of sending letters to your care to my correpsondents in England & in France, but I believe not to send them on Account of the War with you & the Turk: the general situation of the politics of Europe when I left it induces me to think that Messieurs Bourbon will side with the Turk, & perhaps John Bull also. Besides the extra trouble it would give you (should this be the case) there is also an extra danger of the miscarriage of the Letters, as I have nothing but letters of friendship to write a neglect of it is of little importance.

I do not know if Capt Billings will write you by this conveyance: if he does not it will be because he wants time to write a very long letter & because a short one would not do

But to make insects birds, fish stones minerals & plant I venture myself in his behalf to present his compliments to you & to your lady.

Whatever advantage or pleasure I may find in the travels or society of Capt Billings; & I promise much of both to myself, yet the Idea does not fully satisfy me: if one could live a hundred years in the full profession of all the powers—a le bonheure—[27]5 or 6 years spent in branching on this previous to my visiting the other continent would not be so much thought of—but the melancholy remorse of 60 or 70, with 36 substracted from it! And then besides these is another continent still less known than America that demands a visit from me—the Gods have a right for ought I know to shorten my life: but not to curtail my fame because they have invited me to Heaven I will not request a letter from you. I demand one; & refuse me if you dare to do it. direct to me to the adress of Capt Billings.

Farewell.
I have the honour to be
Sir your sincere friend
your much obliged
most obedient
& Most humble Servant

Ledyard

Postscript
Irkutsk Jan 2nd 1788
Capt Billings I did not close at Yakutsk the budget for Petersbourg which give me an opportunity of presenting my compliments to you from here. I am very well we came from Yakutsk here in sledges on the Lena: we were 20 days on the journey. I expect that our courier will be ready to set out in 3 or 4 days time. Capt Billings regrets exceedingly that he has not his Ohotsk collection to send by the Conveyance but he will write to you himself. As for my own budget it is like my heart always open to my friends & contains nothing new or extraordinary to the brave & goods

I would write you something of my travels if I could do it with as much prosperity as good will: I cannot. Whatever observations I may make on this continent they will be indigested & imperfect untill joined with those I hope to make on the continent of America. If I ever return by my intended route to London or Paris I hereby authorize you to demand of me any information you please and assure you at the same time that if for want of friendship to me you should neglect to do so I will positively punish you for it by sending it to you myself without your application.

The genius of my enterprize sleeps for the moment—peace be unto it sleeping or waking: it is an innocent spirit. It is also an Amorous one when at ease, & during this recess from the hot pursuits of fame do not be surprized if among other of its lucubrations you find it sporting in the world of love—not algebraicaly, mathematicaly, nor altogether seriously, but some how platonicaly, by accident, from necessity—I know not how—but it is certainly somehow for I feel this moment a kind of soft sentimental pain that I am sure has originated from a pair of blue eyes I saw at your house: indeed why should I hesitate to say I love her & have so often mentioned in my letters to you: I am not content to be always King: if she was here I would resign my scepter to her. speak kind of Anthony ye who have not seen a Cleopatra

it is not a modern observation that there is in madness itself a pleasure that none but madmen can concieve of. who can despize the chains of love but an anchorite. I feel inclined to be a slave to my german lass. To stoop to rise is the title of a comedy the best I ever read: & I am certain that the man who would not clean the shoes of his mistress would never act with ardour in her arms. Adieu! I pray you to love me—if it is ever so little I shall be thankfull—even a grain of regard from so good a heart as yours will comfort me. pray write to me—by heavens I would sooner receive a letter from you than be king of Denmark

present my compliments to Madme Pallas—her cheerfull & open complaisance to me in the happy moments I spent in your house has procured her my esteem and her sensible good wishes for my happiness makes me aspire to be thought her friend—kiss Albertine for me—I salute the little greyhound—the Thibet gods—the chair tables, & the walls of your appartments—for could they speak they would all declare how pleased I have been among mementos of my quondam bonheur farewell—& farewell those the happy lord of all within

Yours forever

Ledyard

★

To Sir Joseph Banks
25 January 1788; Irkutsk

City of Irkutsk in Siberia
January 25 1788
Sir

My movements are such at present that can only just inform you where I am and that I am well: since writing you last which was from this City I have been at Yakutsk: I went on the river Lena & arrived there on the 18th of Septr in 22 days: I arrived unfortunately too late to pass to Ohotsk: about the middle of November Captain Billings arived then with a part of his command from the River Kovyma. He has not been able to pass the Shalatskoi cape and indeed I believe not to pass very far from the Kovyma towards it

It has even appeared to me ridiculous to attempt it after the voyage of Captain Cook. We are very glad to see each other as old acqauintances & he has very generously offered his service to me having time on my hands at Yakutsk I have accompanied him here we came on the Lena in sledges in 20 days: the journey is 2000 versts & upwards. I am very glad to have escaped a part of the winter at Yakutsk: it is extremely cold there. I found a mercurial thero of no use there by the 25th of November. In Decr clean mercury openly exposed was constantly frozen so as to cut like led. french brandy openly exposed coagulated in $\frac{1}{2}$ an hour: an ounce of clean quick silver openly exposed froze hard in 15 minutes, Cap't Billings had no apparatus with him to ascertain specifically the degrees cold: but judged it to be 38 degrees. In his northern voyage the greatest degree of cold in his Thermometrical diary is $43\frac{3}{4}$. The greatest that has been at Irkutsk this season is 31 by Reaumer. I am not certain whether I shall not accompany Capt Billings in a little excursion during remainder of the winter to the lake Baikal & its environs Perhaps to Kiakta & perhaps to Narhotinsk. In May we return again to the Northward on the Lena to Yakutsk & from there to Ohotsk where we shall do well to arrive before another winter. The summer after is a summer I can give you no account of. But I am afraid Capt Billings will not be able to stand to Sea: if not I shall visit the coast of Korea & the Tschutokoi Indians. The next season I shall most certainly be at Nootka sound. Since my being obliged to stay so long on this continent I am sorry for your sake & for the world in general that I have not a naturalist with me: he would be taken good care of & the journey I have taken & shall take would Afford him an ample field for research. I want to send you many things myself: but for want of an intermediate correspondence— the great distance I am from you, & my rascaly poverty I cannot do it: I am dubious of the arrival of my letters even: I am among a bad People: I cannot tell you how bad they are. The attachment I have to the virtues of the western nations prevents my entering liberaly into society here though there is a great deal of it & a great variety: I can form no connections: except the society of my old Shipmate Captain Billings who is very friendly to me. I am as much alone as I should be on one of the Andes.

This letter goes to Petersburg by a courier of Capt Billings who takes a large collection of subjects in naturalist with him to the admiralty College & Mr Pallas: I believe it is a tolerable good one in zoology and mineralogy: there are also some good fossils & petrefaction the collection of fish is very good: the whole is pretty extensive: in the botanical line he has very little done

The internal geography of this part of the empire will be much improved by his expedition: the northern external parts remain as they were except about the mouth of the Kovyma. The coast of Korea is now the only object in geography that can be pursued by him: that is of little service to the geography of the world: to this empire it is of importance now, & hereafter will be more so. There are a regular series of plans already entered upon by this government to colonize that part of the empire & to establish a maritime commerce there & they are now going rapidly into execution.

farewell.

I have the honor to be with esteem
Sr Your must obt & hble servt

Ledyard

★

On February 1, 1788 in Irkutsk imperial guards sent by Empress Catherine II arrested Ledyard and immediately began to escort him west back across Siberia toward the border with Poland. It had taken Ledyard ten weeks to travel from Moscow to Irkutsk on his own; now, with the power of the Empress behind them, the guards spirited Ledyard that distance in 33 days. After an interview with Petr Passek, the governor-general of the Russian border region, in what is today Belarus, Ledyard reached Poland on March 18. A month later, after traveling through Vilna, he arrived at Konigsburg on the Baltic and booked passage back to London.

I dined Yesterday with a Turkish Lady who told me that the Peasantry of Moldavia tatow themselves & that among them it is a mark of Friendship to wear the same Marks

Informed to day by a German Gentleman who commanded a Russian Regiment in the last War that the Janizaries tatow.[28]

Informed also that the Custom of staining the Nails of the Fingers of a Scarlet Colour is common on the Caspian & black Seas.—I saw one instance of it myself near Kazan. This is a Custom among the Cochin Chinese. I saw it at the Island of Perlo Condor myself.

The Custom among the Russians of calling John the Son of John: Alexander the Son of Alexander &c is a Custom as antient as the antient Jews.

The Scripture Phrase at the Death of a Patriarch is, "& he gathered himself up & died"—"& he was gathered to his people".[29] A Corps at Sandwich Islands is always gathered up, & in the form of some Feetuses in the Womb. &c— Abraham was buried in the Cave of Macpelah, the American Indians also bury their Dead in *Caves*. The artful Custom of dreaming among the American Indians when they want to gain any thing corresponds with Jacobs Dream about the speckled Sheep. Sir William Johnson tells a good Story of this Kind[30]—The Americans are much given to pretended Dreams & both Jacob & an Indian of America have had Impudence enough to father such Dreams upon their Gods.

It is very remarkable that both the Asiatic & American Tartars have the same chaste or superstitious notions of Women during the Menstrual Illness that Laban had in omitting to search for his Silver Gods when hid under Rachel who feigned the Menstruals.

Jacobs Servitude for his Wives exactly correspond with the same Custom universal with the Asiatic & American Indians.

The first particoloured Coat mentioned in History was Joseph's.

The Russians use the word *Benanite* by the way of Reprobation. The Child Lot had by his youngest Daughter was called *Benani*.

The story of Cain's murdering Abel is as true as others of the kind— God said he would put a Mark on Cain. What mark could this have been? It must have been something very distinguishable since those whoever it might be (as well me as another) that met with should know him; but where are his Offspring God has marked them in Vain.

The Otaheite word *Tata* or *Taata*, (since at Otaheite they cannot sound the Letter R,) is analogous in Sound & Orthography to the word *Tartar*. The former sginifies Man in the Otaheite language & in the Tartar language the latter is I think expressive of the same Idea.

I wish I could assert upon better authority than my own Suspicions that Wampum works contain Hieroglyphics. The Scoundrel Chevalier Karamyschev of Irkutsk was the first that I have seen who coincided with me in that Idea. I had purposed to have procured Drawings of the Asiatic & American Wampum but I am I know not how a prisoner to her Majesty of Russia. I have seen the Initials of a Tartars name worked among the Wampum on the borders of his Garment. A people so attached to their Ancestors as the Tartars would naturally endeavor to preserve some memorials of them

My anxious hopes are once more blasted, the almost half accomplished wish! What secret machination has there been? What motive could direct to this? But so it suits her royal Majesty of all the Russians and she has nothing but her pleasures to consult she has no nation's Resentment to apprehend, for no State's, no Monarch's Minister am I, but travel under the common flag of humanity. Commissioned by myself to serve the World at large, and so the poor, the unprotected, wanderer must go where sovereign will ordains. If to death why then my Journey is over sooner and rather differently from what I had contemplated. If otherwise why then the Royal Dame has taken me rather much out of my way, but "I may take another route—" The rest of the world lies uninterdicted.

Detained at every Town I pass thro' by one idle Rascal or another, & the Snuff box Serjeant that guards me now more than any other—"take Physic pomp"[31]—loose your Liberty but once for one hour ye who never lost it that ye may feel what I feel. It gives me. Altho' born in the freest Country in the World, Ideas of its exquisite Beauties & of its immortal Nature that I had never before. Methinks every Man who is called to preside officially over the Liberty of a free People should once—it will be enough—actually be deprived *unjustly of his Liberty* that he might be avaricious of it more than of any earthly possessions. I could love a Country & its Inhabitants if it was a Country of Freedom & for no other reason than because it was a Country of Freedom. There are two kinds of People I could anathematize with a better Weapon than St Peters; those who dare deprive others of their Liberty, & those who could suffer others to do it. Methinks if I was a victorious Prince I would never keep any Prisoners if the People I was at War with fought for Liberty.

The Russian Female Head Dress is Asiatic & of the Turban kind. The Russ Dress is all Asiatic: It is long, loose & of the Mantle kind covering almost every part of the body. It is a Dress not originally calculated for the

Latitudes they at present inhabit. Within Doors the Russian is an Asiatic & without an European.

The Words Turk & Tartar might have been of the same origin. The Turk was a Bucarian roving Tartar.

I am now at Kazan. It is 9 Months since I left it, & I am 9 times more fully satisfied than I was before of some circumstances mentioned in my Diary in June last because fond of the Subjects I have been in pursuit of I was jealous that I might have been rash & premature in some of my Opinions, but I certainly have not been & I feel a double satisfaction in saying so because I have ever thought that the first Ideas of things were the best.

One circumstance alluded to in my Diary is the cause of the difference of Colour in the human Species. I must speak decisively of it—I am fully convinced of its being solely the Effect of natural Causes. I have never extended my opinion & do not to the Negroes. I cannot give publicly an opinion of them; but privately I think of them as I do of the other two Classes of Man which I call in the common Language, the *White people* & the *Indians*. There are many excellent reasons that rise collaterally from my present Voyage to induce me to think so but yet I still wish to have better, because I think they exist as well in Africa to render the Negro blacker than the Indian as in Asia to render the Indian darker than the European, or in Europe to render the European fairer than the other two: or in other Words that the principal Causes exist no where locally, but as much in one quarter of the Globe as another.

The other circumstance alluded to is particularly that national or genealogical connexion, that remarkable affinity of person & manners which exists between the Indian on this & on the American Continent. Of this I must speak equally decisive, & I declare without the least hesitation, with the most absolute conviction, that the Indians on the one & on the other continent are the same people as far as I have seen either. It also respects the origin of the great Tartar Nation & their present history considered as a People of this Continent. I at present feel myself justified in supposing that neither their origin nor present extent as a Nation clearly & remarkably distinct from any other has been ascertained or even well thought of. Albugassi who was himself a noble Tartar has said much the most & best of their origin and something of their extent but not half enough particularly of their extent which in fact he did not know.[32] Like a Soldier he has wrote a kind of Muster Roll of his Country men. I do not remember any thing like Philosophic Research or Information in his History, tho' I read him with Avidity not twelve months since. Among the Voyagers in this Country even the most modern, I have instead of more still less Information. A few vocabularies to lead astray those who would wish to find real Information. & a relation of a few Customs without any remarks upon them is the amount of the whole.

I find nothing material said about this great people by any Writer whatever. The late contest about the contiguity of Asia and America has accidentally struck out a few observations remotely consequential & one now & then finds something Philosophically said of them, but very unphilosophically placed, among Quadrupeds, Fish, Fowl, Plants, Minerals & Fossils.—I am sensible that many reasons are assignable for this neglect both among Travellers & Men in general, but not one or all of them together would be sufficient in my opinion to justify the former; with half the Abilities of the least accomplished among them I should blush to be of the number. Steller ought to have been hung and Le Bruyn burned. Such Travellers in Countries of such immense extent and replete with those circumstances that lead boldly into the most remote History of Man & of Nature have only furnished matter to feed the pampered Vanity of Buffon & of airy Hypothesis.[33]

When the History of Asia & I will subjoin America because it is the latter part of the former, is as well known as that of Europe it will be found that those who have written the History of Man have begun at the Wrong End.

March 12} I am on my Road to Poland & 220 Versts from Moscow—Thank Heaven a Petticoat appears! & thank God the Glimmerings of other Features! How nice this Gradation is & yet as plain as the simplest thing in Nature. But Wampum, or if you will, Beads, Fossils, Rings, Fringes, & easter[n] Gewgaws, are as much here as in Siberia. I find on the borders of Poland that they bury like the Tartars near Kazan among a Tuft of Trees. Women are the Harbringers of an alteration in manners in approaching new Countries.

I am at the City of Neeshna, in a vile, dark, dirty, gloomy, damp Room;[34] it is called quarters; but it is a miserable Prison. The Soldiers who guard me are doubly watchful over me when in a Twon tho' at no time properly so thro' their consummate Indolence & Ignorance, for every day I have it in my power to escape them if I chuse it but tho' treated like a felon, I will not appear one by flight. I was very ill Yesterday. I am emaciated. It is more than 20 days since I have eat & in that time have been dragged in some miserable open Kabitka 5,000 Versts. Thus am I treated in all respects (except that I am obliged to support myself with my own Money) like a vile Convict. Was I guilty of any the least thing against the Country or any thing in it, or was there even a Crime alledged against me, I could suffer with some patience or at least resignation; but when I reflect upon my Innocence not only as to any injury, done or thought of not only to this Country, or to any other, or against human Nature itself, I consider Resignation as Cowardice, nor will I set the base Example, debase my honour, or sin against the Genius of my noble Country. They may do wrong & treat me like a Subject of this Country, but by the Spirits of my great Ancestors, & the ignoble Insult I have already felt they shall not make me one in Reality. It might not make me contented indeed but I suppose it would make me resigned but to be arrested in my Travels at the last stage but one in these dominions where the severe Laws of the Climate and season had unhappily detained me, both of which however I should have braved but for the Restraining courtesy of the Governor [the Commandant]. Seized imprisoned and transported in this dark and silent manner with no cause or accusation but what appears in the mysterious wisdom which is pictured in the face of my Serjeant of course without even a guess at my Destination: treated in short like a Subject of this country. In such a case Resignation would be a crime against the noble Genius of my dear native country.

I had left Moscow in the manner related in some scattered paper in my Port Folio on the 10th of March. It was the time of the equinoxes with them. The Gales were from the East attended with heavy Snow falls three Days. I had them in the Rear as I travelled West. They blew me almost to the City of Polosk which I hoped would have been the End of my unfortunate Voyage as a Prisoner without a Crime—it was not. General Passek to whom I was sent was not there, he was at the City of Mogaloff, 200 Versts (as I imagined) S.E. of Polosk. I could see nor be informed of any thing. The General at Moscow did not know where General Passek was or General Passek was where he ought not to have been. I suspect the former, be it which it will it matters not as to the manner of doing business in this County & the Character of its Officers. The General slumbers on the pillow of Rank & so does the Serjeant; & to know their rank is to know their duty & their Duty their Rank; & ne plus ultra. When the Kabitka stopt in the Street at Polosk I was so weak & ill with fatigue (for the first time of my life) that I fell asleep as I lay, & although carried out of the City to the first post (15 Versts) on the road to Mogaloff over a very bad road I knew nothing of my Fate until I arrived at the Post. When I understood from the Serjeant that I had to go 200 Versts to seek Genl Passek I was frantic; my want of Information left me ignorant of any other Subject to vent my rage against

except the one called Fate which I never could comprehend & could therefore never gain any kind of satisfaction of, but from habit & the custom of
Europe I cursed it wherever it was. I was never before sensible of a weakness of body. I fell down in my rage on the floor & slept until daylight.

Pursued my Journey next day & the following I arrived at Mogaloff.
My reception, detention & departure must be a Subject hereafter.

I left Mogaloff on the 18 of March and arrived at the Barrier Town 90
Versts the same evening—waited in the Street half an hour before called in
to the Majors—from there conducted to the Directors house—alone in an
anti-room there half an hour.—At last the dear moment came that I was conducted over a Bridge across a little River, across the Barrier into the little
Village Tolochin in Poland.35—O Liberty! O Liberty! how sweet are thy
embraces! Having met thee in Poland I shall bless that Country; Indeed I
believe it wants the blessing of every charitable mind. I was conducted for
quarters to the house of a Jew. not being permitted to enter the Dominions
of a people more destitute of principle than themselves they hover about
its boundaries here in great numbers. It was a large dirty house filled with
dirt & noise & children. When my Baggage was brought in, I found I had
been robbed of 5 Roubles that were in a Bag in my Portmanteau. I discovered it to the Russian Lieutenant who instantly set about seeking for it. It
was found in the Boots of the Russian Postillion, & as the Russian Soldier
was guard over me & my Property & was drunk, at the moment (tho' not
before) I suspected him to be an accomplice. I wrote so in my letter to
General Passek. The Russian Officer did me the Satisfaction, without asking or thinking of it myself, to strip & flog the Postillion before me. Thus
was my Voyage in Russia finished as it was begun. I was robbed at Moscow
on my setting out of 50 Roubles, which I lost entirely, & from that time to
this at different times whether in Russia or Siberia I have constantly had
something stolen from me. For the third time only since my confinement
I slept without my Clothes this Night

March 20} This morning I had a hot bath prepared for me. Very dirty,
& fond of the Russian hot Bath it was a great Luxury to me. I was reanimated
after half an hour spent in it.

I received as a present of the Commandant of the Russian Frontier
Village 4 Bottles of a small Wine of some kind, & from the commanding
Officer of the Russ Guard 6 Lemons & some white Bread; which was a
friendly present here, where the bread is very black & coarse, & what is
worse very dear: indeed other things are so also. I had not time to ask the

reason. It is the uncertain boundary of a Queen on the one hand, whose rapacity of Empire is boundless, & on the other by a People who I strongly suspect of all the Vices of Indolence & Vanity. It is besides almost solely inhabited by Jews who are ever nuisances except in places totally Commercial. The Company drank some Wine & smoaked a Pipe with me. The manner of my Deportment toward the Director of the Russian Barrier Village, in my own Empire, as I called it, visibly mortified him, the vain Russian, for his (I will not say his ungenteel but) beastly haughtiness, disdain & impertinence to me the Evening before: but mark the pliability of a genuine Russian—He choaked me with congratulations on my Deliberation from Confinement; bowed, smiled, complimented, lyed, swore & protested with all the ease & grace of his Predecessor Sinon[36]— In the Evening I contracted with a Russian Trader with the Precautions of writing & signing & taking his Passport in my own possession to carry me from this place to Konigsberg in Prussia 600 Versts for 40 Roubles. I received also from General Passek, by express, who had not yet left his generous Solicitude for me, a young Man, as a Servant to interpret for me, & to serve me as long as I pleased having discharged [him] from his own Family expressly for the purpose.

March 21st} In the morning I set out, but still weak & low—we went 50 versts & I stopped in the Evening. I slept in my Kabitka, tho' I wanted much to be in a house that I might undress myself which I find in my weak state is a great refreshment to me, but the Stage houses are not fit for such or hardly any repose.

22d} The Russian Birch Forests have left me. I have at present well grown Pines, Alder, & a few poor Oak Trees. The few Rocks that are scattered above the Snow are Granite. I passed 20 odd round Hillocks 15-to 30 feet high, situated in a Cluster & without Order, between the Skirts of a Wood & the borders of a Rivulet. The Country hitherto is a plain covered with Forests, a few detached houses, & about every 25 or 30 Versts a Town. The Inhabitants are almost [all] Jews, who keep little, very little miserable Shops in them, & they also keep the Stage houses on the Road. The Villages here are as miserable receptacles as the Russian ones on the desart of Barabanskoi. I never saw more poverty nor much more dirt. It is however a proper situation for them; they ought to be placed between the borders of every Nation. I believe it is curious that I am so often exposed to the small Pox without taking it. I was surprized to day as I have been several times before in this Country by being in the same Room where it was in its full force.

23d} We have rain & the roads are gone, we have taken to our wheels. I have been waiting ever since my first arrival at the Frontiers of Poland to be determined if the poor Devils of Peasantry I there meet with were a sample by which I could judge of the whole. The pleasure I have in seeing a good Peasantry is an uniform Ingredient in the pleasures of my Voyage. Besides my Malice against the Empress of Russia & to the wish I had of seeing a good Peasantry here. Without knowing what he was or his people, I became a partizan of the King of Poland, the moment I entered his Dominions. They afforded me Shelter from the persecutions of an unjust & insolent Tyrant. I said to myself in my wrath that supported by such a Peasantry as I supposed the King of Poland had, that I would joyfully fight the best Corps of Beasts the Empress has; but alas with the Peasantry I have Seen I should be content to be King of Poland whatever he is. If their united Efforts will keep me from starving until I can hurry out of the Country I shall be satisfied. They are without exception, not only the poorest Peasantry but the poorest men I ever saw; surely there are better. Those I have seen are wretchedly diminutive and ill formed, ill fed, ill clothed & ill looked. 5 Feet 2, 4, or 5 Inches is the average height of those I have seen; bandy-legged, splay-footed, & knock-kneed; slender built, effeminate Voices, & unanimated Faces. Their Dress is like the Russ except the colour of their Frock which is white. They have the Hair shaved from the head except the Crown. The domestic Animals I have hitherto seen are equally wretched. I wish since there are such Writers in Europe that when they want to expatiate on the history of little men that they would not fly with such malicious illiberality among the Samoiedes & Esquimaux without acknowledging at least one exception to their general System, in their own dear dominions. Reasoning from Theory downward to facts has exceedingly injured truth. Buffon is a well made Athletic Frenchman: how would he look to meet with thousands among the Laplanders Samoiede & Esquimaux that would foil him in any of the manly Exercises, & more I doubt with his Burgundy to boot he should make his appeal to the talents of the mind he would come off, any better. Good Sense is more the result of undisturbed contemplation than of reading, & I leave mankind to draw the comparison between the French and Samoiede in this respect.—I have passed to day above 50 of the same round Hillocks mentioned yesterday only larger these were situated without order in a wood between two little Villages & not more than ¼ of a mile from burying Ground which is like the Mahometan Tartars as I have before observed. These Hillocks must have been the Tumuli of some people. I have remarked also in some parts of Russia. On the road I passed on the Strait Elsineur to Stockholm in Sweden they are very numerous. In some Instances I suppose them to be the remains of deserted Villages as in Russia, tho' there are also some there that are Tumuli in other Instances as in Sweden. I suppose them to be the receptacles of slaughtered Armies. The Grove burying Places have uniformly accompanied me since my arrival on the confines of Poland.

24th March or 4th April N.S.} The Parts of Poland I have hitherto passed constitute a close, thick, wooded Country; little bad Roads & no cultivation except a few small fields round the Houses. I now & then see a Polish Gentleman's House.—Misery!—Oppression how many forms wilt thou assume to lull the wretched to Submission & to harden the hearts of Tyrants! God grant a part of the Christian System at least to be true & that an heareafter shall rectify the absurd Situation in which daring Villainy, & base Temerity have placed my Brethren & my Sisters in this world with respect to each other. I dare not trace this Custom back of one Moses tyrannizing over thousands, for the honour of human Reason I fear it is of very remote Date.

The Insignia of Catholicism are as disgustful here as in Danemarc. A miserable Jesus made with a Hatchet, some old Rags hung round it: the Crucifix yclipt with pincers, a hammer, Nails, spear, a long Pole with a Spunge, & a number of such things carved in Wood & some things that Jew or Gentile never knew. Why is Christ thus rendered the theme of Scandal & Mahomet not—These however are pitiable Weaknesses, but Russian Impudence in professing the Christian Religion & the Worship of a God when they are as arrant Idolaters as history affords—any account of it is still more offensive.

The Jewish Women I observe as I pass along to be very handsome, cheerful, & free, but very filthy.

Having stopped early this Evening, I have an hour of Day light with which I amuse myself in relating my reception with General Passek.

When I arrived at the Generals Door I was in my Kabitka half an hour or more before I was sent for (it was about 4 in the afternoon) I was conducted by an Officer thro' several plain, decent Apartments to his Bed room, & found him sitting in Bed a little indisposed, with a Romish Parson on a Sopha by his Bed conversing with him. The first rencontre of his Eye gave me his Character, & ascertained my Fate.—I am interrupted by the noisy Worship of the Jewish Family where I am. They have lighted their 7 Candles & begun their hymning. They must be obstinate Dogs to repeat with such perseverance a formula that appears to be so very tedious and insipid to them—they yawn, & loll, and stretch themselves, & are very uneasy, but still they will go on. Now I declare that was I to worship as Jew or Gentile, Greek or Barbarian I would worship not, without it was a pleasure to me & no longer than it was a pleasure to me. Thanks be to them they have stopped their Mouths with some Fish Soop—Eat Sons of Jacob & be happy; if I judge right of your appetites by your actions you like eating better than praying; Eat, it is there we all think & act alike.

As a Traveller sees many things, so he thinks of many things & thinks of them in the careless order he sees them. Seeing a Jewess lift up her Eyes in Devotion before the Seven Candlesticks while the others are chanting I am thinking how universally the Element of Fire has constituted a part of the Ceremony of divine Worship. I question if any other Custom will be found so universal. None can be more antient if the Burnt-Offerings of Cain & Abel is the most antient part of human History.

The General received me with a most endearing politeness, begged me to sit by his Side, & asked if I would take some Tea, Coffee, or any other Refreshment. I made choice of some Tea. He addressed me in French & observed to me that the orders of his Sovereign were that I should be conveyed out of the Empire into Poland, & that I was forbid ever to enter it again without permission & that I had hardiment[37] passed thro' it. It was his business to have said how this or something else he had in his Letter must have constituted my Crime—but it seemed by chance that he mentioned the Circumstance of passing *hardiment* thro' Russia. I had motives the most just to demand a full explication of the reasons for the conduct of his Sovereign. If indeed the Empress had treated me with as much politeness as injustice she would have ordered me a copy of a Crime so considerable as to send for me 6000 versts to transport me out of her Dominions & with the insulting Charge never to enter it again without permission.

My Motives were stimulated too by an Indignation I did not hesitate to discover. I told the General that his were the last hands I should pass thro' & if her Majesty had not ordered him to inform me of my Crime she had added an Insult to the rest of her Conduct to me, he said I thought too rigidly of the Affair, & went on to tell me by complimenting his Mistress, as the most wise, amiable, prudent, & humane Sovereign in Europe & concluded for the moment with this most condoling & sensible Remark; that whatever Reasons her Majesty had for her proceedings she had only politely told me that my Visit to her Dominions was disagreeable & desired me to discontinue it. "had I not been waited on to the place of my destination *by a Guard*"? You have not been prisoner; you have not lost your Liberty &c &c. & then begun in Proverbs to tell me "that Sovereigns had long Arms"—I could no more—I rise—Yes by God Mr le General yours are very long Eastward; If your Sovereign should stretch the other Westward she would never bring it back again entire, & I myself would contend to lop it off.

March 25th} I am troubled with Floods, Rivers & bad Roads.

26} I want about 50 Versts or 10 Polish Miles of half my distance to Konigsberg. The Country begins to be more peopled & more cultivated, & the Inhabitants to appear a *little* more personable, but I have not yet seen one Instance of an *approach* to Beauty in either Sex. The Jews form a very curious Contrast with the Poles in this respect, the Women particularly, I have seen but two or three Women that were unhandsome—But they were very much so; The Jewish Women have beautiful Complexions. A fine Skin & as happy a Mixture of Colour as ever I saw; long black Hair which among the Demoiselles hangs down behind in one & sometimes two plaits, the rest is hid, as the Married Women do all theirs under one or more Handkerchiefs. They have large full Jet black Eyes which like all others of that Sort rather surprize than convince me into the Idea of Beauty. They have good Teeth & some very pretty Features. But I am disgusted the Moment I view a horrid clumsy, large coarse dirty Hand; this added to their uniform filth, & now & then the Itch—I know nothing of their shapes; I regret it, but they are disguized under a vile Eastern Dress. The Child of damned Jealousy or damned Superstition called into existence expressly to turn the Eyes of Man from viewing a Work of Nature as expressly formed to attract Attention, Admiration Esteem & Love.—There is a remarkable Gradation in Dress from the East to the West as in other Customs. The tout ensemble leads to a supposition of a very formidable Nature & gives to understand at least that Mankind have long been acquainted together— to say no more about it—There is a *Melange* of Dress here & so of other Customs. The effects of the Geographical situation of its Inhabitants between the Eastern & Western World this is with difficulty described. The Jews are entirely in the Eastern Stile, if I should say *Mosaic* I believe it would be still more proper, & if the antient Izraelites were Slovens as gross as the modern it ought not to prevent my Remark, & I have no doubt they were, for real Cleanliness is ever a Concomitant of real Genius & Science, speaking nationally & almost always so when the observation is applied to Individuals. This leads me to make a bold inference, that the Moderns have more of Genius & Science, than the Antients which I suppose is true. The Poles on the other hand (if I include the Ladies, who I am apt to think are the best judges & examples of Dress & Cleanliness) have more of the European than Asiatic about; but both the Dress & Manners of Europe sit ill upon them. I speak of the Country People of Condition & what they call Nobless, some of whom viz 2 Ladies & 2 Gentlemen are at Dinner at the Table where I am writing. I suppose I do right to take those people & those below them as a standard to judge by, tho' I should be glad to take those of more Fashion, since the Nobless I have seen join another species of Awkwardness to the one already intimated being mere down right Rustics on whom it is probable that the Asiatic Dress would sit as badly. This however little affects the observation when I see huge, coarse Ear-rings, Rings, Bracelets, a dozen strings of coarse Wax Beads of a dull *red*, (the favourite Colour of a rude People) hang about their Necks; Fingers of both hands loaded with coarse Rings, Pieces of Coin or Medals round the Bosom & in short all the Trinkets of one of Solomon's Mistresses.—Indeed there is a rude, unfinished, capricious fantastic Taste that divides both Poland & Russia from the Genius of Europe; & that any one may understand me I will illustrate my observations by remarking that full seven eights of the Merchandize imported (for Russia has hardly any Manufactures except Images in Iron & other Metals, & Poland I believe none at all) into these Countries are of the flimsy, tawdry kind and mostly from France. A Pedlar from thence will make his Fortune in these Countries with his well painted Gewgaws & the refuse of a French Toyship, when an Englishman would starve with an Assortment of the best goods in Europe; & France particularly fits out her Caravans for these parts in the same manner she does her Ships for the Coast of Africa, or the English their's for Hudsons Bay.

27th} Passed many more of those Hillocks.

28} I arrived to day at the City of Vilna, which is the Capital of the province of Lithuania. The first Salutation was by two dirty wretched looking Soldiers from a decayed smoaky log-built Guard house, who wanted to know if I had any Merchandize in my Kabitka—being answered not—they then wanted to know if I had any money to spare. It seems to me that there is a most wretched Discipline in all the parts of the North where I have passed except in Russia In Denmark I have had the Centinels round the Royal Palace as well as elsewhere carry their Arms to me & at the same Moment ask money of me. In Sweden I never had my Trunk examined if I would convey a sixpence or a Shilling into the hands of a Soldier, & here

I have no doubt I could have passed for the same trifle with my Kabitka full of Goods or even with the Grecian Horse.

Vilna begins a new Country; from an unvariegated, miserable, sickly plain my Eye is relieved by Groups of fine romantic Hills & well cultivated Vallies, but it does not compensate for the number of Beggars that surround me. I had one Coup d'Eil[38] at a Group, to day, of Hills that I will visit tomorrow. I am constantly thinking about Hills, or something else of the Kind & as my thoughts are all my own I write what I think without knowing whether it is of Importance or not & leave others to judge of it being convinced only of this that I ought to write if I think so, & that it is better to write many pages in vain than that one of Service to Mankind should not be written.—I make this remark once for all to inform my Friends that I am sensible to my humble Genius but not ashamed of it, & to intimate to them that I wish them to deal with me with the same honest careless freedom I do with them. to be damned is no torment to the Guilty, & to enjoy fame is no happiness to him who is not convinced he merits it

Remark.—I have observed on this as well as all the other Continents I have visited that on approaching the Confines of Land & Sea the surface of the Earth is covered with smooth round Rocks or Stones. The Superficies having apparently been rendered smooth & equal by other causes than mere length of time or its various effects in the situation in which they are & that there is a great Affinity if not a perfect one between Rocks & Stones (thus described) situated at certain Distances on Land from the Sea & those situated at certain Distances in the Sea from the Land: Those on the Land appearing to have had their Superficies formed from the Effects of Water; from the Movement of the Sea; the wash of the Sea; from Currents or Tides.

I do not remember to have observed this on any of the Islands I have visited except new Holland, where however I did not go far enough inland to make the Observation compleat. I must confess that in travelling thro' the interior parts of Countries in a Centrifugal direction, I should as soon recognize them for Marks of an approaching Sea as in coming from Sea towards Land, Sea-Weed for a Land mark & sooner. The observation like most of my others has obtruded itself upon me & has been tormenting me for several Years to take Notice of it; which I confess I do not like & have therefore given it a place here.

Remark—The Beds of large Rivers near their Sources as I view them intimate to me that they have never changed their positions that the Rocks & mountains which confine & direct their Courses now have always done it & that the Chasms in which they run were not caused by the Rivers; the Chasms being Antecedent or at least coeval to them, & that one cause produced the two effects & perhaps at the same time. If Rivers could not form those deep Chasms what could? Why is the peaked, ragged Mountain peculiar to the central parts of Land & why are they Scarrified in the manner they universally are?—The *Flood*.

All Rivers are most rapid at their Source & an Eye accustomed to it will from the rapidity of its Waters & from the elevation of the surrounding Land very nearly Judge his distance from their Source & what sort of Rivers they are Rivers do not meander much near their source; those whose Waters are muddy are very serpentine

Where Rivers begin to wind they begin also to shift their Beds, form & destroy Islands & plains, & conceal & reveal by turns the Fossil World. Nothing is more capricious than their Currents. It requires great Sagacity to trace their deserted Tracks; & a cautious observer often doubts at first view what upon a review he is thoroughly convinced of; their operations are very extensive & in Countries where they are large & numerous they fairly change the Face of Nature. In Siberia I have remarked something like this that I cannot account for—nay more than I have mentioned; for whether they are the cause or not they are certainly the longitudinal boundaries of Climates.—Every River from the Lena to the Wolga is more or less a proof & an example of the last Observation; some of them very positive ones particularly the Yenissy; There even the Vegetable Kingdom is divided & as the Chevalier Karmyschew very pertinently observed to me. There also is the *natural* boundary between Russia & Siberia. The Tomsk is the next instance & after that the Oby: The others are not such Striking Instances but still worthy of remark. I do not for the moment recollect one general & positive Law that those wandering Districts are subject to that however they meander or digress their ultimate courses shall be towards the Poles or if not directly to the Poles, the inclination shall be north & south & vice versa. These are few exceptions to this general Rule & almost all those Rivers which are such, rise under the Equator which I supposed easily accounted for:—I remark also as a Circumstance that appears merely curious to me, that Rivers which have a Northern & Southern course have almost universally the highest Bank on the East Shore, & that those which run E & W have the high bank on the South shore.

As fishing constitutes a part of the Chace a Savage if he has any fixed abode forms it on the banks of Rivers & so will the new settlers of a new Country. Most of the Russian Cities & Capital Towns that lay on the Rout eastward thro' their dominions beginning at Kazan the first after Moscow to Yakutsk the last to the Pacific Ocean, having been first Towns of Tartars are almost all built on the old & present banks of great Rivers. The City of Tobolsk is partly on an old Bed & partly on the high eastern Bank adjoining it at the conjunction of the Irtys & Oby. The Town of Tomsk, exactly like it on an old bed & Eastern Bank of the river Tomsk, in those places the Rivers are very wide. At Yakutsk on the borders of the Lena the River reckoning from an old Bank West to the present high Eastern one has occupied a breadth of 15 English Miles and this one change it is plain to be seen has been formed not by gradual process, but three different Changes somewhat sudden; The Town of Yakutsk being situated on the middle Bed formed by the three Changes & has been built near 200 years. The River here is also full of Islands & appears very wide, therefore thro' its true Channel is but 2 or 2½ English Miles over. This remarkable change in the Lena here is as I have intimated before because it here *winds much* & forms that great & unfortunate turning from N.E. easterly, in which direction it would have joined the Pacific south of the River Anydirskoi to a course NW & N where it looses its useless Stream in an Ocean still more useless than itself.—I must remark however one thing in favour of it, that at its Mouth & the Islands & Sand Banks there formed by the repercuration of an endless variety of tides & currents it affords a rich Endroit to the curious in the fossil Way;[39] after meandering thro' various Countries & Climates with a Depth & Strength of Water sufficient for the purpose, it here leaves a part of whatever it has found in its Way & rolled along with its Stream or forced hither by the Ice; whether Sand, Rocks, Trees, large Mounds of Earth, wrecks of Houses &c.

It is so also with the other Rivers in this Country the same; their united operations in this respect has rendered the confines of the frozen Ocean & the borders of what Naturalists term with the most Philosophic Propriety the Arctic Flats; a repository of Fossils unequalled elsewhere in extent & I doubt not in variety since those Fossils already found by a few very slight visits have given rise to enquiries of the most interesting Nature, Enquiries that Fossils found in Rivers however extensive which roll longitudinally only cannot be supposed to produce, since a difference of Latitude is the greatest cause of a difference of Climate & objects in natural history known, or supposed to be general or peculiar to certain climates, found reposited in Climates different from them, form a Contrast, & this forms Enquiry; & this Enquiry is not about the Epoch of an inglorious Sovereign, nor the change of Empire but the history of Man at large, the Globe itself, & the Ways of God to Man.

It is singular that the Kovima River which is not more than half the Magnitude of the Lena or Yenisey which has its source & which empties itself in Regions still more remote should notwithstanding more abound in Fossils than those two Rivers.

I am much obliged to Captain Billings for this & many other accounts from that quarter, & had not the unprincely Malice of the Empress of Russia impeded my Travels I should have had many more The Circumstance alluded to of the Kovima Fossils affects very much the Argument of a General Deluge in my poor Opinion, I dare not say how much yet; I will however say upon the whole that I am led independent of Opinion & with a very moderate share of self Love to this. Idea viz. "That all parts of the Earth have at some period unknown to me enjoyed the same Climate, that they have consequently [been] accessible to universal and uninterrupted Migration, & that the Fossils found in Climates we now call frigid were natural to them when those Climates were not frigid; & that the reason why we have only fossils to support the Argument is that the Period when this alteration took place is so remote that nothing else remains which has not lost its form in the unfashioned particles of matter & that Substances the least subject to decay are the Fossils we find; I observe it in the parts of Bones we find, the flinty Shin Bone of the Elephant & the Teeth are almost the only parts that are found & many of them almost gone. The Head of a Rhinoceros added to the rich fossil Cabinet of the Empress of Russia by Dr Pallas is the only material exception that I know of, & that is very curious indeed. I could not take my Eyes from it when I saw it; the form is almost minutely entire even to the Skin & the Hair. It is from Siberia the place where it was found, & some Memda respecting it are among my unfortunate papers at Yakutsk neither must I forget to mention several horns in a tolerable state of preservation in Captain Billings [possession] from the Kovyma, but so miserably are we both accoutred in the Knowledge of such things that we could only suppose what Animals they are parts of Viz— the Buffaloe.

They were composed of a Substance black & grey intermixed resembling the colour of Whale Bone & strips of it hanging detached from the Horn, elastic like Whale Bone; the forms of them not particularly different in any respect, as I conceived, from the Horn of an European ox of good size.

It is a pity Men of Science will not or cannot travel themselves & that Fate should so whimsically ordain to sally forth such as I am for example for the purpose of adding to natural Knowledge, & it appears very demonstrable to me that they ought to be hung for staying home as much as I do for going abroad, & that both should be done.

I suppose the history of Fossils to be very interesting; since we find the Subject of it at least in as great abundance in our highest excursions North as in the lower ones South: why not pursue the Enquiry, the research; particularly N.E. from the Ischutskoi Dominions in NE Asia to the contiguous coasts of NW America. Would it not affect the historical Analogy of those remarkable portions of Earth so much the theme of every Species of Philosophy—but the right—(for I feel it in my heart to be impertinent) which is travelling. On whom do I reflect when I say that parts of our Globe altogether accessible to discovery are less known in strict truth than are parts of the Moon since the Optical Improvements of Dr H[unter] & yet we will affect to reason of them in a style of as much familiarity as Hunter with a Skeleton before him.

April 9th} I have been out to see the City of Vilna; it is about ¾ of a Mile in Diameter each Way, situated in a Vale having both within & without a number of round hills; those within have houses on their Tops & those without Castles, now in Ruins. The City has been laid out in the Style Militaire, with its inner & outer Departments—but the whole was dismantled by a Russian Visit—Some of the Houses are very old & one or two Churches, but not a trait in Architecture (in which by accident I have a smattering kind of Knowledge) worth remark. The Style is grecian. It is watered within by a pretty little Stream, is decently built, & for the season of the year & its situation remarkably clean.

I was extremely pleased in my Walk to meet what they call the Directeur of the Town making his rounds personally to superinspect its Affairs. He was on Horseback in a plain Polish Dress & a plain Sabre by his Side & one Horseman in his Suite, he appeared intent upon his Business like a good Officer & a good Citizen. To the expence of Russia & the honour of this Country I declare that a Russian Officer in the same Office (if he went himself) would never have gone on this or any other Duty without his Coach, the exact number of attendents his Rank entitled him to, & then he [would] have drove Phaeton like over every thing he met & returned with the same Information he set out with, but he had been *seen* tho' he saw nothing himself it was enough for a Russian Officer. Vive l'ecclat!

The Jews here have in appearance for I do not think it worth While to ask any questions the sole management of all kinds of Traffick & as there is no kind of Manufacture here as I am accidentally told I leave as a thing disagreable to examine how people support themselves.

What a Pity it is after having seen the Directeur that I have seen three full dressed Polish Ladies—France has marred the Faces of half Mankind & done more mischief with its Rouge than its politics—Their Dress was a bad imitation of the French. With all my eager Glances not one handsome Face have I seen, & but very few well looking Men.—Their Carnival is at hand & I could wish to see it as among their Joan & Darby Nobless one might rencontre at least with something Buxom.[40]

At the town of Yakutsk there are a great number of Russia Merchants or Traders: they are very enterprizing, hardy Men. It is the most remote Russian Town in the North of Siberia & on that Account particularly is the resort as well as residence of those Men from every known Corner of the Country. I was much in their Company. some had been at the mouth of the River Yenesey, others the Lena & others the Kovyma. Among them all there was hardly any place in the North or East where they had not been. They all agreed in the Voluntary accounts they gave me of the great quantities of Drift Wood at the mouths of the Lena & Yenesey. At the Kovyma there is hardly any. their accounts of this matter were that there was almost constantly a thick crowded Mass of Trees floating on the Borders of the Icy Sea & that it extended out for many Versts some said 50 & others more. As an instance of their simplicity for they did not mean it as a compliment, they have often asked me where I thought so much Wood came from since there was none that grew on the Coasts. They also told me that old Russian hunters or Fur Traders for in Siberia those Epithets are indiscriminately used that were then living said that since their Memory the Sea had retired many Versts to the North, in some places 100 Versts, & that those forsaken plains were overspread with old trunk of Trees buried in the sand. A rich, intelligent Merchant there called Popoff & brother to the Popoff mentioned I think in the preface to Dr Pennants Synopsis gave me also the same accounts & added also others the result of his Travels to the Eastward on the American Coast & also among the Kurile Islands on the Coast of Korea & the River

The number & the magnitude of the Rivers in the Russ Dominions which empty themselves into the Icy Sea produce very great changes, & as a change begun by them continually increases until they loose their existence as Rivers in the frozen Ocean so is there the greatest Change because the last.

If I had information sufficiently particular I would dwell on the Subject & go so far as to estimate first of all the quantity of fresh Water they roll into the Mere glaciale, & then the quantity & quality of Earth & vegetable Substances they carry & deposit there. There is but one River in Northern Russia (viz. the Volga which goes into the Caspian) that does not empty itself immediately or collaterally into the Northern Sea, & as most Rivers have Connections with Lakes so have those, & there also of course numbers of Lakes which also pay their Tribute in the same line to the Icy Sea & the princely Baikal among the others. The Column of Water that goes into that Ocean from the Continent by these Conveyances alone would of itself in 12 months form an Ocean equal in solid Contents to the shallow one that at present barely covers the Earth beyond the Latitude of 70 North.—. Also the circumstance of such a quantity of fresh Water in that Ocean I should suppose would merit the attention of the curious since it naturally leads to a reflection on the quantity of Ice there, of its cause, duration, formation, diminution &c Men have supposed that Ocean to be supplied with Ice from those Rivers but if I had not positive proofs to the contrary I confess I should attribute the cause of the quantity of Ice there to the quantity of fresh Water there, which I believe has not been yet thought of except collaterally by Captain Cook whose few observations on the Subject I admire as much as I did his Abilities & good Sense. accustomed to think for himself & rely upon his own Opinion it rendered him equally penetrating, cautious & bold, & without any particular knowledge of the Circumstances I allude to could nevertheless assert that the Waters of that Ocean froze & that it did not receive its Ice from Rivers, & he assigned a very excellent reason for it which is that Ice formed in Rivers floating in that Ocean must necessarily bring along with them Vegetable Substances of some kind. If his Information would have carried him so far as to say that at the Mouths of every great River in Siberia emptying themselves into that Ocean there were Islands, Spits, & Bars of Sand across them that rendered a Communication of Ice to or from the Sea impracticable his Observations would have been perfect. The Mouths of the Kovyma are in 69 & 69.30 N by Captain Billings observation & by his Journal the Ice was 4 & 5 feet thick only. I was induced to think from this Circumstance when first informed of it that it was the effects of a frost for a Season only which made thus thick & no thicker the Ice; but finding on Enquiry both among the Russ & Yakutee that they never saw any Ice thicker (meaning solid transparent Ice) it obliged me to change my Opinion; Join the observations I had made in my own Voyages with theirs & reason about it in the following manner. Having never reflected on the circumstance of Congelation generally & particularly of the thickness of Ice, those observations above alluded to strike me the more forcibly. Born in one of the NW States of America & having also travelled to the NW among our cold Lakes & Rivers in the Winter I do not remember ever to have seen Ice of a greater if so great a solid thickness either on Lakes or Rivers. Northward of the Streights of Bellisle I have seen the high Sea Ice, & so much for America. In Sweden, Lapland, Finland & at Petersburg I never saw any thicker if so thick. Among the Cakes of Ice cut out of the Neva River at Petersburg for the Icehouses I do not think the Ice exceeds this thickness if so thick. At Yakutsk the Ice (for they cannot carry Water) that they bring on their Sledges from the Lena for domestick use in large Casks was not thicker. The Ice Windows there are taken from the Lena & are nothing but clear solid Ice, they are not more than 12 Inches—but then they are cut out in the fore part of Winter. Therefore I do not remember to have seen or heard of any Ice thicker than that at the Kovyma in nearly 70° nor Ice in any other cold Latitude (particularly where the cold approaches towards the fixed degree of Congelation viz. 32½) but what had nearly or for aught I know for certain the same thickness with the Kovyma where by the best observations made by Captain Billings there during a Winters Residence the degrees of Cold were 38°, 40° & so high as 43¾ Degr Except Ocean Ice I have not seen or heard of any but what is about the same thickness in the Countries I have mentioned. Now if the Ice (for Example) on the Neva at Petersburg in 59°½ N is 4 feet thick only & at the Mouths of the Kovyma in 69°½ N. is 5 feet thick only, & if that is the proportional Difference of Cold in 10° difference of Latitude that difference will be an increase of one Inch & the fractions of the two in the thickness of the Ice to each Degree of Latitude. But I can draw new Inferences from this. I pursue the Idea & say that if this proportion does in sort exist that the thickness of the Ice in a River near the Pole would be only 20 Inches thicker, but what can be inferred from this—That Ice in different situations is of different thickness but that the thickness of Ice formed by Congelation *only* in any place whatever is confined to 4, 5 or 6 feet and that all beyond is adventitious accumulation not owing to Frost only, but to Snow Hail, Sleet & far to the Northward heavy mists which fall on it & add rather a coagulated than a frozen conjunctive Mass—It appears to me that an Answer to those Doubts requires rather a comparative Detail of a number of facts to ascertain their Merit or Demerit than a *Coup d'esprit,* or perhaps a Coup d'esprit would destroy them entirely, and let its will be done.

April 10th} To day after Dinner I left Vilna whose Environs on the West Side are very pretty—it is surrounded by the prettiest little Hills & in the prettiest manner I have seen any where I remark some Instance of Country Houses in imitation of the English manner, but I quit it gladly for the Godlike Regions of the West. If I had believed from Information I never could have formed any adequate Idea without the little Tour I have made of the inferiority of the Eastern to the Western World & that so vast a difference could be found in the qualities of the Hearts & even of the Minds of men. If cultivation can produce such effects I see nothing romantic in supposing that the Men of the West may become Angels without Ceremony of dying for it. I have a most horrid post house this Evening, not because it is filled with Smoak, Dirt & noise but a band of Polish peasantry, which word, by the by signifies in every Country that makes use of it entirely to express the lowest order of People *Slaves*, & I cannot bear the sight of one it becomes the occasion of as much uneasiness to me, as Liberty of Happiness. I become interested to think & act for him, & I have not time to do either.

April 11th} Charming Weather for the Season. I cannot find any thing that interests me among the Poles; perhaps it is because I am stupid or inattentive, & I wish as good an apology in their Favour might exist but in my Soul I doubt it. The Jews marry very young here. I saw the Instance to day of a pair the Female 12 & the Male 14 had been two years married from that time and had no Children.

The Custom of the Young Women or Virgins wearing the Hair hanging down & the Married hiding it is very curiously adhered to by the Jews who are tenacious in all their Customs, so that if they had originally been a good People they would now be the best on Earth. The same Custom is also Universal among the Poles, Russians & Tartars. This is another of those Eastern Customs the offspring of Eastern Jealousy. The Moment a Woman is married among them she becomes marked as we do a Horse we have bought. To hide the Hair is to have it cut off & to have cut off the Ears for the same purpose would not have been more ridiculous. Thus has that inoffensive & endearing part of the human Race been ever used by Man; in the early & uncivilized parts of Society. The general observation that Complaisance to that Sex is the truest test of the degrees of civilization is true, but no one thinks it a sentence of Gallantry. There is not a maxim in Rochefaucault nor a Sentiment in Montesque more just.[41]

April 12} I have not before to day approached an open cultivated Country. Roads exceeding bad, only 25 Versts to day.

13th} Roads excessive bad; if all extremes are not incommodious, the extremes in travelling certainly are. I find that 2 or 3 Versts an hour fatigue as mch as flying post 12 or 14. It is however an unfortunate reflection as it respects me for until since my Imprisonment I never knew what this kind of fatigue was & hardly sensible of any other. To day I saw the borders of the Baltic The Jews here have certainly the most of an uniformity of Beauty I have seen. It may be prudently said that they are all handsome. This uniformity only is undoubtedly the consequence of their not commixing with other people; but how they became so uniformly handsome I cannot conceive.—I walked over a burying Ground to day on one of those Hillocks I have so often mentioned. It was an old Burying Ground, remote from a Village, 20 feet high, a grove of trees on it & a great Number of *Graves.* read the 2d book of Kings: Chap: 23—

Mankind have universally agreed in one Sentiment with respect to the dead which is that of tenderness. however agreably this fact may at first strike one, yet examined with Candour it is rather a proof of human Infirmity which in ever Age has been equally exhibited by the Wise & foolish. Ask a Philosopher in Europe if it is a matter of Indifference with him whether he is inhumed after Death & whether so with respect to his best & dearest Friend, It is connected with the Idea of Death itself with many the Ideas are Synonimous. The greatest proof of this Infirmity is ever found like other Infirmities among the least informed of Mankind: If we in Europe doubt this Weakness & particularly of ourselves, let us go where our poor Prejudices will not follow us & appeal to the Customs of the uninstructed Savage we shall there find the Infirmity so great as to produce this most Shameful contradiction, viz "That men take greater care of each other when totally incapable of taking any than when they were capable of doing just the reverse.["] A Misanthropist might very well say that the Circumstance afforded him a proof of consummate Villainy in the Character of Man; I should be fonder of living after Death than an Englishman should I be content to loose one hour of Happiness while living for all that Mankind united could do for me after Death, & think the Man a knave that would excuse himself paying me a Guinea while alive by saying that he would not forget to do it when I was dead; It is like the Conduct of those mighty good & sensible people who are content to see a friend while living appear with a long Beard & a coarse Shirt on, & the moment he is dead send (for the first time) for a Barber & a Ruffle Shirt. Fortunately however our Weakness goes no further.

The Savage is not content with the same Weakness, he carries it much farther: he decorates, inters, & afterwards takes up his dead Friend from the tranquil Couch of Corruption where he lay; carries him however putrified on his back to some place many days Journey distant & reinters him; if occasion afterwards requires it he again repeats the same Ceremony. Dr Bancroft & Mr Carver both give very curious accounts of the matter: the former in Guiana & the latter among the interior Indians of the Northern Parts of America.[42] I have yet never seen anything of the kind so extraordinary. However irrational this Conduct it has been productive of Events as remarkable & interesting as the most rational in the history of Man. He who has seen an Egyptian Pyramid has seen a Monument of human Weakness as well as power. What squabbles has the same weak Sentiment occasioned at different periods among all the antients and particularly the old Scythians, Battles, Triumphs & the Lord knows what.

It is however fortunate that the extremes of Virtue & Vice are so nearly allied; this Vice like others of its Magnitude is productive also of its Virtues. It taught the Scyths the Art of War. Their attention to their dead in various Ways, was what partly occasioned their Retreats, Ambuscades, & Counter-excursions It besides taught them to be more careful of the living & not expose to a rash decision the fate of a Battle, & the lives of Men. Alexander was embarrassed & baffled by this Circumstance. It gave also Courage to the Scyths, a people whose Ideas after Death were only about the Care that should be taken of their Bodies, having this removed by the great confidence they placed in the Survivors had a Stimulative to Valour that a more complicated System of Philosophy or Religion could not give to Armies however it might to a few Individuals: they could never say that Conscience made them Cowards—If the above is an Apology that pleads in its Favour, there is also another Circumstance that pleads in its Favour with me much more. It seems to be intimately connected with the Idea of an after Existence, & as universal as antient is the Custom of extending kindness to the Dead so is the belief of an after existence & I suppose I may say of immortality. The various forms in which those Sentiments have appeared in action operate in no manner against the original Idea. Time itself which produces effects so different in other Matters is here an Argument against itself & strengthens the Idea that I hope will at last destroy it. It had however effects different than the mere weaknesses I have mentioned. It produced among the Scyths also the most abominable Crimes, the same which exist at present among their descendants in America. It rendered their Wars the most bloody cruel & unrelenting among themselves particularly, & cruel Wars beget Wars. It is the black Soil in which Revenge receives its full Vigour; the whole heart became corrupted. Extent of territory, Riches or choice of Pasturage or Grounds for the Chace became at length only pretexts for Wars which had their foundations in mere Revenge & since they are the first people who *eat* their Enemies I see nothing forced in the supposition that should lead me to think it also the Child of Revenge alone. The War Songs to this Day sung among the American Indians have always in them such language as this—We will eat the Flesh of our Enemies & drink their Blood—The Bodies of our *unburied* Friends call out to be gathered up & inhumed."

15th} I this Morning quitted my Russ Conductors whose horses were fatigued & embarked with my demi-gentilhome, demifrizeur & the distressed Girl of Dantzic. I had taken under my protection on board (for the[y] resemble Chinese Junks) some Prussian Waggons. I passed a barrier Town between the very unfortunate or very despicable King of Poland & those of the Rex Borussorum. If human imbecility will have Kings to govern in Gods name let them be men of Genius. The breath of Frederick like the Dew of Heaven has fallen on these parts & I suppose on the whole of his Dominions. The quick Transition I have made of late from Kingdom to Kingdom with a kind of passive attention to their different manners has so habituated me to take notice of every thing I see & ruminate upon them that I believe in my heart nothing escapes me; the most delicate traits are familiar to me, & like an old American Indian Hunter I have Eyes & Ears peculiarly adapted to my Situation. If inspiration was not already a prostituted Theme I should fairly consent to think myself visited with it, & lay aside that rigid mode of thinking & conclusion that Philosophy demands. In the other parts of my Voyage the transition has been so gentle from the different Characters of People different to each other that I sometimes lost the Gradations. A second visit to the same places has convinced me of the Error & I have as well as I could rectified it. There also were others quite abrupt but none of them were so when I compared to the change I mark to day in entering the Dominions of the late King of Prussia: on the Confines of every other Kingdom there has been a Melange of Character of considerable extent within each, forming a kind of Suburb. It has not been so to day I have within the Space of 3 English Miles leapt the great barrier of Asiatic & European manners; from Servility, Indolence, Filth, Vanity, Dishonesty, Suspicion, Jealousy, Cowardice, Knavery, Reserve, Ignorance, Basses d'Esprit & I know not what, to every thing opposite to it, busy Industry, Frankness, Neatness, well loaded Tables plain good manners, an obliging attention Firmness, Intelligence, &, thank God, Cheerfulness, &

above [all] Honesty, which I solemnly swear I have not looked full in the Face since I first passed to the Eastward & Northward of the Baltic. Once more welcome Europe to my warmest Embraces. God the Source of honour can only know my feelings for I cannot describe them: but I remember that after being absent 9 years from my Mother whom I almost adore I did not meet her with greater Raptures than I do thee.

I do not know where to fix the Philosophic Geography of the other parts of Europe, but if my Vanity should ever tempt me to do it I should be sure of one spot to fix the foot of my Compass. There is something singularly decisive in the limits here marked by the great Frederick. I wish to God he had been a Tartar; his rich Genius would not have cursed all Asia with the useless Conquests of the half formed Zengis Chan, but would have chased from that ignominious & almost useless quarter of the World with equal address & vigour the baneful Sources of those Vices which have even to this very day retarded the bold & noble advances made by the Sons of Europe to a state of Society only worthy of mankind, & if I dare to subjoin the approbation of God.—I know not whether this is digression any more than I am certain whether I ever wrote a Line regularly; but this change in manners is also accompanied by that of Dress which has this singularity attending it, that it has an Analogy more extensive than of manners, & more easily traced; at least equally striking is the change of Features & of Person. There is a Delicacy of Feature peculiar to the Asiatic, it is almost uniform; the European variety is not more remarkable. Perfect Beauty is undoubtedly among both; but an Incongruity of Feature is not among the Asiatics. The Arabian Horse in the Subordinate Scale of beings is not a more distinct Species of Animal compared with the multifarious Species of that Animal among us than the Asiatic & European Man. To make the change I speak of more striking I am among the people most commonly known by the national appellation of Dutch, who compared with every other people I have seen are in strict Justice grotesque & humbly & who have a common Character more different from the Asiatic than any of their European Neighbours. The Analogy between the Mind & Body forms the most excellent Data to reason from of human manners, & I can easily conceive why an infinite Variety of Features should exist among a people whose Education, pursuits, Enjoyments, & Thoughts are as various, & I can as easily assign those reasons for the difference between the European & Asiatic. When I speak comparatively of the Whole there are not two persons in Europe who think, & act, & live alike & their Features are as different &

so are their Bodies. In Asia the Cause & the Effects are reversed. I have, for example remarked the uniformity of manners among the Jews (who are here Asiatics) & I have also remarked an uniformity of Beauty among them— why do I leap so suddenly among the humbly Dutch, & a variety of Knowledge, Pursuits &c &c

Death is the most remarkable and interesting Event in the history of Man & all the Animal Creation. Whatever the Ideas of Man have been respecting it or whatever Customs have followed from those Ideas they are the most to be depended on as Guides that will not deceive us or mislead us in investigating the Character of Man, or our Researches into other parts of Philosophy. Life which is but an opposite Event will not furnish more matter for such a Subject, indeed I believe not so many. It is only a circumstance that gives birth to the other & the beginning or Cause of which we have no proofs so positive as of Death, & for this & other reasons it becomes if not less interesting more the Subject of Ceremony. If we take the Date of our Existence from the History of Adam (& we are fond of doing it) we shall find but one remarkable Ceremony antecedent to the circumstance of Death which gave immediate existence to Millions this was the Ceremony of Sacrifice; but this the moment Death appeared lost its Independence & became a tributary Ceremony to it.—

But I am a poor Peasants' Son
uninstructed—& I write alone
I have none to help me.

There seems to have been very little difference in point of Knowledge among Men before the Epoch of the Deluge & a long while after & the most informed among those were very ignorant; & yet this little difference in the possession of a better kind of Ignorance rendered the Objects of it sometimes Objects of adoration to others. This Sentiment compared with ours of learned Men at this Day will shew the difference between the Knowledge of the present Epoch & those remote ones. The comparison will not only be curious but [will] afford a Data for interesting Investigations. Customs that existed before the Deluge as well as since are now in full force. They originated in times of profound Ignorance, Error & Supposition & like an old Disease are not shook off even in Europe. Many give literal Credit to antedeluvian Tales & like an Epicurean Fop are willing to suffer the excruciating pains of the Gout because their Predecessors did the same, Inspiration (for instance) was a custom of thinking of certain great Men before the Christian Epoch or the harbingers of that Event, an argument that first afforded refuge to Villainy or ingenious Despair, and afterwards like other things, said to be divine; I wish it may be true that God ever inspired Man, & I also wish that Man had not inspired himself first.

If is a mortifying Reflection that the farther back we trace a custom, the greater proofs it gives us of the antient Ignorance & Weakness of Mankind. We see Genius sometimes in our earliest history, but its operations like a misguided Tempest ruined itself by its own force & the same Talents that should have mounted & conversed with reason at the feet of God—descended as far below & lost themselves in a contrariety of mere puerile Riddles. The present cultivated State of the human Mind in Europe is a proof that this reversed Situation of the Understanding at the period mentioned might have been, without the intervention of some unnatural Cause, or of a cause supernatural, for in truth I cannot conceive how any other could produce such an effect any more than I can conceive that the Sublime Points of knowledge of the present European can be the sole effects of natural Causes. God did not create the mind of Man so imperfect as its earliest operations declare it to be, or its operations would not be so perfect as they at present are. Did God at any period withdraw his assistance from Man in the pursuits of Knowledge; if he did was that the reason of his Ignorance. Has man sinned as mentioned under the Moral of the Apple in Eden. How could any Man in a State of Ignorance know himself to be so. We say at present that to be sensible of our Ignorance is to know to a Negative Exactness how wise we are; which is a proof of our Wisdom. could Moses reason thus? He has wrote thus & yet we know that he was uninformed, *beastly*, & Savage, was this Inspiration.

In leaving Vilna the Postillion begged I would not................ the young Woman I had with me in the Kabitka for if I did the Horses would certainly be taken with Sickness—One of the many Instances of Russian Superstition & let me subjoin that after all, this is a Thief & robbed my Portmanteau of 2 Roubles—& this at the moment of departure from him, & the last View I had or ever wish to have of Russia was of a Thief; & a man void of all principle because I had but a few hours before dealt generously by him, & also, which forms the strongest Trait in a Russian Character; a Man whose power to dissemble can only be equalled by his Countrymen for at parting he came uncovered before me with all the good Wishes & good Looks of sacred Honesty & Charity. This good Christian also who carried his Images with him and worshipped them at every post, this good Catholick also who would not suffer a starving Lutheran or any one else to cut his Bread during Lent with a Knife however cleaned that had touched Flesh.

Let no European put entire Confidence in a Russian of whatever Condition and none at all in the lower & middle Ranks of People.

PART IV

THE EGYPTIAN JOURNAL AND LETTERS
JUNE 1788–JANUARY 1789

✴

In May 1788 Ledyard turned up in London, 18 months after he had left the city to begin his world tour. Five weeks later he again departed on another adventure. Backed by a new organization, the African Association, he headed, via Paris and Marseilles, to Egypt in hopes of exploring the interior of Africa and finding the source of the Niger River.

✴

To Isaac Ledyard
June 1788; London

To Monecca.

I was last evening in the Company with Mr Jarvis of New York who I accidently met in the city & invited to my lodgings:[1] when I was in distress in Paris he behaved very generously to me, & as I do not want money at present tho no doubt I shall some other time, I had a double satisfaction in the recontre & invitation I gave him, being equaly happy to see him & to pay him 100 livres which I never expected to be able to do & I suppose he did not think I ever should himself. [[but in this mortal life one is always disappointed & beriddled some way or another]]. If he goes to N York

as soon as he told me he expected to do I shall trouble him with this letter to you & some others to your address for my other dear friends. The Last
time I wrote you was from hence two years ago nearly: but I suppose you
heard from me at Petersburg by a Mr Franklin of N York—indeed I think
I wrote you from Petersburg: I ought to have done it. I promised to write
you from the remote parts of Siberia: I promise every thing to those I love
& so does fortune to me sometimes but we reciprocaly prevent each other
from fulfiling our engagements & she left me so poor in Siberia that I could
not write you because I could not franc the Letter. You are already acquainted
with the intent of the voyage I have been 2 years past engaged in: the history of it I cannot give you nor indeed the world: parts of it, both would
comprehend approve, & I suppose admire, & parts of it are incomp[r]ehen-
sible because undescribable: if I had you by the hand it would however not
be so: we have a language of our own, & you so well know my soul that
should language fail in the communication you would still understand me.

I had penetrated thro Europe & Asia almost to the Pacific Ocean:
but in the midst of my career was arrested a prisoner of state to the Empress
of Russia by an express sent after me for that purpose: The motives of the
Empress in arresting me are found upon examination to have been a mixture of jealous envy & malice. I passed under a guard a part of last winter
& spring: was banished the Empire, & conveyed by a guard to the frontiers
of Poland 6000 miles from the place where I was arrested & this journey
was performed in 6 weeks: cruelties & hardships are tales I leave untold.

I was disappointed in the pursuit of an object on which my future
fortune entirely depended, as well as my immediate existence. I know
not how I passed thro the Kingdoms of Poland & Prussia or from thence
to London where I arived the begining of the present May.

Dissappointed, ragged, penniless: and yet so accustomed am I to
such things I declare my heart was whole. My health for the first time had
suffered from my confinement, & the amazing rapidity with which I was
carried thro the unlimited wilds of Tartary & Russia—but my liberty
regained, & a few days rest among the beatuifull daughters of Israel in
Poland re established it & I am now in as full bloom & vigour as 37
years will afford any Man—Jarvis says I look much older than when he
saw me at Paris 3 summers ago which I readily believe, an american face
does not wear well like an american heart.

From my acquaintance in London my arival was anounced to a Society
of Noblemen & Gentlemen who had for some time been fruitlessly enquir-

ing for somebody that would undertake to travel throughout the continent of Africa. I was asked & consented to undertake the tour. The society have appropriated a sum of 1500 guineas to defray the expences of the Journey. I dine with them collectively this day week, finish the affair & within the month shall be on the move. My route lays from here to Paris, to Marseilles, across the Mediterranian to Alexandria, to Grand Cairo in Egypt & to Mecca on the Red sea: beyond is unknown & my discoveries begin; where they will terminate or how you shall know if I survive.

As we have now at London no Embassy & as I know of now certain medium of conveyance I cannot certainly promise you letters from Asia or Africa: I can only say that I will write you from grand Cairo if I can find a conveyance

Should Mr Jarvis conclude on going to Am[erica] before I leave town I shall send you some tartar curiosities: if not, I am not Certain that I shall have that pleasure. If I can (& I shall strive hard for it) I will also send you a transcript of the few rude remarks I have made in my last tour: with respect to the history of man, the hints I have give from circumstances & facts that have come within my personal knowledge you would find totaly new & extremely interesting: they form an excellent data for investigation: but are better in my hands than any other because no other Man has seen as much of Asia & America, & the analogy of the histories of these two continents form one of their greatest beauties: they would be charming additions to the happy retirement Mr Jarvis tells me you lead on long Island: & your abilities might also improve them into an importance with Mankind: now if I should not send them after saying so much of them it would be a pretty commence & if Jarvis goes not it is most probably I shall not.

My seeing Jarvis has been as good almost as a visit to N York: his account of our family & friends has been minute & faithfull as far as he knows them, & he is pretty well acquainted with them. Nothing in the history of them all has affected me so much as the mercantile misfortunes of your worthy brother & my dear cousin B: surely the race is not to the swift or the battle to the strong: did the pyramids of Egypt wc I shall soon see, cover hearts as worthy as his I should no more stile them monuments of human imbecility: I should worship before them. Mr Jarvis has not been able to give me an exact acct of his situation: I only understand that he has failed in business & retired to Jersey where I think he ought to stay for the world is absolutely unworthy of him: I do not say this because he is my cousin & shared with you the earliest attachments of my heart: these are things I feel, & that the world has nothing to do with any more than it ought to have with him. They are compliments his enimies would make him if he had any. I never knew so much merit so unfortunate. I cannot reflect upon his fat unimpassioned; & unprejudiced against the world. He should retire: if barely comfortable it will be enough for he cannot go from dignity. Embrace the brave fellow for me, & my cousin his wife & her dear little ones—God bless them. Remember me to all my Jersey friends. I am a bankrupt not to them alone: I am one even to myself: but I am not without hopes that a liqu[i]dation on all sides may take place.

I am at present somewhat known to fame & by accident to money: it is but little yet, & whether it will be more or less—to make use of English wit is more or less uncertain. My heart is on your side of the Atlantic. I know the charms on Long Island: the additional ones your residence on it adds to it the neccessity of a few pence: & the sweet accordance of recubans sub tegmine fagi.[2] do not think that because I have seen much & must see more of the World I have forgot America: I could as soon forget you,—my dear Ben—myself—my God.

My Travels have brought upon me a numerous correspondance which added to the employments of my new enterprize really embarrass me. I am alone in every thing and in most things so because nobody has ever been accustomed to think and act in Travelling matters as I do. If I should not be able to send you any transcript from my Travels you will please accept of these two observations of mine, they are the result of extensive and assiduous enquiry and entirely my own; and they are circumstances that will perhaps afford you some satisfaction and such of your curious and learned friends as you may please to communicate them to. They are with me well ascertained facts. The first is that the difference of colour in the human Species, as the observation respects all but the Negroes (whom I have not yet visited) originates from natural causes. The next is that all the Asiatic Indians called Tartars, & that all the Tartars have formed the later armies of Zingis Khan together with the Chinese are the same people; and that the American Tartar is also of the same family: the most ancient and numerous people on Earth; and what is very singular the most uniformly alike— I have been to Day with Mr Jarvis and he leaves London in three Days time the consequence of which is I can send you no transcripts from my writings: I shall [send] you however by him my Siberian Dresses—they are such as I have worn thro' many a scene and glad to get them—I send them to you to remember me by: if you choose to present them or any of them to your Society of Arts and Sciences do so.

The Surtout coat marked No 1 is made of the Rein deer skin & edged with the dewlap of the moose: perhaps you will wear this yourself in winter: it is made for a riding coat & I have rode both horses & deer with it- but you are some how strangely like the english not fond of fur dresses. The Cap No 2 is made all of the Siberian red fox & is also a traveling cap. the form is entirely Tartar The Cap No 3 is a Russian made cap consisting of white ermin & bordered with blue fox skin: it cost me at Yakutsk on the banks of the great river Lena 25 roubles which is 4 guineas & one rouble. The surtout cost 70 roubles. the fox skin cap 6 roubles.: the gloves marked No 4 are made of the feet of the fox & lined with the Tartar hare & cost 5 roubles. The Tartar froc No 5 is the only one of the kind ever brot to Europe: the form & stile is truely Tartar: it was made a present to me and comes from the borders of the frozen ocean at the mouth of the River Kovima Latd 69-39. N. it is made of a spotted Rein deer calf (& the surtout is also the calf) the dark border is a dark skin & as they are rare among the Rein deer so it is there put for ornament the edging is the same as the surtout: you will observe on the inside of the skin a number of spots: these were occasioned by a small insect bred there from the eggs of a species of fly & which together with the vast numbers of musquestoes obliges this charming animal to migrate annualy N & S. as the seasons require & particularly [for] the conveniences of bringing forth its young. The boots No 6 are made also of the Rein deer skin & ornamented with European cloath. The form is Tartar they cost 8 robles: the socks for the boots No 7. are made of the old rein deer skin: they are worn the inside of the boots with the hair to the feet; with or without stockings: these were made a present to me & came from the borders of the frozen ocean: the cloak No 8 which they are wrapt up in was made in London I traveled on foot with it in Danemarc Sweden Lapland Finland & the Lord knows where: in opulence & poverty I have kept it slept in it, eat in it, drank in it, fought in it, negociated in it: it has been thro every scene my constant & faithfull servant from my departure to my return to London & to give it an asylum for I have none here I send it to you—lay it up as soon as I can I will call upon you for it & lay myself up with it. I have mentioned the prices of the above articles to give you an Idea how dear fur dresses are even in the remotest parts of the vast dominions of Russia.

These cloaths were not all that I wore last winter in Siberia: I wore many more & froze my nose & ears after all. You have no Idea of the excessive

cold in those regions. by experiments I made at Yakutsk (which by the by
I desire you to be geographically acquainted with) I found on Novr 19th
my mercurial Thermr froze. In December I found by observations repeated
that 2 ounces of clean quicksilver openly exposed froze hard in 15 minutes
by a watch: strong coniac brandy coagulated. by a Thermr graduated by
Reaumer & filled with rectified spirits of wine I had 39½ deg. On the borders of the frozen ocean a Capt Billings had the winter before last 43¾ deg
by the same Thermr

I observed in those severe frosts that the air was condensed as it is with
you in a thick fog: the Atmosphere is frozen respiration is fatiguing: all exercise must be as moderate as possible. ones confidence is placed alone on the
fur dress it is a happy law of nature that in such intense colds there is seldom any wind: if there is it is dangerous to be abroad: those who happen
to be, lay down on the snow & secure themselves so. In these seasons
there is no chance. the animals submit themselves to hunger & security &
so does Man. There are no wells at Yakutsk by experiment they freez 60 feet
deep. People of these regions are therefor obliged to use Ice or snow: they
have also ice windows: glass is of no use to the few who have it. The difference of the state of the air within & without is so great that they are covered on the inside with several inches of ice & in that state are less luminous
than ice: the timber of the houses splits & opens with loud crocks. the rivers
thunder & open with broad fissures—all nature groans beneath the rigor-
ous winter Just at the turning of this cold season I travelled last winter 2,600
verst about 1950 english miles on the river Lena.

I am sorry Mr Jarvis goes out of town so soon to day is Saturday & he
calls on me on Tuesday to take the things for you & to take leave o f me. I have
not time to do any thing & it happens that just at this moment I am the busiest
with the African society: among other things, I want to send you a copy from
my Sweedish Portrait at Somerset house[3]—I have one by me, but it is an old
stupid devil of a thing [[& looks exactly like Avery the taylor on Groton bank]]
it was taken by a boy, who is as dumb & deaf as the portrait- he is however
under the patronage of Sr Joshua Reynolds the English Raphael. The boy was
sent to me by a country Squire who accidently got acquainted with me at an
Inn where I lodged in London & who has taken a wonderfull fancy to me
& begs to hang me in his hall—this one is yet unfinished, & so is the one for
the Squire—they are done in water & are mere daubings

Jarvis says our Trumbull is clever & advises me to get him to copy
the Sweedish drawing which is not only a *perfect* likeness but good

painting[4]—If I do according to his advice it cannot be soon & indeed I should not trouble you or myself about this shadow of Josephus was I persuaded of presenting him to you hereafter in substance

I shall not have time to settle my affairs, before Jarvis goes if it is to-morrow for to Morrow I must be with the African Committee—I must tell you what this African Committee is. Some few weeks only before my arival now at London a number of Gentlemen had been talking somewhat in earnest about exploring the Continent of Africa. My arival has made it a reality. An Association is formed & a Comittee balloted from it last week for the management of the affairs of it. The Comittee chosen are a Mr Cerke a Mr *Beaufoy,* Lord Rawdon Sir Joseph Banks & the Bishop of Landaff.[5] The Society consists at present of 200 Members. It is a growing thing, & the King privately promoting & encouraging it will make its objects more extensive than at first thought of. The king has told them that no expence should be spared: the subscriptions are then altered from any fixed sum to such sums as exigencies may require; & one or two other Gentlemen are going in behalf of the Society to travel in & about the dominions of civilization in Africa—exclusive of myself who nobody will follow—& to tell you the truth cannot. Mr Jarvis is this morning going

adieu yrs always
Josephus
NB Mr
Jarvis will not
take the 100 livres of me
I believe you will hear from me again soon

✳

To Isaac Ledyard
London, June 1788

June 1788
To Monecca

I suppose that my Letters & curiosities sent by Mr Jarvis are now half way over the Atlantic. This is a little postscript that I leave to the care of his brother in town. Inclosed with it is a poor portrait of me taken by the dumb boy mentioned in my other Letter: if it was anything like painting I would desire you to keep it: as it is I beg you to send it to my mother who will be as fond of it as if done by Guido:[6] it is the only thing I ever presented the dear woman who gave me being & presided over my infancy. I would have sent it framed if the opportunity permitted me to do so.

[[I also send you a penciled sketch of coats of arms. No 1 are arms that I think I remember to have seen on Grandfathers old Chaise— I remember the motto well: that, however is arbitrary. As my god fathers & god mothers advanced me, I saw on Aunt Seymours mantle tree peice arms somewhat like them to the name of Ledyard. In the Heraldry books here they are to the name of Legar—or as it would be in french le Gar. But there is no kind of historical analogy between the crest & motto, which is very beautifull. No 2 are the arms of the Ledyard—or Lediard (for I can find no such name as Ledyard) & of the Sutton family of the english county of Wilts: joined by some circumstance the scollop quarters being the Sutton. No 3 are the Ledyard or Lediard arms indistinct from the Sutton: field sable: cross pattee in gold with gules or stars: the crest a silve ? Lion with gules in his right paw— it is good & honorable: difficilia et pulchra might be wrote under such a crest with propriety

I know not how the orthographical difference of Ledyard & Lediard has arisen: it is but little, & if a french name easily accounted for, as we use the y very often where the french use the i. It is a french name by its orthography & in french would be wrote le diard. I think I remember in a conversation between grand father & Aaron Bull about pumpkin beer that the former said the faimily (meaning ours) came from Normandy in france: the name is in france & England: in the former it is spelt Lidiard: here Lediard. why with us Ledyard I know not: be it which it may I am right in being yrs]]

Let ye postscript come in here
Josephus
P.S. June 29th 1788
I set out to Morrow morning
for France. Adieu!

★

To *Thomas Jefferson*
4 July 1788; *Paris*

To Thomas Jefferson
Mr Ledyard presents his compliments to Mr Jefferson—he has been imprisoned and banished by the Empriss of Russia from her dominions after having almost gained the pacific ocean. he is now on his way to Africa to see what he can do with that continent. he is ill with a cold & fever or he would have waited on Mr Jefferson with Mr Edwards.[7] he is with perfect respect & affection Mr Jeffersons most humble & obt servant.
Hotel d'aligre
rue d'orleans
4 Juile

★

To *Thomas Jefferson*
July 1788; *Paris*

To Thomas Jefferson
To his Excellency Thomas Jefferson Esquire
Embassador for the United States of America
Sir
When men of genius want matter of fact to reason from it is bad, though it is worse to reason without it: it is the fate of genius not to make, or to misapply this reflexion, and so it forms theories: humble minds admire these theories because they cannot comprehend them, & disbelieve them for the same reason
Simplify the efforts & attainments of all the antient world in science & it amounts to nothing but theory: to a riddle: the sublime of antient wisdom ws to form a riddle: & the delphic god bore the palm: Men had then great encouragement to do so: they were made priests prophets, kings & gods: & when they had gained these distinctions by riddles it was necessary by riddles to preserve them.
Men have since tho but very lately & not yet universaly sought impartialy for truth & we now a days seek truth not only for its own enchanting beauty,

but from a pinciple tho not more valuable yet more generous viz the pleasure of communicating it to one another. The soothsayers, magicians prophets & priests of old would think of us as errant fools as we think them knaves

In my travels I have made it my rule to compare the written with the living history of Man, & as I have seen all kinds of men so I have not hesitated to make use of all kinds of history (t[ha]t I am acquainted with) in the comparison: & I give in many cases as much credit to traditions as to other history: implicit credit to none nor implicit credit to inferrences that I myself draw from this comparison except rarely; & then I am as sure as I want to be. Thus I know & feel myself above prejudice: Moses, Albugassi & the writers of the last 20 years are all alike to me as to what I am seeking for: I would only understand if I could what Man has been from what he is: not what he may be hereafter tho all mention the tale. I would also know what the earth has been from observing how it is at present: not how it may hereafter be, Man I am, but I declare to you that in this temper of mind & from the information incident to the extent & nature of my travels I find myself at my ease concerning things which some cannot & others will not believe that are of considerable importance; & I will tell you in a very few words what some of them are—I wish I had time to mention them all, or if I do that it was more in detail.

Sr I am certain (the negroes excepted because I have not yet personally visited them) that the difference in the colour of Men is the effect of natural causes.

Sr I am certain that all people you call red people on the continent of America & on the continents of Europe & Asia as far south as the southern parts of China are all one people by whatever names distinguished & that the best general one would be *Tartar*

I suspect that *all* red people are of the same family. I am satisfied myself that America was peopled from Asia & had some if not all its animals from thence.

I am satisfied myself that the great general analogy in the customs of Men can only be accounted for but by supposing them all to compose one family: & by extending the Idea & uniting customs, traditions & history I am satisfied that this common origin was such or nearly as related by Moses & commonly believed among all the nations of the earth. There is a transposition of things on the globe that must have been produced by some cause equal to the effect which is vast & curious: whether I repose on arguments drawn from facts observed by myself or send imagination forth to find a cause they both declare to me a general deluge

I am yr Excellencys most humble
& most gratefull friend

Ledyard

*

To Thomas Jefferson
Alexandria; 15 August 1788

Alexandria in Egypt August 15th 1788
Sir

As I go to Cairo in a few days from whence it will be difficult to write to you I must do it from here tho unprepared: I must also leave my Letter in the hands of the Capt (who engages to deliver it to Mr Cathalan at Marseilles [in] 4 or 5 weeks—I am in good health & spirits & tho prospects before me respecting my enterprize flattering this with wishes for your happiness & am eternal remembrance of your goodness to me must form the only part of my Letter of any consequence except that I also desire to be remembered to the Marquiss la fayette, his lady, Mr Short & other friends. Deducting the week I staid at Paris & 2 days at Marseilles & [I] was only 34 days from London to this place: I am sorry to inform you that I regret having visited Mr Cathalam & of having made use of your name: I shall ever think tho he was extremely polite that he rather strove to prevent my embarking at Marseilles than to facilitate it, for his bandying me about among the members of the Chamber of Commerce he had nearly—& very nearly lost me my passage—& in the last ship from Marseilles for the season. He knew better: he knew that the Chamber of Commerce had *no business* with me & besides I only asked him if he could without trouble *address me to the Capt of a ship bound to Alexandria*—nothing more.

Alexandria at large forms a scene wretched & interesting beyond any other that I have seen, poverty, rapine, murder, tumult blind bigotry, cruel persecution, pestilence.

A small town built on the ruins of antiquity—as remarkable for its bare & miserable articheture as I suppose the place once was for its good & great works of this kind. A pillar called the pillar of Pompey, & an Obelisk called Cleopatra are now almost the only remains of such great Antiquity—they

are both & particularly the former noble subjects to see & contemplate &
are certainly more captivating from the contrasting deserts & forlorn
prospects around them. No man of whatever turn of mind can see the whole
witht retiring from the scene with a "sic transit gloria mundi"[8]—but I have
not begun yet to view those scenes so affecting in the history of unfortunate man: & why they unfortunate?—who can feel the interrogation: who
deny the fact: who divine the course. To be the more counfounded I am
going to Cairo—from there perhaps thro scenes embossed with riddles
still more mortifying.

 Untill I arrive there I must bid you adieu & have the honor to be with
perfect esteem

 Sr
 Your much obliged
 & affectionate hble servt

 J Ledyard
 P.S. I send this to the care of Mr Cathalan—& if I can will write you
again from some quarter

       ✶

To Thomas Jefferson
10 September 1788; Cairo

Grand Cairo Sept 10th 1788
Sir,
 I wrote you a short letter from Alexandria and addressed it under cover
to Mr Cathalan & sent it to Marseilles by the same vessel I came in from
Thence to Egypt where I arived the 5th of August. I begin this letter without knowing when I shall close it or when I shall send it—& indeed
whither I ever shall send it: but I will have it ready in case an opportunity
should offer. Having been in Cairo only 4 days, I have not yet any thing curious or particularly interesting to begin with: indeed you will not expect
much of that kind from me. my business is in another quarter & the information I seek totally new: any information from here whatever would not

be so was I possessed of it. At all events I shall never be entirely without a subject when it is to you I write: I shall never think my letter a bad one when it contains the declarations of the esteem I have for you: of my gratitude & of my affection for you & this notwithstanding you thought hard of me being employed by an english association which hurt me very much while I was at paris You know your own heart & if my suspicions are groundless forgive them since they proceded from the jealousy I have, not to loose the little regard you have in times past been pleased to honour me with. You are not obliged to esteem me, but I am obliged to esteem you, or to take leave of my senses & confront the opinions of the greatest & best characters I know of: if I cannot therefore address myself to you as a Man that you regard I must write to you as one that regards you for your own sake & for the sake of my country which has set me the example.

I made my journey from Alexandria by water & entered the western branch of the mouths of the River Nile into the River. I was 5 days coming on the river to Cairo but this passage is generaly made in 4, sometimes in 3 days.

You have heard & read much of this River—& so had I: but when I saw it I could not concieve it to be the same—it is a mere mud puddle compared with the accounts we have of it: what eyes do travellers see with—are they fools or rogues. For heavens sake hear the plain truth about it: first with respect to its size: plain comparisons in such cases are good: as you know the river Connecticut—of all the rivers I have seen it most resembles it in size: & having only a little wider may on account better compare with the river Thames. This is the mighty the sovereign of rivers—the vast nile that has been metaphored into one of the wonders of the world—let me be carefull how I read—& above all how I read antient history!

You have read & heard too of its inundations: it is a lye: the banks of this river were never entirely over flowed much more the meadows round it. If the thousands of large & small canals from it & the thousands of men & machines employed to communicate by artificial means the water of the nile to its meadows is the inundation meant it is true—any other is false. It is not an inundating river. I came up the River the 20th of August & about the 30th of August the water is at its height ie the freshet: when I left the river its banks were 4 5 & 6 feet above water & here in town I am told that they expect the nile to be 1 or 2 feet higher only—at the most. this is a proof if I wanted one yt the banks of the nile are never overflowed. I have made a subject of it & transmited my observations to London: there I have said much at large about it: in a letter I cannot do it.

I saw three of the pyramids as I passed up the River but they were 4 or 5 leagues off. If I see them nearer before I close my letter & observe any thing about them that I think will be new to you, will insert it. It is warm weather here at present, & but for the north winds that cool themselves in their passing over the Mediterranean Sea & blows upon us we should be sadly situated: as it is I think I have felt it hotter at Philadelphia in the same month.

The city of Cairo is about half as large as Paris—and by the aggregate of my informations contains 700,000 inhabitants: you will therefore anticipate the fact of its narrow streets & will concieve it necessary also that the houses are high: in this number are included 100,000 of the Coptics or antient egyptians—& there are Christians: there are also many other christian Sects here from Damascus, Jerusalem, Aleppo & all parts of Syria.

With regard to my voyage I can only tell you for any certainty that I shall be able to pass as far as the western boundaries of what is called Turkish Nubia—and at a Town called Sennar—you will find this town on any chart—it is on a branch of the nile.⁹ I expect to get there with some surety— but afterwards all is dark before me: my design & wishes are to pass in that parrelel across the Continent. I will write from Sennar if I can. You know of the disturbances in this unhappy & forlorn country—& the nature of them. The Beys revolted from the Bashaw have possession of upper i.e. southern Egypt & are now encamped with an army pitifull enough about 3 miles southward of Cairo: they say—Bashaw come out from your city & fight us—& the Bashaw says come out of your entrenchments & fight me. You know that this revolt is a stroke in Russian politiks. Cairo is a wretched hole & a nest of vagabonds. nothing merits more the whole force of Burlesque than both the poetic & prosaic legends of this country. Sweet are the songs of Egypt on paper—who is not ravished with gums, balms, dates, figgs, pomegranates with the circassia & sycamores witht knowing that amidst this ones eyes ears mouth nose is filled with dust eternal hot fainting winds, lice bugs mosquetoes spiders flies—pox, itch leprosy, fevers, & almost universal blindness.

I am in perfect health & most ardently wish you yours. make my compliments to all my friends & particularly to the Marquis la fayette should [he] be with you.

Sr your sincere friend
& most humble & obedient Servant
J Ledyard

★

To *Thomas Jefferson*
15 November 1788; Cairo

To his Excellency T. Jefferson Esqr Embassador from the United States of
America to the Country of France
Cairo Novr 15th 1788}
Sir

 This is my third Letter to you from Egypt & I shall address it under
cover as I have my others to Mr Cathalan at Marseilles: above all things that
respect you have my constant and ardent wishes for a good state of health.
The rest you can command. I hope Mr Short is well & Madme Barclay &
family. I should certainly write to the Marquis de la Fayette if I knew
where to find him. I speak of him often among the French at Cairo. But if
our news here with respect to the Affairs of France is authentic, he would
hardly find time to read my Letter if his active spirit is employed in the conflict in proportion to its powers

 It is possible however that my compliments may reach him; & I
most humbly request that it may be by your means. Tell him that I love him
& that among the french patriots at Cairo they call on the names of
Souffrein & la Fayette, the one for point blanc honesty & the other as the
Soldier and Courtier The old veteran in Finance & civil economy (Mr
Necker) is welcomed to the helm the same plaudits that attend on that
event.[10]attend those who have damned to destruction the ecclesiastic that
preceeded him.

 I have been at Cairo three months & it is within a few days only that
I have had any certainty of being able to succeed in the prosecution of my
voyage: the difficulties that have attended me have occupied me day &
night: I otherwise should not only have wrote to you oftener; but should
have given you some little history of what I hear & see. My excuse now is
that I am doing up my bagage—& most curious bagage it is—for my journey;
& that I leave Cairo in 2 or 3 days. Perhaps I should not have pleased you
if I had wrote you in any detail. I know your taste for Ancient history I think:
it does not comport with what experience teaches me. There are besides your
many fine minds in the West in the same situations. The enthusiastic avid-

ity with which you search for treasures in Egypt, & I suppose all over the East will, & ought, in justice to the world & your own generous propensities—to be modified, corrected & abated, when—you hear the truth. I should have wrote you the truth and it is dissagreeable to hear the truth when habit has accustomed one to hear falsehood. You have the travels of Mr Lavary in this country. Burn them. Laugh at the elegant loquacity of writers like Thucidides. The sublime poetry of Homer has nothing to do with historic facts. Leo, Heroditus, & Diodsiculus never traveled themselves, & lived besides in epochs very unfriendly to history.[11] Without entering into an investigation that would be too long for my Letter I cannot tell you why I think all historians have written more to satisfy themselves than others. I am certainly very angry with those who have written of other countries when I have travelled as well as of this & of this particularly: they have all more or less decieved me: and they are the more blameable because I am (I suppose like others) inclinable by the common operations of the imagination to decieve myself in reading history & therefore stand in double need of truth. In some cases it is perhaps difficult to determine which does the most mischief: the selflove of the historian, or the curiosity of the reader: but both together have led us into errors that it is now too late to rectify.

You will think my head is turned to write you such a letter from Egypt but the reason is I do not indend it shall be turned:

If I had been life deceived & was in any other country I shall not write thus. I have read but little of Egypt and have heard less but this little is beyond what I see—every thing is exaggerated:

I have passed my time disagreeably here. Religion does more mischief than all other things. In Egypt it has always done more than in all other places. The humiliating situation of Frank would be insupportable to me—but for my voyage. It is a shame to the sons of Europe that they suffer this arrogance at the hands of a banditti of ignorant fanatics. I assure myself that even your curiosity & love of antiquity would never detain you in Egypt 3 months

I have from here SW about 300 leagues to a Black King: there my present conductors leave me to my fate—beyond (I suppose) I go alone. I expect to cut the Continent across between the parralels of 72° & 20° N Lat. I shall if possible write you from the Kingdom of this Black gentleman. If not; do not forget me in the interim of time which may pass during my voyage from thence to Europe—& as probable to France as any where. I shall not forget you. Indeed it would be a consolation to think of you in my last moments.

Be happy. I have the honor to be with esteem & friendhsip yr Excellency's most obedt & most humble Servant
    JLedyard

✸

Ledyard's journal from his sojourn in Egypt was returned to Henry Beaufoy in London. In 1790 Beaufoy edited and compiled the Proceedings of the Association for the Promoting the Discovery of the Interior Parts of Africa, *within which he printed the following excerpts from Ledyard's journal.*

Ledyard spent two weeks in Alexandria and five months in Cairo. He died in January 1789 of dysentery and impatience and was buried in an unmarked grave.

A traveller, who should, by just comparisons between things here and in Europe, tell his tale; who, by a mind unbewitched by antecedent descriptions, too strong, too bold, too determined, too honest, to be capable of lying, should speak just as he thought, would, no doubt, be esteemed an arrant fool, and a stupid coxcomb.—For example, an Englishman who had never seen Egypt, would ask me what sort of a woman an Egyptian woman was? If I meant to do the question as much justice by the answer, as I could in my way, I should ask him to take notice of the first company of Gypsies he saw behind a hedge in Essex; and I suppose he would be fool enough to think me a fool.

August 14th. I left Alexandria at midnight, with a pleasant breeze North; and was, at sun-rise next morning, at the mouth of the Nile, which has a bar of sand across it, and soundings as irregular as the sea, which is raised upon it by the contentions of counter currents and winds.

The view in sailing up the Nile is very confined, unless from the top of the mast, or some other eminence, and then it is an unbounded plain of excellent land, miserably cultivated, and yet interspersed with a great number of villages, both on its banks and as far along the meadows as one can see in any direction: the river is also filled with boats passing and repassing—boats all of one kind, and navigated in one manner; nearly also of one size, the largest carrying ten or fifteen tons. On board of these boats are seen onions, water-melons, dates, sometimes a horse, a camel, (which lies down in the boat) and sheep and goats, dogs, men and women.—Towards evening and morning they have music.

Whenever we stopped at a village, I used to walk into it with my Conductor, who, being a Musselman, and a defendant from Mahommed, wore a green turban, and was therefore respected, and I was sure of safety:—but in truth, dressed as I was in a common Turkish habit, I believe I should have walked as safely without him. I saw no propensity among the inhabitants to incivility. The villages are most miserable assemblages of poor little mud huts, slung very close together without any kind of order, full of dust, lice, fleas, bed-bugs, flies, and all the curses of Moses: people poorly clad, the youths naked; in such respects, they sank infinitely below any Savages I ever saw.

The common people wear nothing but a shirt and drawers, and they are always blue. Green is the royal or holy colour; none but the descendants of Mahommed, if I am rightly informed, being permitted to wear it.

August 19th. From the little town where we landed, the distance to Cairo is about a mile and a half, which we rode as asses; for the ass in this country is the Christian's horse, as he is allowed no other animal to ride upon. Indeed I find the situation of a Christian, or what they more commonly call here a Frank, to be very, very humiliating, ignominious, and distressing: no one, by a combination of causes, can reason down to such effects as experience teaches us do exist here: it being impossible to conceive, that the enmity I have alluded to could exist between men;—or, in fact, that the same species of being, from any causes whatever, should ever think and act so differently as the Egyptians and the English do.

I arrived at Cairo early in the morning, on the 19th of August, and went to the house of the Venetian Consul, Mr. Rosetti, Chargé d'Affaires for the English Consul here.[12]

After dinner, not being able to find any other lodging, and receiving no very pressing invitation from Mr. Rosetti, to lodge with him, I went to a convent. This convent consists of Missionaries sent by the Pope to propagate the Christian Faith, or at least to give shelter to Christians. The Christians here are principally from Damascus: the convent is governed by the Order of Recollets: a number of English, as well as other European travellers, have lodged there.

August 21st. It is now about the hottest season of the year here; but I think I have felt it warmer in the City of Philadelphia, in the same month.

August 26th. This day I was introduced by Rosetti to the Aga Mahommed, the confidential Minister of Ismael, the most powerful of the

four ruling Beys: he gave me his hand to kiss, and with it the promise of letters, protection, and support, through Turkish Nubia, and also to some Chiefs
far inland. In a subsequent conversation, he told me I should see in my
travels a people who had power to transmutate themselves into the forms of
different animals. He asked me what I thought of the affair? I did not like
to render the ignorance, simplicity, and credulity of the Turk apparent. I told
him, that it formed a part of the character of all Savages to be great
Necromancers; but that I had never before heard of any so great as those which
he had done me the honour to describe; that it had rendered me more anxious to be on my voyage, and if I passed among them, I would, in the letter
I promised to write to him, give him a more particular account of them
than he had hitherto had.—He asked me how I could travel without the language of the people where I should pass? I told him, with vocabularies:—I
might as well have read to him a page of Newton's Principia.[13] He returned
to his fables again. Is it not curious, that the Egyptians (for I speak of the natives
of the country as well as of him, when I make the observation) are still such
dupes to the arts of sorcery? Was it the same people who built the Pyramids?

I can't understand that the Turks have a better opinion of our mental
powers than we have of theirs; but they say of us, that we are *a people who
carry our minds on our fingers ends:* meaning, that we put them in exercise
constantly, and render them subservient to all manner of purposes, and with
celerity, dispatch, and ease, do what we do.

I suspect the Copts to have been the origin of the Negro race: the nose
and lips correspond with those of the Negro. The hair, whenever I can see
it among the people here, (the Copts) is curled; not close like the Negros,
but like the Mulattoes. I observe a greater variety of colour among the human
species here than in any other country; and a greater variety of feature than
in any other country not possessing a greater degree of civilization.

I have seen an Abyssinian woman and a Bengal man—the colour is the
same in both; so are their features and persons

I have seen a small mummy;—it has what I call wampum work on it.
It appears as common here as among the Tartar. Tatowing is as prevalent
among the Arabs of this place as among the South Sea Islanders. It is a little curios, that the women here are more generally than in any other part
of the world tatowed on the chin, with perpendicular lines descending from
under the lip to the chin, like the women on the North West Coast of
America. It is also a custom here to stain the nails red, like the Cochin
Chinese, and the Northern Tartars. The mask or veil that the women here

wear, resembles exactly that worn by the Preists at Otaheite, and those seen at Sandwich Islands.

I have not yet seen the Arabs make use of a tool like our axe or hatchet; but what they use for such purposes as we do our hatchet and axe, is in the form of an adze, and is a form we found most agreeable to the South Sea Islanders. I see no instance of a tool formed designedly for the use of the right or left hand particularly, as the cotogon is among the Yorkertic Tartars.

There is certainly a very remarkable affinity between the Russian and Greek dress. The fillet round the temples of the Greek and Russian women, is a circumstance in dress that perhaps would strike nobody as it does me; and so of the wampum work too, which is also found among them both.

They spin here with the distaff and spindle only, like the French peasantry and other in Europe; and the common Arab loom is upon our principle, though rude.

I saw to-day (August 10th) an Arab woman white, like the White Indians in the South Sea Islands, Isthmus of Darien, &c. These kind of people all look alike.

Among the Greek women here, I find the identical Archangel head-dress.

Their music is instrumental, consisting of a drum and pipe, both which resemble those two instruments in the South Sea: the drum is exactly like the Otaheite drum; the pipe is made of cane, and consists of a long and short tube joined: the music resembles very much the bagpipe, and is pleasant.—All their music is concluded, if not accompanied, by the clapping of hands. I think it singular, that the women here make a noise with their mouths like frogs, and that this frog-music is always made at weddings; and I believe on all other occasions of merriment where there are women.

It is remarkable, that the dogs here are of just the same species found among the Otaheiteans.

It is also remarkable, that in one village I saw exactly the same machines used for diversion as in Russia.—I forget the Russian name for it. It is a large kind of wheel, on the extremities of which there are suspended seats, in which people are whirled round over and under each other.

The women dress their hair behind exactly in the same manner in which the women of the Calmuc Tartars dress theirs.

In the History of the Kingdom of Benin in Guinea, the Chiefs are called Aree Roee, or Street Kings. Among the Islands in the South Sea, Otaheite, &c. they call the Chiefs Arees, and the great Chiefs Aree le Hoi. I think this curious; and so I do that it is a custom of the Arabs to spread a blanket when they would invite any one to eat or rest with them.—American Indians spread the beaver skins on such occasions.

The Arabs of the Deserts, like the Tartars, have an invincible attachment to Liberty: no arts will reconcile them to any other life, or form of government, however modified. This is a character given me here of the Arabs.

It is singular that the Arab Language has no word for Liberty, although it has for Slaves.

The Arabs, like the New Zealanders, engage with a long strong spear.

I have made the best inquiries I have been able, since I have been here, of the nature of the country before me; of Sennar, Darfoor, Wangara, of Nubia, Abyssinia, of those named, or unknown by name.[14] I should have been happy to have sent you better information of those places than I am yet able to do. It will appear very singular to you in England, that we in Egypt are so ignorant of countries which we annually visit: the Egyptians know as little of Geography as the generality of the French; and like them, sing, dance, and traffic without it.

I have the best assurances of a certain and safe conduct by the return of the caravan that is arrived from Sennar; and Mr. Rosetti tells me that the letters I shall have from the Aga here will insure me of being conveyed, from hand to hand, to my journey's end.

The Mahometans in Africa are what the Russians are in Siberia, a trading, enterprizing, superstitious, warlike set of vagabonds, and wherever they are set upon going, they will and do go; but they neither can nor do make voyages merely commercial, or merely religious, across Africa; and where we do not find them in commerce, we find them not at all. They cannot (however vehemently pushed on by religion) afford to cross the Continent without trading by the way.

October 14th. I went to-day to the market-place, where they vend the Black slaves that come from towards the interior parts of Africa:—there were 200 of them together, dressed and ornamented as in their country. The appearance of a Savage in every region is almost the same!—There were very few men among them: this indicates that they are prisoners of war. They have a great many beads and other ornaments about them that are from the East. I was told by one of them that they came from the West of Sennar, fifty-five days journey, which may be about four or five hundred miles. A Negro Chief said, the Nile had its source in his country. In general they had their hair plaited in a great number of small detached plaits, none exceeding in length six or eight inches—the hair was filled with grease, and dirt purposely daubed on.

October 16th. I have renewed my visit to-day, and passed it more agreeably than yesterday; for yesterday I was rudely treated. The Franks are prohibited to purchase slaves, and therefore the Turks do not like to see them in the market. Mr. Rosetti favoured me with one of his running Chargé d'Affaires to accompany me: but having observed yesterday among the ornaments of the Negros a variety of beads, and wanting to know from what country they came, I requested Mr. Rosetti, previously to my second visit, to shew me from his store samples of Venetian beads.—He shewed me samples of fifteen hundred different kinds: after this I set out.

The name of the country these Savages come from is Darfoor, and is well known on account of the Slave Trade, as well as of that in Gum and Elephants teeth.

The appearance of these Negros declares them to be a people in as savage a state as any people can; but not of so savage a temper, or of that species of countenance that indicates savage intelligence. They appear a harmless, wild people; but they are mostly young women.

The beads they are ornamented with are Venetian; and they have some Venetian brass medals which the Venetians make for trade. The beads are worked wampum-wife. I know not where they got the marine shells they worked among their beads, nor how they could have seen white men. I asked them if they would use me well in their country, if I should visit it? The said, "Yes:"—and added, that they should make a King of me, and treat me with all the delicacies of their country. Like the Egyptian women, and like most other Savages, they stick on ornaments wherever they can, and wear, like them, a great ring in the nose, either from the cartilage, or from the side: they also rub on some black kind of paint round the eyes, like the Egyptian women. They are a sizeable well-formed people, quite black, with what, I believe, we call the true Guinea face, and with curled short hair; but not more curled or shorter than I have seen it among the Egyptians; but in general these Savages plait it on tassels plaistered with clay or paint. Among some of them the hair is a foot long, and curled, resembling exactly one of our mops. The prevailing colour, where it can be seen, is a black and red mixed. I think it would make any hair curl, even Uncle Toby's wig, to be plaited and plaistered as this is.[15] This caravan, which I call the Darfoor caravan, is not very rich.—The Sennar is the rich caravan.

October 19th. I went yesterday to see if more of the Darfoor caravan had arrived; but they were not. I wonder why travellers to Cairo have not visited these slave markets, and conversed with the Jelabs or travelling Merchants of these caravans: both are certainly sources of great information.—The eighth part of the money expended on other accounts, might here answer some good solid purpose. For my part, I have not expended a crown, and I have a better idea of the people of Africa, of its trade, of the position of places, the nature of the country, manner of travelling, &c. than ever I had by any other means; and, I believe, better than any other means would afford me.

October 25th. I have been again to the slave market; but neither the Jelabs (a name which in this country is given to all travelling Merchants) nor the slaves are yet arrived in town—they will be here to-morrow. I met two or three in the street, and one with a shield and spear.

I have understood to-day, that the King of Sennar is himself a Merchant, and concerned in the Sennar caravans. The Merchant here who contracts to convey me to Sennar, is Procurer at Cairo to the King of Sennar: this is a good circumstance, and one I knew not of till to-day. Mr. Rosetti informed me of it. He informed me also, that this year the importation of the Negro Slaves into Egypt will amount to 20,000.—The caravan from the interior countries of Africa do not arrive here uniformly every year—they are sometimes absent two or three years.

Among a dozen of Sennar slaves, I saw three personable men, of a good bright olive colour, of vivacious and intelligent countenances; but they had all three (which first attracted my notice) heads uncommonly formed: the forehead was the narrowest, the longest, and most protuberant I ever saw. Many of these slaves speak a few words of the Arab language; but whether they learned them before or since their captivity I cannot tell.

A caravan goes from here (Cairo) to Fezzan, which they call a journey of fifty days; and from Fezzan to Tombuctou, which they call a journey of ninety days.[16] The caravans travel about twenty miles a day, which on the road from here to Fezzan, one thousand miles; and from Fezzan to Tombuctou, one thousand eight hundred miles. From here to Sennar is reckoned six hundred miles.

I have been waiting several days to have an interview with the Jelabs who go from hence to Sennar. I am told that they carry, in general, trinkets; but among other things, soap, antimony, red linen, razors, scissars, mirrors, beads; and, as far as I can yet learn, they bring from Sennar elephants teeth, the gum called here gum Sennar, camels, ostrich feathers, and slaves.

Wangara is talked of here as a place producing much gold, and as a kingdom: all accounts, and there are many, agree in this. The King of Wangara (whom I hope to see in about three months after leaving this) is said to dispose of just what quantity he pleases of his gold—sometimes a great deal, and sometimes little or none; and this, it is said, he does to prevent strangers knowing how rich he is, and that he may live in peace.

ENDNOTES

✴

PART I: A JOURNAL OF CAPTAIN COOK'S LAST VOYAGE

[1] The message in the bottle, although rich with romance in such a lonely place, did not last long at Kerguelen. In 1796 sailors on a U.S. ship found the bottle, with three messages (Kerguelen's, Cook's, and one from a third captain) and took it with them.

[2] The entire quotation, as well as most of the previous two paragraphs and the succeeding paragraph, is an almost exact reproduction from John Rickman's 1781 book. Rickman does not reference the source of his quoted material on Kerguelen.

[3] Only Rickman and Ledyard, among all journal keepers, mention this incident. Ledyard's pithy statement about the international language of love is his, not Rickman's.

[4] A phrase that time has not made understandable, sons of Mur could refer to the Mur River, which flows through Austria and Hungary, or Mur, the son of a Sumerian god Enlil, the god of the air and dawn (until he was banished to the underworld).

[5] Much of the next 18 paragraphs of description of Tahiti relies heavily upon John Hawkesworth, who edited a three-volume account of the voyages of Byron, Wallis, Carteret, and the first Cook voyage in 1773. Ledyard dipped into Hawkesworth for phrasing, content, and anaylsis, and his table of vocabularly came from a longer list in Hawkesworth. Ledyard acted as a good editor, streamlining Hawkesworth, but in the end there was too much blatant plagiarism.

[6] Hawkesworth wrote, "In their motions there is at once vigour and ease; their walk is graceful, their deportment liberal, and their behavior to strangers and to each other affable and courteous."

[7] Hawkesworth wrote, "After meals, and in the heat of the day, the middle-aged people of the better sort generally sleep; they are indeed extremely indolent, and sleeping and eating is almost all that they do."

[8] Up from the throat, through the lips, with the palate, and through the teeth.

[9] Much of this paragraph is derived from Hawkesworth's ideas about language.

✳

PART II: LETTERS FROM EUROPE

[1] In America Ledyard formed a fur-trading company with Robert Morris, the Philadelphia financier; in Lorient he worked with a merchant named Berard.

[2] Then—mount

[3] Ben Uncas was the famous 17th-century Mohegan leader.

[4] The brothers Daniel and Theodorick Fitzhugh, tobacco farmers from Virginia, left Paris in October 1785. Jefferson lent them 600f.

[5] Thomas Barclay was the first U.S. consul to serve abroad. He was consul general in France beginning in 1782. In 1786 Barclay, succeeding where John Lamb could not, negotiated the first U.S. treaty with a non-European nation (Morocco). He was absent from Paris on this mission from January 1786 onward.

[6] John Lamb, a neighbor from Groton, Conn., was the first envoy to the Barbary States, but he failed to secure either a treaty with the dey of Algiers or the release of American prisoners held there.

[7] Ledyard was probably refering to Æsop's Fable of Hercules and the Waggoner: A man was driving a heavy load along a muddy road. At one point his wheels sank into the mud, and the more his horses pulled, the deeper the wheels sank. The driver dismounted and knelt beside his horses, praying to Hercules. Suddenly, Hercules appeared and said, "Get up and put your shoulder to the wheel." The moral: The gods help those who help themselves.

[8] David Franks stayed in Paris from October 1785 to January 1786. Like Ledyard, he was a friend of Jefferson's who benefited from the Virginian's hospitality. Jefferson gave Franks 200f in September 1785 after Franks was threatened with imprisonment for past debts. Franks accompanied Barclay to Morocco for the negotiations with the sultan.

[9] Charles Gravier, Count de Vergennes, was the French foreign minister.

[10] Andrew Hodge, a Philadelphia merchant, married Anne Ledyard, the daughter of Ledyard's grandfather and his second wife.

[11] The feast day of the Virgin Mary is usually celebrated on September 8.

[12] In May 1773 Ledyard canoed from Hanover, New Hampshire, to Hartford. Coos refers to a region of the upper Connecticut River valley. It originally referred to an offshoot tribe of the Abenaki, the Coashaukees; a New Hampshire county is now named Coös.

[13] Ledyard's uncle and guardian Thomas Seymour was mayor of Hartford from June 1774 to May 1812. His wife Mary was the younger sister of Ledyard's father.

[14] The feast day of St. Cloud is usually celebrated on September 7.

[15] The reference might be to Henry Fielding's *The History of Tom Jones*: "Then Kate of the Mill tumbled unfortunately over a tomb-stone, which catching hold of her ungartered stocking inverted the order of nature, and gave her heels the superiority to her head."

[16] Benjamin Ledyard married Catherine Forman in January 1775.

[17] Eleanor Forman, the sister-in-law of Ledyard's first cousin Benjamin Ledyard, married Philip Freneau, the poet and failed biographer of Ledyard.

[18] Nathaniel Barrett, a Massachusetts merchant, left Paris in February 1786.

[19] The houyhnhnms were wise horses in *Gulliver's Travels*.

[20] Small bag or package.

[21] David Humphreys, a Connecticut native, Yale graduate, poet, and aide-de-camp to George Washington, was a secretary to the American delegation in France. He later was minister to Lisbon and Madrid.

[22] George Nugent-Temple Grenville, the Marquis of Buckingham, was a former Lord Lieutenant of Ireland and home secretary.

[23] "By heaven, methinks it were an easy leap/To pluck bright honor from the pale-faced moon,/Or dive into the bottom of the deep,/Where fathom-line could never touch the ground,/And pluck up drowned honor by the locks." Shakespeare, *Henry IV*.

[24] Isaac Ledyard married Ann McArthur in March 1785.

[25] Friedrich Melchior, Baron von Grimm was the famous minister from the Duchy of Saxe-Gotha; the Chancellor of the Exchequer was William Pitt, the Younger.

[26] Sir James Hall, a Scot, was then in his mid-20s. He later became a leading geologist.

[27] Tippoo Sahib was the sultan of Mysore in southern India from 1782 to 1799.

[28] Typical of the editing of Ledyard's original letter, here the transcriber

excised a section, leaving just a note in parentheses "After some Reflections on unprincipled Libertinism the Letter proceeds."

[29] This was the battle of Quiberon in 1759.

[30] Jean Pierre Blanchard was a famous balloonist. On January 7, 1785, Blanchard and Dr. John Jeffries, a Harvard graduate, made the first flight over the English Channel, traveling from Dover, England, to Calais, France. Eight years later he made the first balloon ascent in America, flying from Philadelphia into New Jersey.

[31] Of his age.

[32] William Short was a Virginian protégé of Thomas Jefferson's, acting as Jefferson's private secretary. He died in 1849, one of the last person alive at that time to have known Ledyard well. The poor widow and her two copper coins is from Mark 12:42-44 and Luke 21:2-4—"Truly, I say to you, this poor widow has put in more than all those who are contributing to the treasury. For they all contributed out of their abundance; but she out of her poverty has put in everything she had, her whole living."

[33] William S. Smith, a Princeton man and aide to George Washington during the war, was the secretary to the American legation in London. In June 1786 he married Nabby Adams, the daughter of John and Abigail Adams.

[34] In November 1786 in London Sir Joseph Banks, William Smith, John Walsh, a longtime fellow of the Royal Society, former M.P. and veteran of the Indian colonial service, John Hunter, a Scottish surgeon, fellow of the Royal Society and collector of skeletons, and William Seward, the famous anecdotist and friend of Edward Bancroft, signed a subscription totaling £7-7-0 for Ledyard.

[35] To present me on my knees before him. I adore his generous heart.

[36] "...at the moment, I think as he does about the government of this country here. Everything is a cabal, even on the streets. Fortunately for me I understand well to give some punches."

[37] Jefferson broke his right wrist in September 1786.

[38] He is refering to the Nadowessioux or the Sioux and the Chippewa.

[39] While in Russia, Ledyard used the Gregorian Old Style calendar 11 days behind the Western Julian calendar. On March24 / April 4, 1788 Ledyard in his diary switched back from Old Style to New Style.

[40] Louis Philippe, Count de Segur, was the French ambassador in St. Petersburg.

[41] Grand Duke Paul, the son of Empress Catherine II.

★

Part III The Siberian Journal

1 A mile is about two-thirds of a verst; or 104.5 versts equals one degree of latitude.

2 Here as elsewhere, Ledyard deliberately left a blank space in his journal. According to Philip Freneau, the compiler of his *Life & Letters* manuscript, Ledyard intended to later fill them up "when conveniency and leisure would permit." However, when Ledyard was arrested he lost some of his journals that might have contained the missing segments. Regardless, he was so pressed for time during his short stay in London following the Russian journey, that he never was able to fill in many of the blanks.

3 Samson Occum was the first Indian student to study under Eleazar Wheelock, the "Sanguine Divine" who later founded Dartmouth.

4 Kayenlaha was the name of the young Indian teenager who lived with Lafayette in Paris for two years. Mount Ida is a Greek mountain associated in ancient times with Zeus.

5 Sir, I wish you a good trip.

6 In 1731 the French scientist Rene Antoine Ferchault de Reaumur fixed the freezing point at zero degrees and the boiling point at eighty degrees. Thus, −30° R would equal −35° Fahrenheit.

7 The sea dog is the seal.

8 Man of the woods.

9 Saloon.

10 Adam Laxmann was a district police officer and son of Erik Laxmann, a Finnish naturalist and chemistry professor who owned the glass factory Ledyard visited at Lake Baikal.

11 Denham was a well-known 17th-century Irish-born poet in London. From "Cooper's Hill": "My eye, descending from the hill, surveys/Where Thames amongst the wanton valleys strays;/Thames, the most lov'd of all the Ocean's sons/ By his old sire, to his embraces runs,/Hasting to pay his tribute to the sea,/Like mortal life to meet eternity."

12 Lesser gods.

13 Here I switch from the *Life & Letters* transcript to the Henry Beaufoy transcript entitled "John Ledyard Original Manuscript Journal of his Journey towards Eastern Siberia and Kamchatka. 1787." Much of Ledyard's description of the Tatar's face on page 180-182 comes from the *Life & Letters* transcript.14

14 Otiosity: leisure, indolence.

15 Ledyard is refering to Thomas Sherlock, the bishop of London from

1748 to 1761; John Tillotson, the archbishop of Canterbury from 1691 to 1694 and dean of St. Paul's Cathedral who married Oliver Cromwell's niece; and Laurence Sterne, the pastor and novelist. All three men published best-selling collections of their sermons.

[16] The Billingsgate fish market was a raffish Thames-side institution in southeast London,

[17] Journellement: daily.

[18] Mercury freezes at–38° Fahrenheit, or at about –31° Reaumur.

[19] Thomas Pennant, a Welsh naturalist, fellow of the Royal Society and friend of Peter Simon Pallas and Sir Joseph Banks, was most well-known for his History of Quadrupeds (1781) and Arctic Zoology (1785).

[20] In 1717 Alexander Pope published the love poem "Eloisa to Abelard:" They were star-crossed lovers who, unable to marry, spent their lives separated. "How oft, when pressed to marriage, have I said/Curse on all laws but those which love has made?/Love, free as air, at sight of human ties/Spreads his light wings, and in a moment flies."

[21] Jonathan Carver, a Connecticut army captain, explored the upper reaches of the Mississippi River valley. His memoir, Travels through the Interior Parts of North America in the Years 1766, 1767, and 1768 was dedicated to Sir Joseph Banks and published in 1778. Like Ledyard, Carver often plagiarized other authors' works.

[22] This is about –65° Fahrenheit.

[23] See I Samuel 18:20-29. David killed 200 Philistines and gave their foreskins to King Saul as a dowry to marry his daughter Michal.

[24] While in St. Petersburg, Ledyard drew 20 guineas on the account of Sir Joseph Banks through Brown & Porter, an English merchant firm in town.

[25] Christian Bering, a member of the Billings Expedition, was the nephew of Vitus Bering.

[26] Groton, Connecticut, Ledyard's hometown, is at 41° latitude.

[27] With luck.

[28] The yeniceri, or Janissaries, were an elite Turkish army corp that were a powerful polticial force in the Ottoman Empire from the 14th century until 1826.

[29] See Genesis 35:28-29. Much of the material following also refers to Genesis—Laban and Rachel (31:25-55), Joseph and his coat (37); Lot (19); and Cain and Able (4).

[30] William Johnson was the British Superintendent of Indian Affairs from 1755 to 1774 and ended up owning more than 400,000 acres of land in New York State.

31 Shakespeare, *King Lear*: "Take physic, pomp,/Expose thyself to feel what wretches feel,/That thou mayst shake the superflux to them/And show the heavens more just."

32 The 17th-century Khivan ruler Abulgazi Bagadur wrote a nine-volume *History of the Turks*.

33 Georg Wilhelm Steller was a German-born naturalist on Bering's second expedition. As the first European naturalist to explore the flora and fauna of the North Pacific, he described animals that later became named Steller's Jay, Steller's sea lion, Steller's sea cow, and Steller's eider. Peter Simon Pallas later edited and published his journals. Cornelius de Bruyn was a Dutch painter and traveler who wrote popular books at the turn of the 18th century on the Holy Lands, Asia, and Europe.

Georges-Louis Leclerc, Comte de Buffon was a French scientist best known for his 36 volume *Histoire naturelle, générale et particulière* (1749-1788).

34 Ledyard is writing from Nizhni Novgorod.

35 Talachin, Belarus, is on the Drut River.

36 Sinon was the Greek warrior who, pretending to have deserted his compatriots, persuaded the Trojans to bring the wooden horse into Troy. Virgil, *Aenead*: "Now hear how well the Greeks their wiles disguis'd;/Behold a nation in a man compris'd./Trembling the miscreant stood, unarm'd and bound;He star'd, and roll'd his haggard eyes around,/Then said: 'Alas! what earth remains, what sea/Is open to receive unhappy me?/What fate a wretched fugitive attends,/Scorn'd by my foes, abandon'd by my friends?'"

37 Boldly.

38 Glance.

39 Recupercuration: a repeated crossing; endroit: place.

40 The most well-known poem by Saint John Honeywood, a Massachusetts native and Yale man, was "Darby and Joan": "When Darby saw the setting sun,/He swung his scythe, and home he run,/Sat down, drank off his quart, and said,/'My work is done, I'll go to bed.'"

41 François, duc de la Rochefoucauld was a 17th-century French aristocrat famous for his maxims: "*Nos vertus ne sont, le plus souvent que des vices déguisés.*" Our virtues are usually only our vices in disguise. Charles-Louis de Secondat, Baron de Montesquieu, was an 18th-century French intellectual and critic.

42 Edward Bancroft, a Massachusetts doctor, lived in Dutch Guiana in the 1760s before moving to Paris and spying for the British government during the American Revolution.

*

PART IV THE EGYPTIAN JOURNAL AND LETTERS

1 James Jarvis was an American coin minter and family friend.

2 Virgil, *Eclogues*: "Stretching out at your ease under the shade of a beech tree."

3 Carl Fredric von Breda, a Swedish painter studying under Sir Joshua Reynolds, did the portrait of Ledyard. It originally hung in Somerset House, the new palatial government building on the Thames.

4 John Trumbull, a Connecticut acquaintance of Ledyard's, was one of the leading painters of the post-Revolutionary War era.

5 Cerke is probably Andrew Stuart, a lawyer and M.P. who served on the Board of Trade; Henry Beaufoy was the Quaker son of a London wine merchant, a committed abolitionist and a Whig M.P.; Lord Rawdon was a young army officer destined to become Governor-General of India; and Richard Watson, the Bishop of Landaff, was a chemist and fellow of the Royal Society.

6 Guido Reni was an early 17th-century Baroque painter from Bologna. Ledyard probably saw his paintings in the Louvre, where 20 of his pictures reside.

7 Alexander Edwards, a South Carolina man, was visiting Jefferson at the time.

8 So the glory of this world passes away. The phrase is used at papal installations.

9 Sennar was a kingdom in present-day Ethiopia, with its capital on the Blue Nile.

10 Andre de Bailli, Suffren de Saint-Tropez was the famous French admiral who secured victories over the British Navy in the Indian Ocean during the American Revolution. Jacques Necker, from Geneva, was Director-General of Finance from 1776 to 1781 and 1788 to 1789.

11 The Leo Ledyard is refering to is probably Leo Africanus. Born Al-Hasan Ibn Muhammad in Granada, Leo was educated in Fez and traveled throughout northern Africa and the Middle East in the sixteenth century. His *Description of Africa, Della descrittione dell'Africa et delle cose notabili che iui sono, per Giovan Lioni Africano*, appeared for the first time in 1550. It had a whole section devoted to Egypt. Both Thucydides and Herodotus were fifth-century BC Greek historians.

[12] Carlo Rosetti was a longtime adviser to the Beys of Egypt. The English Consul was George Baldwin, who was one of the first people to attempt to bring the India trade through Suez.

[13] In 1687 Isaac Newton published the three-volume *Philosophiae Naturalis Principia Mathematica,* which contained his laws of motion and gravity.

[14] Darfur is in present-day western Sudan. Nubia was a vast ancient kingdom in present-day northern Sudan. Wangara was a mythical, wealthy African kingdom thought to be located in present-day Ghana.

[15] In Laurence Sterne's *Tristram Shandy,* Vol. IX, chapter two, Corporal Trim desperately tries to get Uncle Toby's old wig in order: "it curl'd every where but where the Corporal would have it; and where a buckle or two, in his opinion, would have done it honour, he could as soon have raised the dead." The French term *boucle* refered to the side curls of a wig.

[16] The Fezzan is a region in the Sahara in present-day Libya. Timbuktu is in present-day Mali.

ACKNOWLEDGEMENTS

✷

My gratitude goes to my literary agent Joseph Regal and to Kevin Mulroy, the editor-in-chief of National Geographic Books. Lisa Thomas spent two years honing the idea and shepherding the widely-flung materials into print. Her patience, imagination, and editing skills made for a perfect collaboration. Deep appreciation goes to Penny Dackis, Melissa Krause, who did a wonderful job of transcribing Ledyard's scrawl, Judy Klein who copyedited the manuscript with diligence, and Carl Mehler who created the two marvelous maps.

In composing this book, I stood on the shoulders of a number of dedicated Ledyard historians, especially Sinclair H. Hitchings, James Kenneth Munford, and Stephen D. Watrous.

I am very thankful for the assistance I received and permission to use materials from the following institutions that hold Ledyard material.

Rauner Special Collections Library at Dartmouth College: the Siberian journal and letters dated February 1786, 8 April 1786, 8 August 1786, 16 August 1786, 18 August 1786, November and December 1786, 20 December 1786, 5 January 1787, 20 August 1787, June 1788 and 4 July 1788.

National History Museum in London: letters dated 18 October 1787, December 1787 and 2 January 1788, and 25 January 1788.

New-York Historical Society: letters dated July 1785, summer 1785, 25 November 1786, 19 March 1787, 15 May 1787, 29 July 1787, 22 October 1787, June 1788, 15 August 1788, 10 September 1788 and 15 November 1788.

Library of Congress: letters dated 7 February 1786, 7 July 1786 and July 1788.

I thank the many people whose support was essential. In particular, Debbie and Jim Zug who read through the manuscript and made, as always, helpful suggestions, and Rebecca and Livingston Zug, whose hearts are as big, beautiful, and strong as St. Paul's Cathedral.

National Geographic
Adventure Classics

★

20 Hrs., 40 Min.: Our Flight in the *Friendship*
Amelia Earhart
ISBN: 0-7922-3376-X
$14.00 U.S./$22.00 Canada
Amelia Earhart's high-spirited account of her first crossing of the Atlantic by airplane in 1928, as a co-pilot aboard the *Friendship*, rich with autobiographical information and a discussion on the future of flight—including the important role she expected women to play.

The Adventures of Captain Bonneville
Washington Irving
ISBN: 0-7922-3743-9
$15.00 U.S./$24.00 Canada
Capt. Benjamin Louis Eulalie de Bonneville, U.S. Army, explorer, fur trapper, and trader, was one of the most colorful figures in the history of the American West and an irresistible subject to Washington Irving, who purchased the captain's journals and wrote this engaging historical account of Bonneville's death-defying experiences across the American West.

The Adventures of Theodore Roosevelt
Theodore Roosevelt
Edited and with an Introduction by Anthony Brandt
0-7922-9346-0
$16.00/23.00 Canada
Adventure Classics series editor Anthony Brandt focuses his attention on

Roosevelt's robust and adventurous spirit, and treats readers to an engaging assortment of Roosevelt's far-flung adventures including African safaris, ranch life in the American West, and a peril-filled trip down Brazil's legendary River of Doubt. Drawn from Roosevelt's numerous journals, letters, articles, and books, *The Adventures of Theodore Roosevelt* is an unforgettable chronicle of the life of a naturalist, outdoorsman, and gifted reader and writer, who also happened to be the 26th President of the United States.

The Cruise of the *Snark*
Jack London
ISBN: 0-7922-6244-I
$13.00 U.S./$21.00 Canada

In 1907 the author of *The Call of the Wild* and *The Sea Wolf* decided to undertake his own grand adventure: a seven-year, round-the-world cruise aboard the *Snark*. From Hawaii to the Marquesas to the Solomons to Bora Bora, the story of the voyage is one of excitement and spirit, occasional leaks, and London's own hilarious attempts to understand the mysteries of navigation.

The Exploration of the Colorado River and Its Canyons
John Wesley Powell
ISBN: 0-7922-6636-6
$14.00 U.S./$21.50 Canada/£8.99 U.K.

John Wesley Powell, the legendary one-armed pioneer, led the first expedition down the Colorado River into the Grand Canyon. Powell and his crew faced forbidding rapids and scarce food, all of which are documented in thrilling detail in this harrowing saga of strength, determination, and perseverance.

Inca Land
Hiram Bingham
ISBN: 0-7922-6194-I
$14.00 U.S./$22.00 Canada

In 1911, Yale University scholar Hiram Bingham set off for Peru with the goal of climbing Peru's highest peak. Along the way discovered Machu Picchu, an ancient Inca stronghold high in the mountains. Bingham's wonderfully literate account of the extraordinary find is preceded by an engaging description of his own freewheeling adventures in Peru.

THE LAST VOYAGE OF CAPTAIN COOK
The Collected Writings of John Ledyard
Edited and with an Introduction by James Zug
ISBN: 0-7922-9347-9
$16.00 U.S./$23.00 Canada
A firsthand account of the last voyage and murder of Captain Cook, one of
the earliest crossings of Siberia, and personal correspondence with Thomas
Jefferson are among the treasures to be discovered in this unprecedented
collection. John Ledyard may be the greatest and least-known traveler in
the history of the United States. James Zug, author of *The American Traveler*,
vividly brings this 18th-century traveler to life with an introduction and
annotated text.

THE JOURNALS OF LEWIS AND CLARK
Meriwether Lewis and William Clark
ISBN: 0-7922-6921-7
$16.00 U.S./$25.00 Canada/£9.99 U.K.
This newly abridged and edited edition of Meriwether Lewis and William
Clark's unprecedented a two-year, 5,000-mile journey through the heart of
the unknown American West to the Pacific Ocean includes a modern
English "translation" that corrects the duo's famously poor spelling and
grammar, making for a truly readable account of the journey.

MY LIFE AS AN EXPLORER
Sven Anders Hedin
ISBN: 0-7922-6987-X
$16.00 U.S./$25.00 Canada/£9.99 U.K.
An adventurer with a capital "A," Sven Hedin explored the parts of Asia
marked "unknown" on the maps of the 19th and early 20th centuries. His
delightful memoir is filled with dangerous situations, the discovery of
lost cities, and exotic lands and people, all brilliantly illustrated by
the author.

THE NORTH POLE
A Historical Reader
Edited and with an Introduction by Anthony Brandt
0-7922-7411-3
$15.00/$22.00 Canada

The fascinating saga of tragedy and triumph in the quest to reach the North Pole is expertly told in this sweeping history of the quest for the North Pole. Series editor Anthony Brandt deftly presents the story of the exploration of the Arctic through selected passages from explorers, interweaving the words of the adventurers with his own contextual material and expertly carrying the story from the 15th century to the 20th. Featuring selections from Frijtdof Nansen, Adolphus Greeley, Robert Peary, and dozens more.

The Oregon Trail
Francis Parkman
ISBN: 0-7922-6640-4
$14.00 U.S./$21.00 Canada/£8.99 U.K.

The first historian of the American frontier left his home in Boston in 1846 to travel west with the Conestoga wagons along the Oregon Trail. Parkman encountered a truly wild land fraught with danger, starvation, and marauding Indians, all of which he recorded in the classic account of America's move west.

Sailing Alone Around the World and The Voyage of the *Liberdade*
Joshua Slocum
ISBN: 0-7922-6556-4
$13.00 U.S./$21.00 Canada

Joshua Slocum's 1899 account of the first solo voyage around the world has been treasured by sailors for more than 100 years. This Adventure Classics edition of Slocum's thrilling chronicle of raging storms, threatening pirates, and treacherous reefs includes another harrowing tale of hardships along the coast of South America.

Scrambles Amongst the Alps
Edward Whymper
ISBN: 0-7922-6923-3
$14.00 U.S./$22.00 Canada/£8.99 U.K.

Before thermal clothing, even before reliable ropes, Edward Whymper braved the Alps with energy and determination as he pioneered modern mountaineering. This classic account of his adventures recounts Whymper's many attempts to climb the Matterhorn and the shocking tragedy that befell his companions when they finally achieved their goal.

THE SILENT WORLD
Jacques Cousteau
ISBN: 0-7922-6796-6
$13.00 U.S./$19.50 Canada
This 50th anniversary edition of Jacques Cousteau's thrilling memoir includes his charming story of the invention of SCUBA from spare automobile parts in the 1940s and details the adventures that followed as he and his team tested the limits of endurance and pioneered ocean exploration.

THE SOUTH POLE: A HISTORY
OF THE EXPLORATION OF ANTARCTICA
Featuring Shackleton, Byrd, Scott, Amundsen, and more
ISBN: 0-7922-6797-4
$15.00 U.S./$22.50 Canada
Through the words of the famous—and not so famous—explorers the challenges and hardships of reaching and exploring the South Pole are documented through journals, ship's logs, and personal accounts that tell the extraordinary story of the exploration of the frozen continent.

THE TOMB OF TUTANKHAMUN
Howard Carter
ISBN: 0-7922-6890-3
$14.00 U.S./$22.00 Canada
The 1922 discovery of the undisturbed tomb of an Egyptian pharaoh gave the world its first glimpse into the splendor of ancient Egypt. Carter's account, published for the first time as a single volume, deftly conveys his own amazement as he uncovers priceless treasures, including the pharaoh's intact mummy.

TRAVELS IN WEST AFRICA
Mary Kingsley
ISBN: 0-7922-6638-2
$14.00 U.S./$21.50 Canada/£8.99 U.K.
Defying Victorian conventions, Mary Kingsley traveled alone to West Africa in 1893. Kingsley was often the first European to enter remote villages, but she made fast friends with the tribes she encountered while collecting priceless samples of flora and fauna. Kingsley's engaging book records numerous obstacles and challenges, including a hilarious encounter with a panther. She faced each one head-on, and always dressed as a lady!

Voyage of the *Beagle*
Charles Darwin
ISBN: 0-7922-6559-9
$13.00 U.S./$21.00 Canada

Charles Darwin's 1845 account of a five-year journey to South America as the naturalist aboard the HMS *Beagle* is a wonderfully told tale of a marvelous journey, rich with vivid descriptions of the natural world, the observations of which would lead to the publication of *Origin of Species*.

The Worst Journey in the World
Apsley Cherry-Garrard
ISBN: 0-7922-6634-X
$16.00 U.S./$25.00 Canada/£9.99 U.K.

While Robert Falcon Scott and his party set off on an attempt to be the first men to reach the South Pole, Cherry-Garrard and companions set off in search of the never-before-seen breeding grounds of the emperor penguin, a miserable assignment that the author dubbed "the worst journey in the world"—until he returned and discovered the shocking fate of his expedition's leader.

To Order National Geographic Adventure Classics
visit your local bookstore or log on to:
http://www.nationalgeographic.com/books.